Kurt Jackson

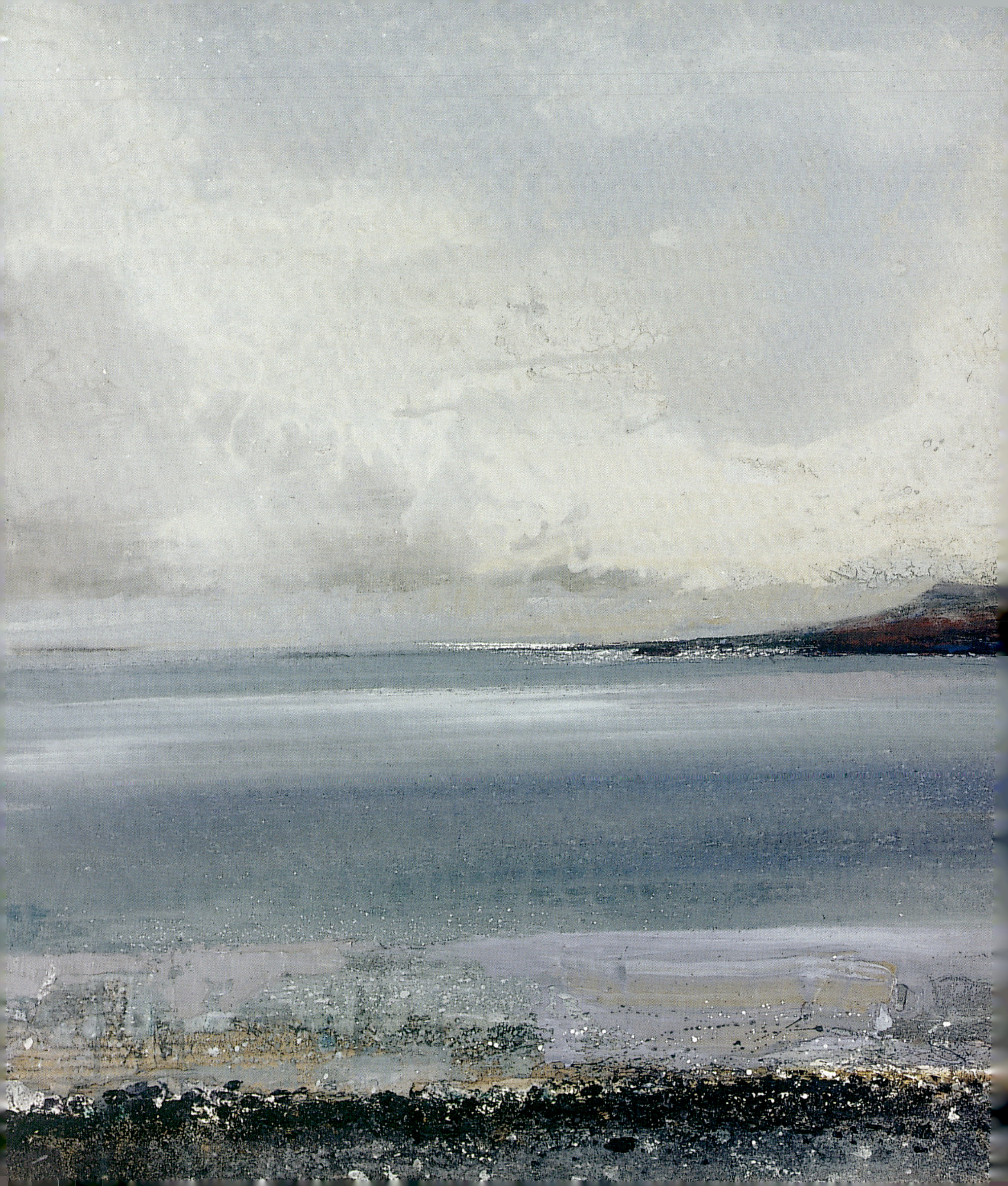

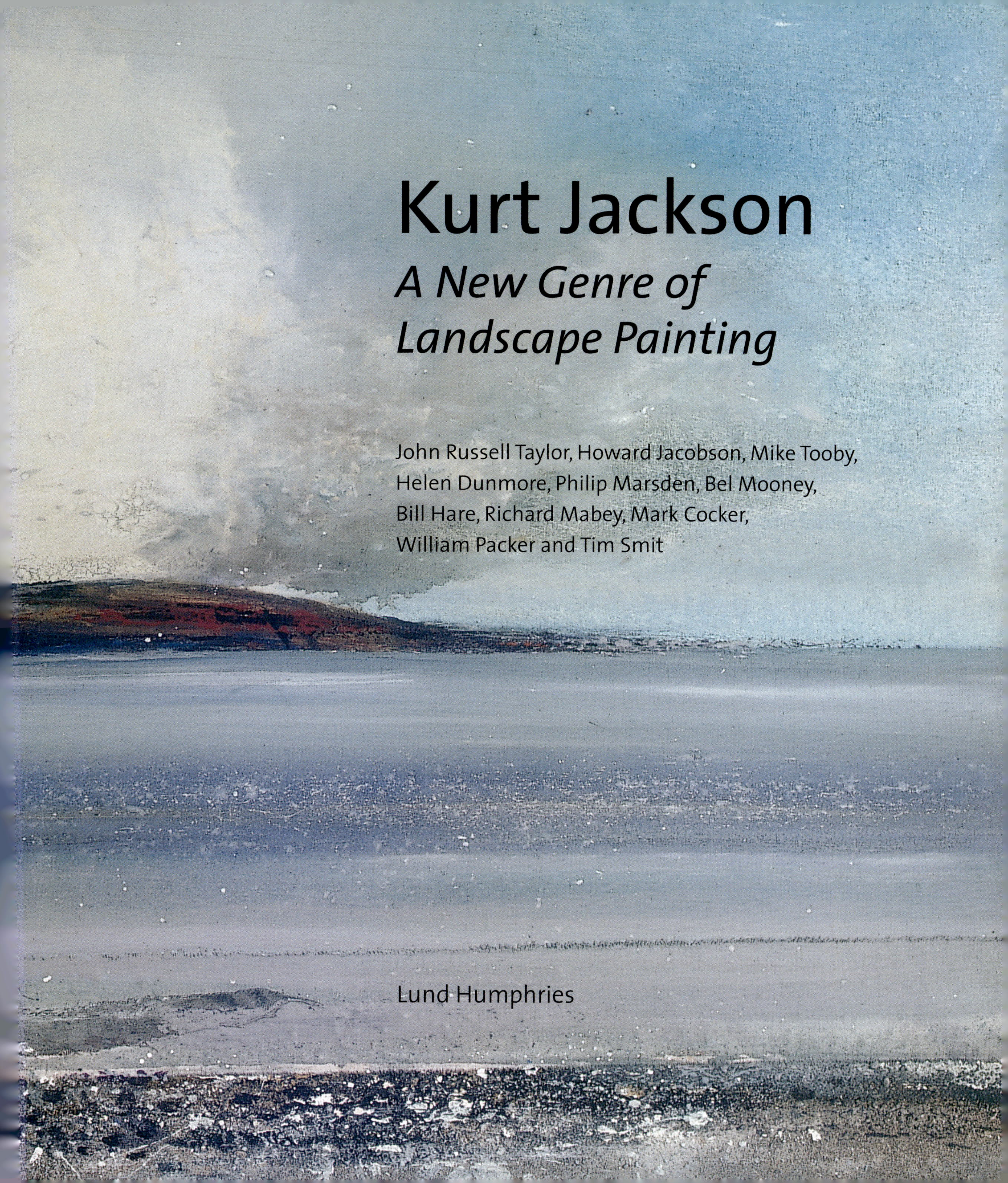

Kurt Jackson

A New Genre of Landscape Painting

John Russell Taylor, Howard Jacobson, Mike Tooby,
Helen Dunmore, Philip Marsden, Bel Mooney,
Bill Hare, Richard Mabey, Mark Cocker,
William Packer and Tim Smit

Lund Humphries

First published in 2010 by Lund Humphries, in association with The Lemon Street Gallery

Lund Humphries
Wey Court East
Union Road
Farnham
Surrey GU9 7PT

Lund Humphries
Suite 420
101 Cherry Street
Burlington, VT 05401-4405
USA

www.lundhumphries.com
Lund Humphries is part of Ashgate Publishing

British Library Cataloguing-in-Publication Data:
Jackson, Kurt.
Kurt Jackson : a new genre of landscape painting.
1. Jackson, Kurt--Criticism and interpretation.
2. Landscape in art. 3. Ecology in art.
I. Title II. Taylor, John Russell.
759.2-dc22
Library of Congress Control Number: 2009935161

ISBN: 978–1–84822–041–6

Edited by Nicola Homer
Designed by Kevin Brown at park44.com
Set in The Sans
Printed in Thailand

Titlepage: Detail of *Samson from Rushy Bay, Bryher, 2003* (plate 30)

Contents

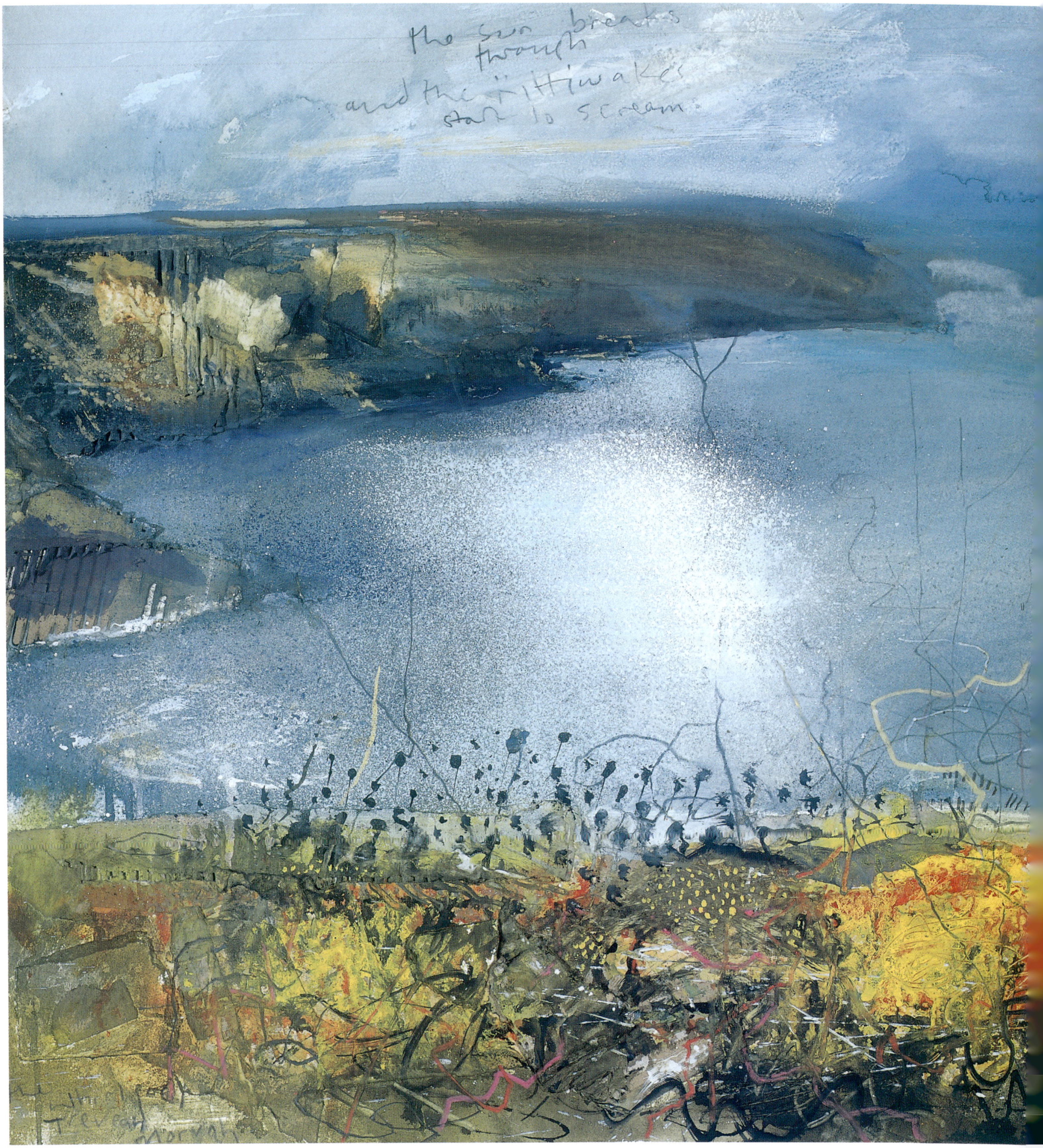
the sun breaks through
and the kittiwakes
start to scream

Foreword: Kurt Jackson, Visionary Observer

John Russell Taylor

1
The sun breaks through and the kittiwakes start to scream. The Whirlpool, Trevean, Morvah, March 2006
Mixed media and collage, 57 × 61 cm (22.5 × 24 in)

It is a common assumption that artists must be either modern or traditionalist, and never the twain shall meet. Kurt Jackson, happily, is living proof that this is not true. Few contemporary artists are more vividly aware of the tradition from which they come. In fact, Jackson spent his earliest years as an artist painting landscapes which were unmistakably in the great British tradition – albeit, like much other twentieth-century art, viewed through Post-Impressionist lenses.

So much for the traditionalist in him. But there are two caveats to that. The first is that, with few exceptions, the sights that caught the eye of classic landscapists such as J.M.W. Turner and John Sell Cotman in their time appear very different today, and so the way they are painted is almost bound to be dramatically different. The second is that Jackson is inevitably caught in the bind that Salvador Dalí, of all people, most clearly defined: 'The one thing we cannot help being, however hard we try, is a modern artist.'[1] In other words, an artist working at the beginning of the twenty-first century, even if they wanted to be an exact imitator of one of their artistic idols from the past, inevitably is permeated by the tone of their own time.

This is why 'creative forgeries' after a while look more like the art of their own time than that of the period they are pretending to belong to. Whatever they looked like when they were first painted, Han van Meegeren's forged paintings of Jan Vermeer, for example, now strike us as feeble 1930s religious art. Not that Jackson ever had any desire to indulge in slavish imitation of his forebears: he is one of the great originals of British painting. But no one comes from nothing, and we can see where he is coming from quite easily. What no one can guess – probably what even he cannot guess – is where he is going.

This no doubt has something to do with his curious origins as a painter. Both his parents were painters, which can have an adverse effect on a child's future as a professional artist, both through a fear of not living up to the parents' standards and expectations, and through possible discouragement from parents who know all too well the snags and pitfalls of taking up such a career. However, none of this seems to have been the case with the Jacksons: his parents travelled a lot as part of their work experience, and generally took Kurt with them. When he was one month old they travelled to Africa, and lived there for some time while Kurt's father taught in a North Nigerian art school on the edge of the Sahara – an experience which shaped his young mind with images and tangible relics of Africa. Slightly later, once they had returned to England, the family travelled a great deal every year: 'long journeys camping, wandering round the Continent, my father painting and the rest of us having a great time'.[2]

Jackson's early memories find him watching with casual interest while his father painted, largely in watercolours *en plein air*, thinking it looked to be an interesting thing to do. His parents at every opportunity encouraged him in this interest, clearly regarding it as natural, if not quite inevitable, that he should turn out to be an artist. There was always generous praise when he did well, and his father's Quaker work ethic automatically made Jackson assume that he should exceed the formal demands of his teachers, putting in a linocut or a collage when a simple drawing would have been sufficient.

He was born in Blandford, Dorset, and spent much of his childhood in not-quite-rural Hertfordshire (when the family was not travelling), playing with his friends in water-meadows, wooded lanes and overgrown fields, but with dual carriageways and housing estates only just out of sight. While a schoolboy there, and in Cornwall during the 1960s and early 1970s, he developed a passionate interest in natural history, and might well have turned in that direction for a profession. In the event, he was simultaneously offered places at St Albans College of Art to study painting and at Oxford University to take a degree in Zoology. He chose Oxford largely because of the fuss that was made, at school and even at home, about the prestige and possible value of the Oxford offer.

Although Jackson's teenage interest in the observation of nature continued, he rapidly realised that a degree course at Oxford was far too academic for him, requiring him to spend a lot of time studying things at a microscopic level or considering in theory exotic species that he had never even glimpsed in life. Consequently he claims to have spent most of his time in Oxford attending classes at the Ruskin School of Drawing and Fine Art, or painting in the nearby countryside. It was perhaps inevitable that finally the painting should win out over

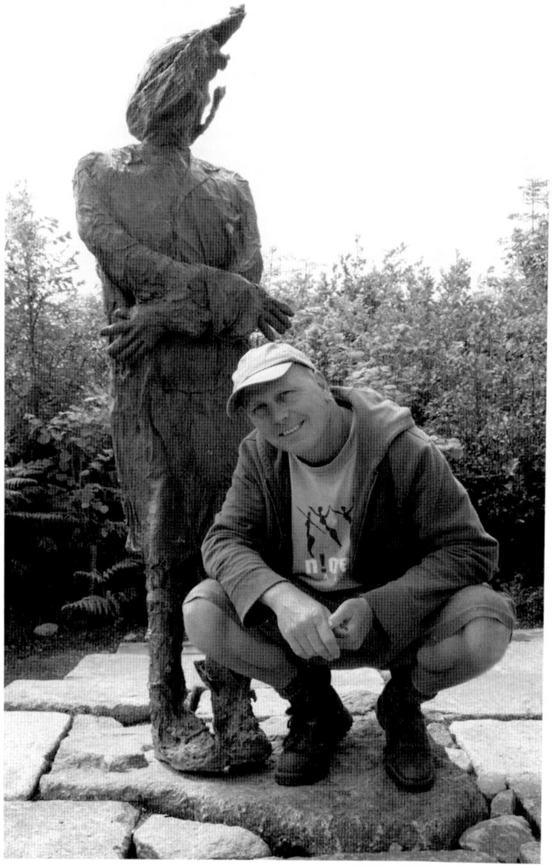

2
***Breezy*, 2009**
Bronze, 198 × 66 × 56 cm (78 × 26 × 22 in)

Zoology as his chosen way of life, but clearly for a landscape painter it must have been a shaping factor that not only did he respond passionately to the visual stimuli in what he saw, but also that he knew from the first very precisely what he was painting.

This, with a concomitant concern over ecology and the environment, manifested even before they became intellectually fashionable subjects, has been important in all his work. Of course, such concerns have long – at least since the beginning of the Romantic Movement – been part of the English tradition. As soon as anyone could say, as the nineteenth-century English poet Walter Savage Landor said of himself, 'Nature I loved, and next to Nature, Art', conceptions of the sacredness of nature, and therefore fears for its safety, became a virtually inalienable part of the English artistic psyche. So in this sense too Jackson is a traditional artist.

Then again, it all depends what you mean by 'traditional'. From some points of view it might seem to be an insult, or at least a severe limitation laid upon Jackson, to call his art traditional. That is, if you regard traditional art as locked into the past and diametrically opposed to innovation of any kind. On the other hand, it has become a commonplace of art criticism to see Henry Moore as the last in a line that goes straight back to Michelangelo, yet no one would regard him and his sculpture as antiquated and obscurantist. He represents simply the latest development and extension of a great humanist tradition that is still a living, changing thing.

This is exactly the sense in which Jackson is a traditional painter. You cannot see any of his paintings – large or small, oil, acrylic, watercolour or mixed media – without being aware of a great underlying body of tradition, a tradition which clearly includes Turner's later, more abstracted works, Constable's more private watercolour sketches, and elements of Impressionist and Expressionist ideas on landscape as they have filtered into the mainstream of British art. That may be an important part of it. But these are only the foundations on which Jackson's personal style is built. It is evident, for example, even in the simplest, most direct of the plein air watercolour studies, that Jackson has been aware of and digested the art of some New York Abstract Expressionists and, even more so, since they are closer to his own generation, the German so-called Neo-Expressionists like Anselm Kiefer (*b.*1945). Hence the frequent incursion in Jackson's work of apparently random dashes and blobs of colour, which cannot be explained in terms of detailed observation but are very important in conveying the spirit and feeling of the scene as they strike the observing artist. Then there is his developing interest in the quasi-sculptural application of non-painting elements to the surface of his canvases. Sometimes it may be incorporating the material observed – such as sand or pebbles – to 'represent' itself. Sometimes it is a metaphor, or even a sort of pun, as in his Cornish painting *Catch the Light* (2002–3), where the catching of the very present but wholly impalpable light is conceived almost literally as something that could be done, with a real fishing net attached to the front of the canvas.

And there is yet another important element of Jackson's art which is wholly untraditional. I mean, of course, his use of scribbled inscriptions, along with more formal printed words and phrases. One can readily find apparent parallels in contemporary art, from Cy Twombly (*b.*1928) to Tom Phillips (*b.*1937), not to mention twentieth-century uses closer to Jackson's Cornish home, as in the early works of Ben Nicholson (1894–1982). Even earlier, the device occurs (though not, probably, for deliberate artistic effect) in the elaborately annotated landscape drawings and watercolours of Edward Lear – though these were meant entirely as preparatory studies, *aides-memoires* for when or if he decided to base a major formal oil painting on the subject. They were certainly never intended to be publicly shown.

In the twentieth century, what had been a practical preparation became a deliberate artistic stratagem. Some of the later twentieth-century examples – the printed words in works by Ruskin Spear (1911–90), later taken up by artists such as Tom Phillips, R.B. Kitaj (1932–2007) and David Hockney (*b.*1937) – seem to chime with Jackson's practice. His delight in scrawling almost graffiti-like inscriptions across his landscapes and seascapes is likely to remind us of Cy Twombly (who applies graffiti-like scribbles to his painted surfaces in a rather similar fashion and also, at one period, painted tempestuous seascapes hovering forever on the brink of abstraction). This is an important point in relation to Jackson's oeuvre. There is probably no single work that could be mistaken for an out-and-out abstraction: the landscape basis is always patent. But sometimes it is a very close thing. One feels, looking at these extraordinary works, that the documentary element – making some kind of record of what is before the artist's eyes – is important, but it is only one strand. Equally present are how the artist feels about what he sees, and how, at some deep, instinctive level, he apprehends the spirit of time and place.

If this sounds slightly mystical, that is not too wide of the mark. Not, possibly, that Jackson himself would see it that way. Curiously, as the son of two artists-cum-art teachers, he managed to avoid ever being formally trained in art. Reading zoology at Oxford sounds very no-nonsense and scientific. Immediately after

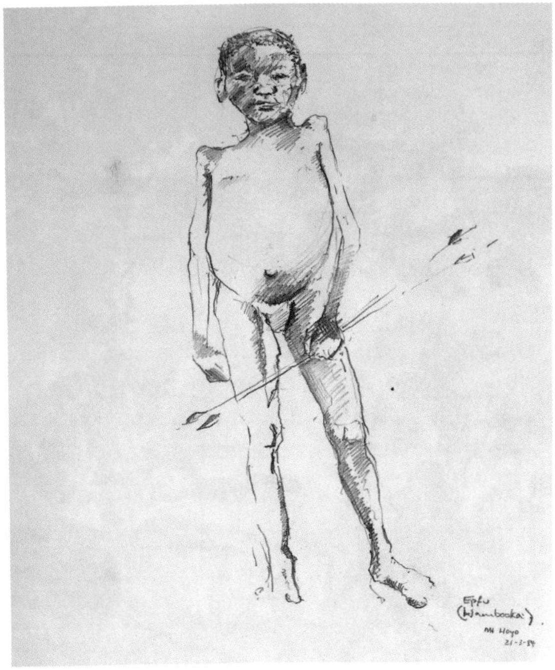

3
Epfu [Wambooka]. Mount Hoyo, Congo, 21/3/84
Pencil, 25 × 18 cm (10 × 7 in)

graduation he and fellow zoology student Caroline set off on a sort of gap year, trekking the length and breadth of Africa. And then, just as if it were the most natural thing in the world, they settled in Cornwall, began to grow a family, and he started to paint in earnest.

The process, for him, is clearly obsessive. His whole life, including wife, children and general lifestyle, is intimately bound up with the making of art. He has tended, ever since fixing on his life-choice of painting, to work in coherent projects, worrying at a subject until he feels that he has teased out all that he can from it – though he insists that no subject is ever sucked completely dry of possibility. Consequently he has done intensive series of paintings concerned with, for instance, specific mines and quarries, usually reflecting the changing face of life in Cornwall. Frequently he has been the last man in before the business closed down completely, so that the documentary aspect of his work has been important in its own right, though never more important than the sheer aesthetics.

Jackson has always been incredibly prolific, and has had a dazzling profusion of one-man shows since his first, at Cambridge University in 1984, as well as participating in numerous group shows since 1982, when he exhibited alongside his father and brother at the Maltings Gallery in Wheathampstead, Hertfordshire.

The Cornish work, even from before he joined the Truro gallery, has generally fallen into distinct and organised series. The urge to travel embraces home territory as well as abroad, which has resulted in a number of projects connected with physical journeys within the peninsula. In 1995 it was 'Painting the Path of the Sun', in 1997–98 'Crossing the Peninsula', in 1998–99 'The Tinner's Way', in 2000 'A3071. The Road to St Just', and in 2001–02 'The Long Field', which was based on a year-long microscopic scrutiny of a specific field not far from his home. By this time the process had been formalised into 'Kurt Jackson's Annual Cornish Project'. The series 'Porth' in 2004 stood slightly apart, and was so large that it occupied simultaneously Newlyn Art Gallery (for the larger paintings) and Messum's (for the rest). But the main series continued through the exhibitions 'The Cornish Estuary: An Heyl Kernewek' (2004), 'The Cornish Hedge: An Ke Kernewek' (2005) and 'Ponds, Pools and Puddles: Pollow, Lynnow ha Lagennow' (2006) – note the titles in Cornish, and indeed the texts in Cornish in the catalogues of the shows concerned – right up to 2008's 'Tamar Project'.

Ever active, in recent years Jackson has also engineered independent bouts of intensive painting not only close to home in Cornish apple orchards, but in French olive groves, walnut orchards, cork oak and chestnut forests, and Spanish almond groves. He notes: 'I feel at home in woodlands, content and fascinated, intrigued by all that coexistence of life forms – a web of fauna and flora.'[3]

He feels that his travelling helped to shape his attitude to nature: 'How you view Nature depends on how you see yourself fitting into it.'[4] In his case, that is somewhere between comfort and total awe. Or, more precisely, his attitude fluctuates between the two extremes. Another experience that crystallised his awareness of this was a trip he took to the Amazon with two friends, when he was twenty. They went deep into the jungle, hours away from any human habitation, and for more than a month slept in hammocks slung between the trees. During that time they felt perfectly at ease, as though this were Eden. Then one night he woke up to a terrifying noise, unimaginably loud and completely inexplicable. In the morning they discovered that their chosen plot had been invaded by Howler monkeys. It was their distinctive roaring, produced from their enlarged voice boxes and louder than any sound a human could produce, which had so terrified him, though surprisingly his two companions had not even woken up. He admits that he does not seem to have been in any actual danger, but from that point he was so frightened that he had to stay in a clearing and would not enter the deep jungle again.

All the same, the fascination with the wilderness remained. Even though his love of Cornwall persists and retains a central role in his work, there is no denying that there is little or no true wilderness remaining in the county. But at least, if Jackson is looking for a wilderness that is (or should be) awe-inspiring as well as seeming at times relatively domesticated and comfortable, one does lie close at hand: the sea. Jackson believes:

> That's why I often paint the open sea with no land visible: the last wilderness here is the sea. You can look out there to the Atlantic and there is no visible sign that we have done anything to it, although we know we have. That's the fascination I have with it, and why I paint it over and over again – big expanses of open sea and open sky. At the same time you can look at wilderness on a micro-scale, peering into the bottom of a blackthorn hedge where again there's no visible sign of the effects of human activity. That can be equally exciting to me. When I'm painting I often try to get myself into a place where I'm totally surrounded by rocks on a beach or cocooned by gorse.[5]

Mike Tooby, former director of Tate St Ives, after seeing a show of Jackson's once asked him if he considered himself a Conceptual Artist. That made him smile, but

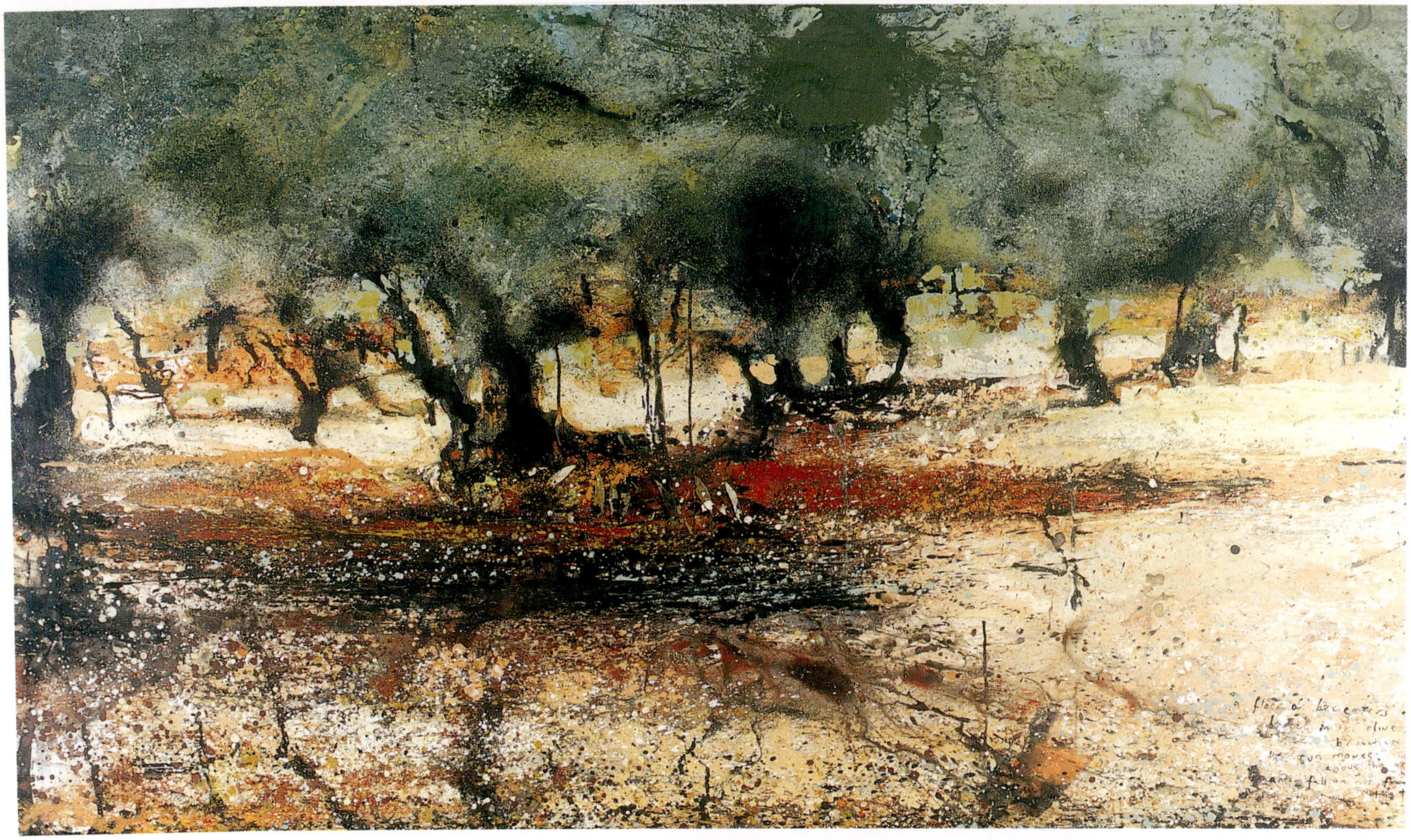

4
A flock of bee eaters above, breeze in the olive branches, the sun moves above the grove, ants fall on me from the trees, 2004
Mixed media on canvas, 121 × 197 cm
(47.5 × 77.5 in)

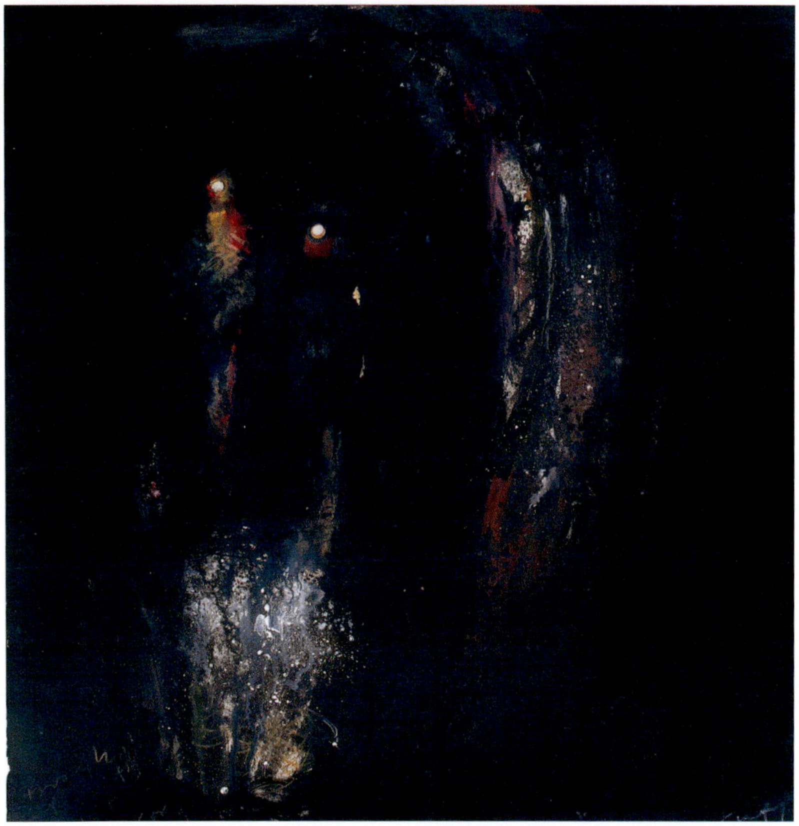

5
Through Deep Adit into Geevor, June 2007
Mixed media, 61 × 57 cm
(24 × 22.5 in)

it is perhaps not entirely surprising: the answer is that he does not see himself that way, but he might well. The Cornish projects, especially those that revolve around a long walk or a minute scrutiny, sound, and indeed are, rather like the artistic walks undertaken by Richard Long or Hamish Fulton. Except that when those artists come home with the results of their perambulations, these tend to be physical relics – pebbles, feathers, twigs – along with photographs and neatly printed scripts outlining or commenting on their itineraries. Jackson is not immune from this tendency. He records that during his childhood rambles he would often bring back a feather or a bone that he had found and do little sketches of it, carefully annotated, while at times subsequently, especially around the year of *The Long Field, December 2001* (plate 113), he would make little sculptures or assemblages of similar relics. But primarily, he did as he has always done: just painted. Though not, of course, without evolution.

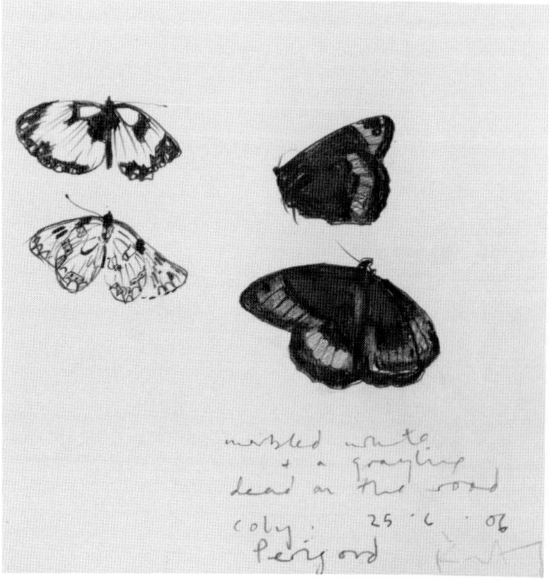

6
Butterflies, Perigord, France, 25/6/06
Pencil, 25 × 25 cm (10 × 10 in)

Because they are so systematic, the annual projects are an excellent index of his development, both technical and, for want of a better word, spiritual. During their extended trail through Africa after graduation, not only did Kurt and Caroline decide that they wanted to live together and raise a family, but he decided, beyond a shadow of a doubt, that he wanted to live the rest of his life as a full-time artist. He had, as we have seen, been painting from a very early age, ever since he was given his first box of watercolours. But most of his painting in his teens was closely dependent on his interests in natural history: he might even, conceivably, have gone on to be a biological illustrator, though even then it seemed to him a bit too sterile and academic to merit his serious consideration.

Jackson's decision to become a full-time artist was a bold one to take on his postgraduate voyage across Africa. The move to Cornwall in 1984 was due to the artistic tradition thriving in the far west. While Boscastle, the village where they first settled and lived for some five years, was quite separate from the centres of artistic activity around St Ives and Newlyn, he did, however, have artist friends there – Chris and Ros Thomas – and pays generous tribute to the influence they had on him, 'particularly in teaching me how to enjoy paint'.[6]

Up to this point, it should be remembered that watercolour was Jackson's principal medium. An important part of his development over the next few years was to be his mastering of other media, notably acrylic and oil, and the broadening of his ideas on what could and could not be regarded as art. To begin with, most of what he exhibited was still in watercolour, which entailed certain extra freedoms as well as extra limitations. The limitations were mostly to do with scale: conventionally, watercolours were expected to be on a relatively small scale. But otherwise, with the unlikely example of Edward Burra (with his oil-like solidity of colour) before them, watercolourists might reasonably feel that aesthetically they were free to attempt whatever they wanted to. And the freedoms could be considerable.

Jackson's childhood habit of painting, very accurately, his finds from field and stream, and annotating them with quasi-scientific details, had at least accustomed him to combining image and text. Of course, the annotated biological or botanical drawing has a long history behind it, going back as far as Leonardo da Vinci, if not further. But this history stands a little aside from the tradition of fine art, and so, in the late twentieth century, the incorporation of texts in free-standing paintings was still pretty bold and unconventional. While Jackson's sketchbooks tended from the start to be annotated – since one function of sketchbooks is to act as *aides-memoires*, a scattering of words may prove a helpful supplement to the captured images – it is not quite clear when he began to incorporate inscriptions in his mainstream works as a deliberate stratagem. Certainly they occur in the paintings of the South Crofty Tin Mine he did early in 1995, but there the spectator cannot be completely certain whether they are the artist's invention or merely a record of inscriptions he saw below ground.

In any case, the tin mine paintings seem in various ways uncharacteristic. For one thing, they represent darkness, with the figures of the miners picked out in little pools of light, whereas normally (despite one or two astonishing paintings of sea and coast by moonlight) what we overwhelmingly associate with Jackson is dazzling colour, in blazing sunlight. Furthermore, we do not usually expect such a central emphasis on the human inhabitants of a Jackson scene, even though the dramatis personae for this little drama remain sketchy and distant.

If this is thought to suggest that Jackson is in some way anti-social, he would – in some sense – admit to it. He prefers, indeed positively needs, to work in isolation. However, the fact remains (and I think we would realise this even without any background knowledge of Jackson's motivation) that the miners and their predicament were of crucial importance in inspiring the tin mine series. Jackson was drawn to the subject by the suspicion that the South Crofty Tin Mine, the last operational mine in Cornwall, was fated soon to close – a suspicion which rapidly proved to be correct. Not that Jackson's art is ever narrowly political. He says himself that his attitude to the miners – like his attitude to the fishermen he has often painted following their calling, or worked alongside, recording the moods of the sea which constantly challenges them – is deeply ambiguous.

With both the miners and the fishermen he feels deep sympathy for their immemorial traditions of labour, and their sufferings when they are taken away from them by mine closure or fishing restrictions. At the same time, he knows that both callings intervene in the natural order of things, and that the ecological effects of this intervention are sometimes malign. Mining undoubtedly led to the complete deforestation of Cornwall, and the destructive effects of over-fishing on the sea itself as well as the fishermen who do it are plain for all to see. Which side to take, when one can see the virtues and drawbacks of both? Nature he loved, and next to Nature, Art... Or does Art finally come first?

Almost all of these works are still watercolours, or mixed media in which watercolour plays a dominant part. As early as 1987 we find also paintings in oils or combining oil paints with collage, generally on board or occasionally, evocatively, on driftwood. If watercolour was something Jackson learned at his father's knee, it seems that his early attempts at oil painting had something to do with the influence on him during the Boscastle years of Chris and Ros Thomas, who not only taught him by example how to enjoy paint, but encouraged him to greater boldness in his exploration of the media available to a painter.

He learned from the Thomases not to be afraid to take his time over painting, although it was built into his DNA (and no doubt a consequence of his primary experience as a watercolourist) that he rejoiced in being a fast worker, catching the fleeting impression as it fled. If slow-drying oils posed a problem, an answer was at hand with the rapid development of acrylics. When they first came on to the art supply market, artists appreciated their speed (when they did not mistrust it), but felt that they were lacking in variety and subtlety compared with oils. Rather rapidly these objections were overcome, and by the end of 1994 Jackson had begun to recognise the advantages of working in a medium that could be indistinguishable from oils yet applied with the speed and fluency of watercolour. In any case, he was turning increasingly to mixed media, which could mean all sorts of unpredictable combinations of such different media as lay to hand in the heat of creation – though seldom as radical as 'granite dust and bitumen on filter paper', which is the description attached to one of the paintings he did of Carnsew Granite Quarry, near Penryn, in January 1998.

Vital to the proper understanding of all this is the question of Jackson's style in watercolour. Despite the amount of precise biological and botanical illustration he produced in his teens, the earliest works we now know are impressionistic. Indeed, in many ways the execution is quite traditional, involving virtuoso use of

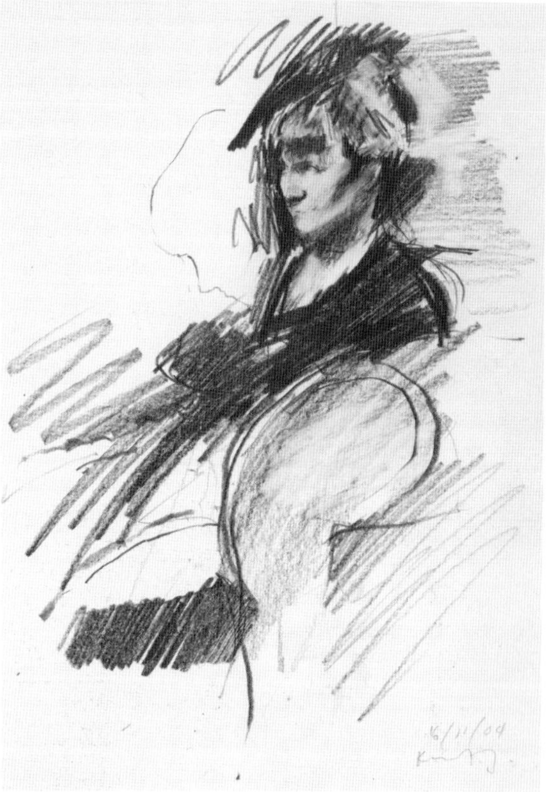

7
Caroline, 16/11/09
Pencil, 30 × 20 cm (12 × 8 in)

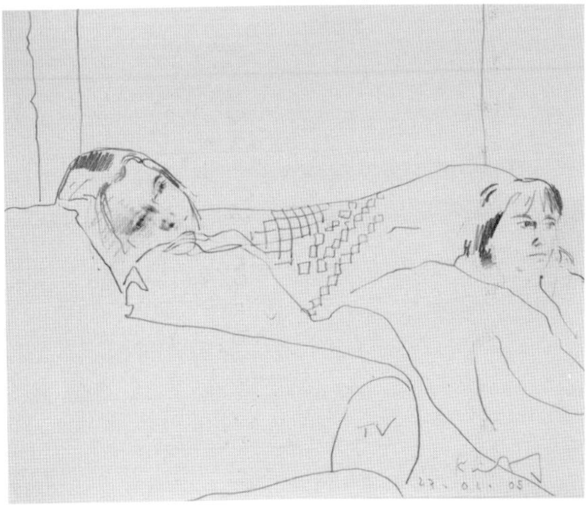

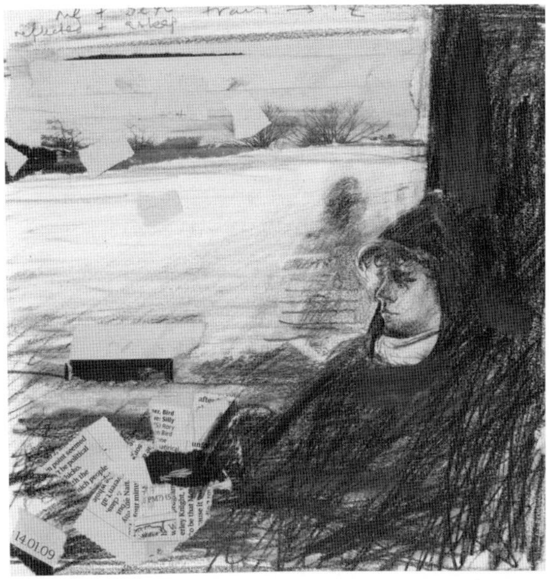

8 (top)
Chloe and Zinzi, 27/1/05
Pencil, 21 × 26 cm (8 × 10 in)

9
Seth asleep, my reflection, train, 2009
Pencil and collage, 25 × 25 cm (10 × 10 in)

watercolour washes, along with admittedly (and increasingly) more unusual elements, such as surface scratching and other pigments dribbled on to the painted surface. Jackson himself says on this aspect of his work: 'I see myself as part of the English landscape tradition but I want to go about it in a modern way – in the use of materials, for instance. Turner's watercolour sketches I adore. Lately I have been rediscovering Constable's sketches – incredibly avant-garde for their time.' At the same time (by 1999) he points to the influence of such contemporary or near-contemporary artists as Barbara Rae (*b.*1945), whose landscapes triggered his use of acrylic; Joan Eardley (1921–65), whose influence on him came not only from 'those fantastic seascapes', but also from her studies of Glasgow street children, and particularly her use in them of integral texts; and Robert Rauschenberg (1925–2008) with his bold mixing of materials – 'a genius at mixing media, I think'.[7]

Why should Jackson be interested in mixing media anyway? Primarily it must be his naturally questing spirit, which constantly asks 'What if?' But also he has a constant interest in a variety of artists and what goes right or what goes wrong for them. One of the recurrent problems he has noted is that of falling into a routine that can soon become tired and overworked. He thinks that this situation often arises when an artist develops a particular, distinctive technique, and achieves a personal success with it. As soon as a particular way of doing things becomes recognised as the hallmark of a given artist, there is the danger that he or she will come to feel trapped in it or, perhaps worse, not recognise the entrapment. Many of the personal problems experienced by Patrick Caulfield (1936–2005) arose from his evolving a very distinctive style and achieving great success with it while still at college. He was, in a sense, damned if he did and damned if he didn't: when he ventured to do something different, people said 'That doesn't look like a Caulfield', while if he stuck to his tried-and-true style, they said, 'Same old stuff!'

Jackson senses the need to avoid this trap. And one way to do so, for him, is to experiment with, or at least remain constantly open to the possibilities of, the actual media he works in. Possibly he feels that getting into a rut is a danger for him (given his ever-burgeoning inventiveness, few others would be likely to think so) because he likes to paint in series, and even paint precisely the same subject, over and over again. In an extreme form, this would surely apply to a lengthy series he painted in one day (18 June) in 1997. He had become amused and intrigued by his observation that all the souvenir shops in Cornwall seemed to have the same small selection of postcards on sale. Acting on this observation, he bought some fifty of the same postcard, showing 'the Crowns' (the largest surviving buildings of Botallack Mine) on Botallack Cliff, viewed from the opposite cliff – which happened to be the nearest to where he then lived. Armed with these and a range of acrylic paints he set himself to painting over the card image precisely what he saw, in terms of light and colour, every half hour of the day.

The idea of making these basically uniform, though in practice very diverse, pictures could well look like some kind of a rut, if a very limited one. But Jackson makes no bones about his delight in returning again and again to the same subjects, on and around his home territory. His point is that it never is the same subject: every moment of every day presents the same basics in a different light. But another safeguard against self-replication is the attitude Jackson sees in Rauschenberg: 'He finds a way of making paintings and then produces a series of works by that method: then somehow he invents a whole new way of working and starts afresh.'[8] No one is likely to query Jackson's enterprise in this field. Even his collection of postcard paintings was in its way an experiment, and was certainly a new approach to landscape painting in Jackson's career up to then, something he had never done before – and very probably would never do again. But the constant potential for change remains. And the changes that occur are a comforting mixture of the deliberate, the accidental and the unavoidable.

Probably the last class is the most important. In 1999 Jackson himself observes, with an air of slight surprise:

> When I looked for early examples of my work ... I was struck by how different the work looked then. I think the paintings have become more complex. There's far more diversity in the way I use the paint, in the way I make marks. there's more mixed media now. At one time I tended to use watercolour in a traditional way – I'd think 'Don't use white, don't use black'. But then I thought 'Who makes these rules?' and now I use as many different types of white and black and dark grey in as many different combinations as I need.[9]

This readiness, largely unconscious, to try new things and go in new directions is still a mark of Jackson's talent. Apart from his experiments with different media and different combinations of media, he has taken to making more radical changes and additions to his repertoire of techniques. One of these is his extensive development in his use of words as an integral part of his paintings. Another is his very striking use of large and significant objects applied to the surface of his larger and more ambitious paintings. The use of words has gradually evolved from incidental annotations on informal watercolours to elaborate inscriptions that are clearly meant to be read and taken into account by the spectator, as well as being of necessity a vital part of the composition. These are sometimes written in Jackson's usual handwriting (as opposed to stencils, rubbings and so on), implying, perhaps, some very personal significance to what is written. The words frequently embody the momentary observations of the painter while he paints. In the mid-1990s they seemed to get longer and longer, as a final mark applied to a painting after it had been in all other respects completed.

There is, too, another class of addition. It occurred to Jackson in around 2000 that it would be interesting to take rubbings of road and path signs he encountered as part of the local Cornish landscape. He also saw how these could form a natural-seeming part of his landscape paintings – or how they could point to how disruptive this sort of signing could be: 'By taking a painting of, say, the open sea and collaging in a rubbing of a sign saying "No Parking" in the foreground, I hope that it might produce in the viewer some sense of how inappropriate and intrusive it seems to me.'[10] On the other hand, some of the inscriptions invite us to enter further into the soul of Cornwall, by plugging us into the notionally extinct but nowadays much studied and revived Celtic language of Cornwall, as in Jackson's 2004 sequence of large paintings under the general (Cornish) title 'Porth'.

As to the physical adhesions, such applications began in a small way by the addition of sand and small pebbles to some of the early seaside pieces. As well as the colour and composition, Jackson has always been fascinated by the texture of paintings, and these were carrying such a fascination one stage further, beyond the imaginative evocation of natural textures and into literal re-creation. But by the time of 'Porth' Jackson had moved forward from such fringe activities to the incorporation of a whole fish net or a complete, albeit paint-covered, fisherman's waterproof. Similarly, the German painter Anselm Kiefer included bales of hay in his work, indicating that this sort of technique was very much in the air around the turn of the twenty-first century. An aware artist as Jackson could hardly have remained immune from such influences.

Jackson has, when pressed, described the pattern of a normal day's work. He emerges as a modern equivalent of the kind of Victorian novelist who assigned themselves a set timetable for writing each day. (Famously, Trollope once completed a novel halfway to Birmingham on a train, and had initiated another before he arrived.) Jackson blames or credits the Quaker work ethic inherited from

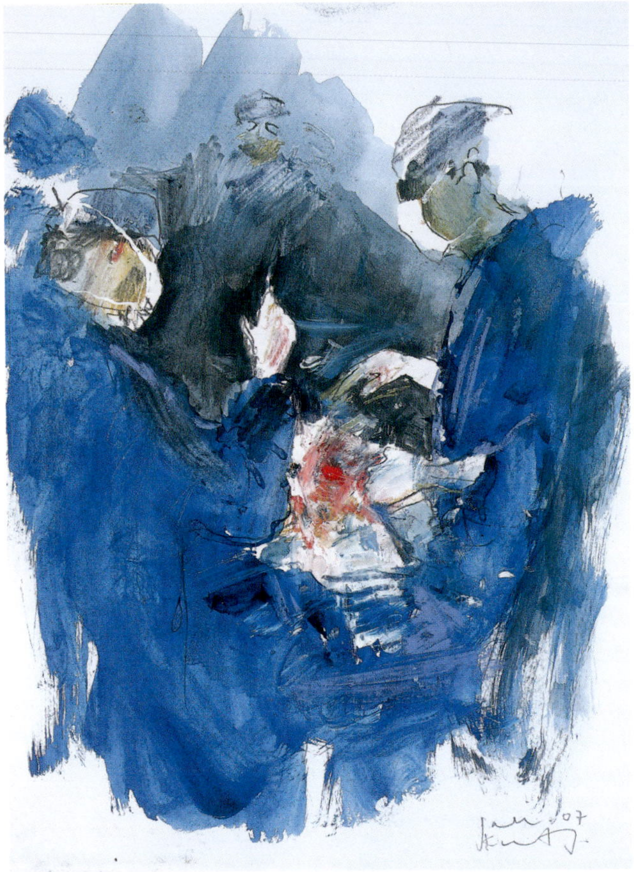

10
Scalpel, January 2007
Mixed media,
42 × 29.5 cm
(16.5 × 11.5 in)

his father for his compulsion to paint every weekday from dawn to nightfall. The weekends are in principle reserved for his family, though sometimes he admits they do not withstand the blandishments of a compelling subject.

While Jackson's drawings and watercolours are always made *en plein air*, his larger works are often, but not always, created in the traditional manner – working in a studio from sketches made on the spot. On many of his walks he has actually made a study every few yards as he has progressed. All this is vital background to one of the most important, possibly crucial, series in Jackson's painting career to date, that of 'Porth', memorably shown at Newlyn Art Gallery early in 2004. Although Jackson was no stranger to the use of lettering of some sort in paintings, this group demonstrated the first consistent use of it through a whole coherent series. In these works he also went one stage further by attaching large and significant objects – such as paint tins, natural found objects, clothing and footwear – to the painted surface and incorporating it into the painting. 'Porth' is the Cornish word for a cove or bay, and the whole series arose from Jackson's experience of a specific cove, very close to where he lives in St Just. This is called on Ordnance Survey maps 'Priest's Cove' but, as Jackson points out, it should actually be 'Priest Cove'. It has nothing to do with priests in any shape or form, being what language experts call an onomastic fantasy – wording that evolves out of an aural misunderstanding. The name has in fact, as indicated in an inscription running right across one of the Porth cycle of paintings, evolved from the Cornish words identifying the place as St Just's 'porth', so the current name is really tautological.

Be that as it may, the effect of the one location, with its outlying islets, is quite palpable in the giant mixed-media canvases that make up the series. They all start with Jackson looking out to sea (from what is very nearly the most westerly point of Britain), and taking in, on a factual level, the water and the light playing on it, the distant horizon *chimérique*, the movement of the waves breaking on the shore, and the shapes and textures of the shore upon which they break. But that is only stage one. From there the physical scene is deconstructed and put together again in the artist's mind, and on to canvas in the studio. The process is not so peculiar when you remember that the Chinese way of painting a landscape is for the artist to take it in at leisure, then turn their back on it to paint its essence from their own inner eye. Similarly, in Jackson's practice the scene is reduced to its essentials in the artist's memory and imagination, then re-created in painting form – and sometimes built up even further by inscriptions and adhesions. Jackson has an acute eye, a focused intellect (he did not train as a

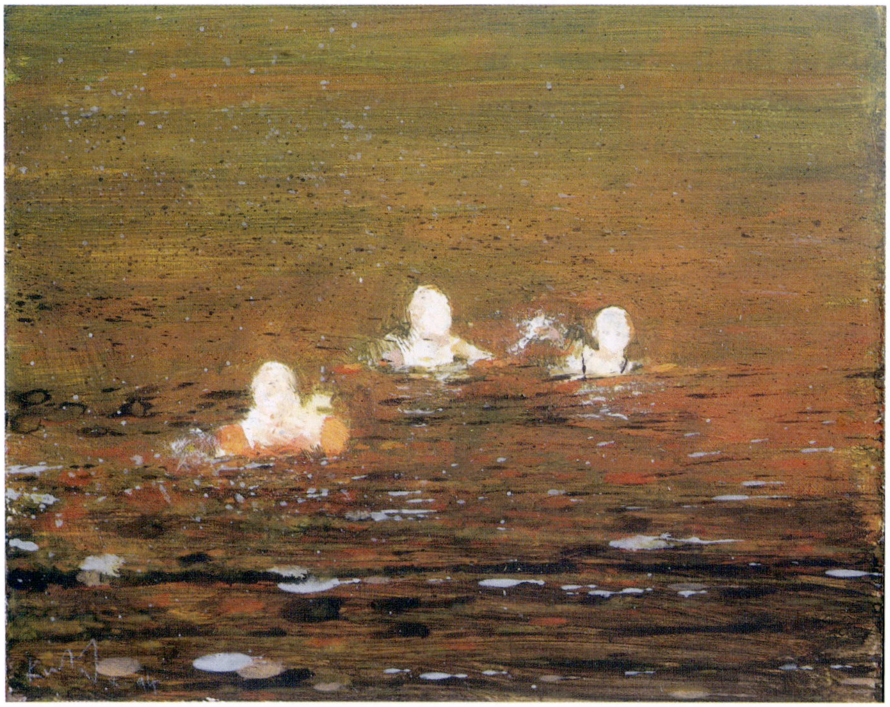

11
L'Etang, 1994
Acrylic on board, 14 × 18 cm (5.5 × 7 in)

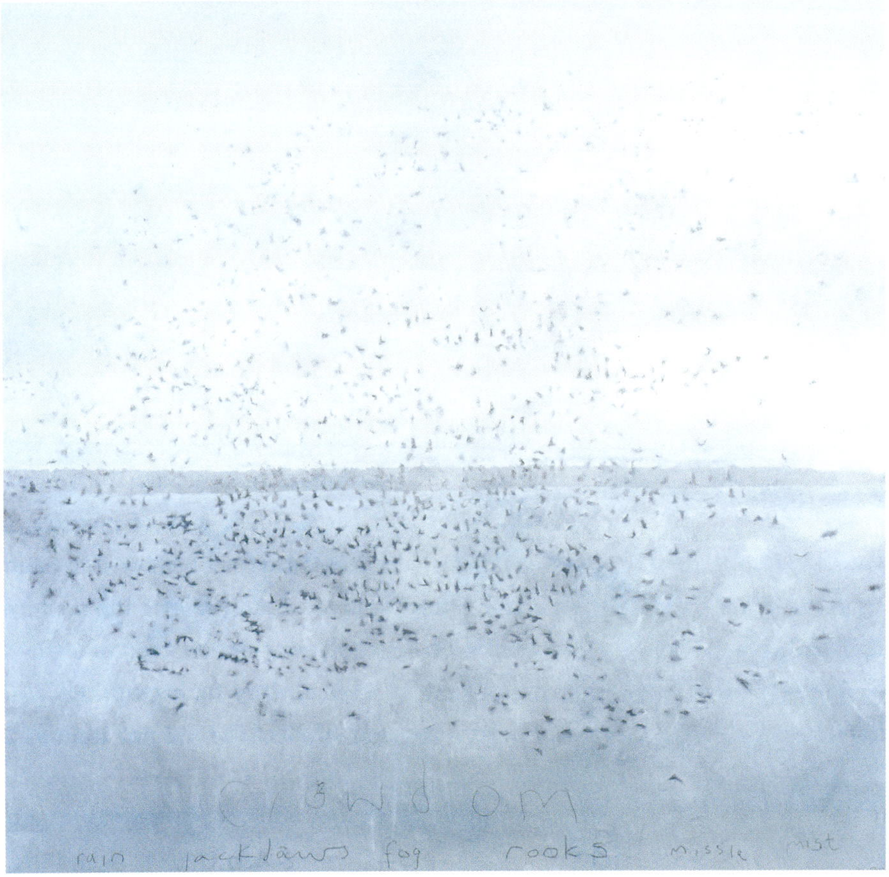

12
Crowdom – rain, jackdaws, fog, rooks, missle, 2007
Oil on canvas, 152.5 × 152.5 cm
(60 × 60 in)

scientist for nothing), and an intense, instinctive bond with the land and sea around him.

This bonding may seem to be peculiarly intense when it takes place on what has come to be in effect his native soil, but he still has much of the traveller about him. Though he may be ideally happy at home, that does not preclude an occasional desire to open himself to other scenes, other atmospheres. These always have some significance to him beyond the immediate, visual charms. Jackson has recently been returning to regular painting grounds in Europe (France, Spain and Greece). To casual acquaintance these exotic landscapes, with their rich earth-browns and amazing bursts of warm and pale colour, have found their ideal evoker and interpreter, but naturally there is a lot more to it than that. The areas lovingly revisited are those where Jackson would regularly go with his painter parents when he was a child, and he has always been fascinated by the stories beyond the vision: the still untamed rivers of France, so unlike our own dawdling, domesticated streams, and the olive groves which signify to Jackson a hard peasant economy that has long disappeared from England.

These tough and dynamic paintings seem at first sight to show a different side of Jackson's artistic nature, plugging him into a very different place in art history – one closer to an Abstract Expressionist violence of expression than to the contemplative calm of much of his Cornish work. As Harold Monro puts it in one of his poems, 'Summer is raging through the frantic country'. But ultimately the forces behind the art are the same: concern (human and ecological) coupled with a preoccupation with local myth and tradition, beyond and supporting all the specifically aesthetic criteria that matter to all artists. Heart and mind and, dare one say, soul are here and elsewhere, inextricably fused in Jackson's art. We are all the beneficiaries.

That much is plain. But it still leaves some mysteries to be illuminated. We know what Jackson does, but it is still unclear how he does it and why he does it that way. As to the 'why', we have Jackson's own self-definition:

> I see myself as primarily a contemporary plein air painter – part of a long tradition, but hopefully trying to find new approaches and maybe pushing at the boundaries and interpretation. For me producing a painting involves three main factors. Firstly, the experience of being in situ (the environment, nature, my involvement in my surroundings); secondly, the mark-making, the surface, the painterliness of the painting; and finally the picture of the painting – the part that illustrates what is in front of me/around me. These are all equally important and therefore a small quick spontaneous sketch can be as valid as a large piece which has had many months invested in it. The figure usually appears in my work only as a means of showing scale or to give a feeling of emptiness within the landscape. Exceptions to this occur when portraying my own family or with some of the recent projects of people working/living in the landscape. I am not sure about how I make decisions on the use of media, which is probably why I enjoy using mixed media frequently.[11]

Some of the processes are self-evident. Many of the smaller works are initiated and completed face to face with their subjects, completely in accordance with classic Impressionist theory. But even Monet did not do exactly what he said he did: many of his major works might well have been initiated on the spot, but more often what began *en plein air* would then lie around in his studio for months or even years, being taken up again from time to time and worked on until he was totally satisfied. (This was especially true with his series, such as the paintings of Rouen Cathedral or of grain-stacks, or of the Thames viewed from the Savoy Hotel, because he wanted them to hang together as a series, with the right degree of correspondence and dissonance among them.)

With Jackson it is often the same: he works his large paintings over and finalises them in his St Just studio. But by no means does this apply to all. Sometimes the evidence is on the canvas itself: the inscription is a sort of diary entry evoking the process as it is engaged in. For example, *Dry white limestone River Calavon* (2003) has various inscriptions, among them this:

> breeze through shimmering poplar leaves
>   (sequins)
> insects land to drink from the canvas
> one cicada singing lazily
> and the shadows move in the heat

It is clearly a description of where he is painting while he is actually painting there.

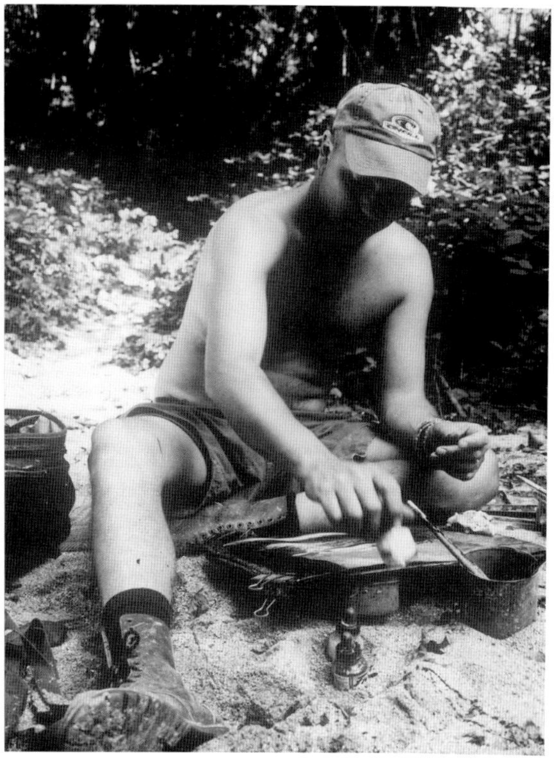

13
In the Pyrenees, 2000

At his 2009 London show, numerically so large that it required two Cork Street galleries to contain it, there was shown a fascinating film of Jackson working in the course of one day in a tree-lined meadow somewhere in France. The excitement of this lay not only in the insight it offered into the way he paints, or at least must sometimes paint, but the fact that one could turn immediately from the video screen to the painting itself. What immediately strikes one, given the evident control of the finished work, is the sheer pace of creation in the film: as Jackson attacked (I use the term advisedly) the large square of linen staked out on the grass before him, I for one kept thinking of the famous film of Jackson Pollock 'action painting' in his studio, darting and whirling as paint scatters around him. Except that Pollock was producing an abstract, following its own rules as it evolved beneath his feet, while Jackson was representing something – the forest vegetation just the other side of the sunlit meadow. And, one would gather, doing it all in one day's sunlight, entirely on the spot.

The whole show was provocatively entitled 'Forest Gardens', an apparent contradiction in terms but totally appropriate in terms of Jackson and his personal attitude to Nature and Art, and the proper relation between the two. Not only as an academic zoologist, but as a practical ecologist and frequent, if usually incidental, worker in the orchards of Cornwall, the chestnut forests of France and the almond groves of Spain, he had a special psychological entrée to the forest scene. In particular, he was perfectly placed to see the forests not only as the sort of wild place they are generally perceived to be by the layman, but as a unique collaboration between nature and humankind.

This view was vividly present in the works exhibited in London at Messum's early in 2009 and painted in the previous two years. 'Nature', in Cornwall certainly and in most of France and Spain (obviously in some places, obscurely in others), is inevitably shaped by man. Jackson, though a committed conservationist, is unusually clear about what he wants to conserve. It is not a question of removing every trace of man from nature, which would be impossible anyway. Jackson recognises that what is to be sought is balance, a recognition of the interdependence between the various factions in play. This sounds – and is – highly rational, but it does not in any way impede the ecstatic side of Jackson's pantheistic vision.

'Nature he loved, and next to Nature, Art?' In Jackson's work the two are inseparably fused, held in a magical balance which takes the breath away. Jackson is an inspired artist but also, and perhaps just as importantly to him, the best possible representative of the ideals that underlie what the world is trying to do to preserve itself in this new Age of Anxiety.

Notes

1. Brooke, Brian and Taylor, John Russell, *The Art Dealers*, Hodder & Stoughton, 1969, p.139.
2. Mallett, Francis, *Kurt Jackson: Paintings of Cornwall and the Scillies,* White Lane Press, Plymouth, 1999, p.10.
3. Maybey, Richard, *Forest Gardens,* Messums, London, 2009, p.8.
4. Mallett, Francis, *Kurt Jackson: Paintings of Cornwall and the Scillies,* White Lane Press, Plymouth, 1999, p.5.
5. Ibid, p.5.
6. Ibid, p.17.
7. Ibid, p.22.
8. Ibid, p.22.
9. Ibid, p.22.
10. Ibid, p.28.
11. *Kurt Jackson: New Paintings,* Messums, London, 2000, introduction.

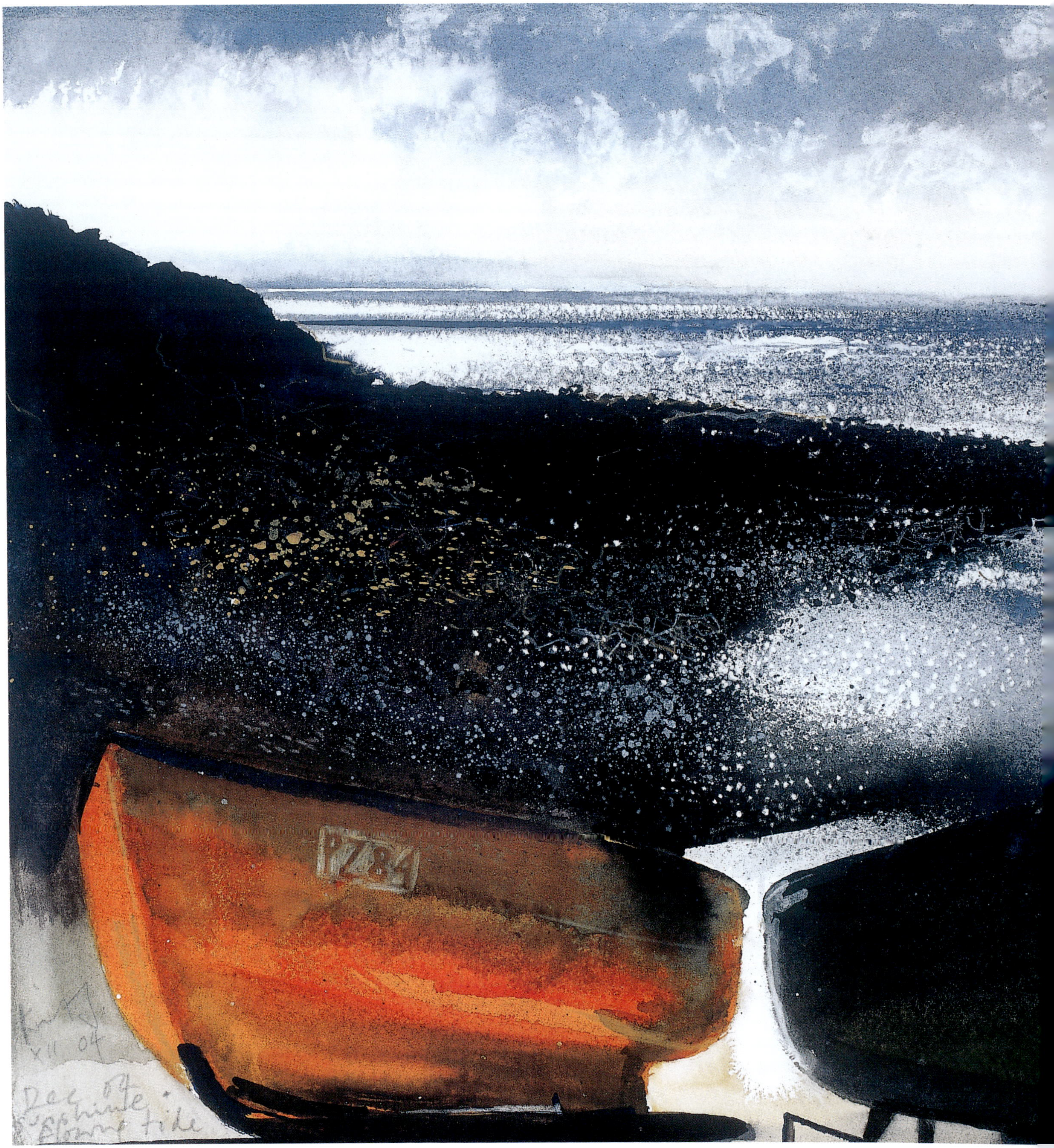
PZ84
XII 04

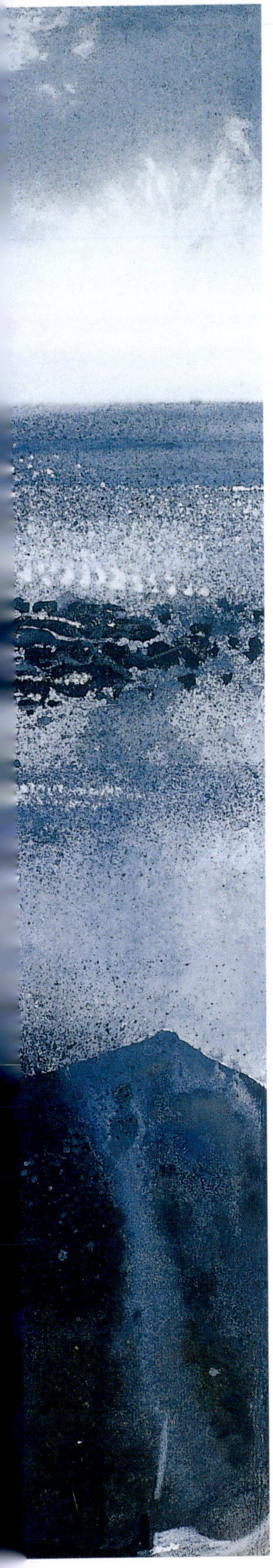

14
Sunshine and flowing tide, December 2004
Mixed media, 29 × 31 cm
(11.5 × 12 in)

1 The Beauty
Howard Jacobson

'The one thing I am not embarrassed by is beauty', the artist Kurt Jackson tells me as we slither up the wet slate out of which Boscastle harbour seems to have hewn itself. Which is just as well. Boscastle, to my eye, is as beautiful as a place gets if you like your beauty harsh. 'Chasmal' was Thomas Hardy's word in the poem 'Beeny Cliff'. 'What if still in chasmal beauty looms that wild weird western shore', he wrote, not as a question but rather as an expression of human futility, when he returned to Boscastle in anguished old age, devoured by regret.

Boscastle is not an easy place in which to live, but it calls back everyone who leaves. Remote, greyer than the Atlantic Ocean against which it is braced, the water drip-dripping from its rocks, as though it is slowly giving back the flood that overwhelmed it two summers ago (although, in truth, it has been dripping here forever), Boscastle makes a mockery of time.

Jackson and I both lived here in the 1980s, and we have come back to meet each other for a day, to talk about his work, but just as much to talk about old times. In fact, we did not know each other well despite the fact we were immediate neighbours. He lived in a little rented cottage on one side of the road, at the point where the village street gives out into the harbour, whereas I assisted in the running of a craft shop and tearooms in the Old Mill opposite. He, young, barely out of Oxford, where he had met his wife Caroline, was teaching himself to be a painter; I, the better part of a generation older, was publishing my first novel.

We ran the risk, both of us, of parochialism: the local painter and the local writer. Occasionally, in the summer months, you would see one of his landscapes leaning against his cottage wall, with a price sticker on it, and you would hear the visitors discussing whether it was a good likeness of the Valency Valley or not, and whether it was worth what he was asking. Meanwhile, my novels were for sale in my shop, alongside the guidebooks and the picture postcards and the pressed-flower cards. We provided a touch of local colour for the tourists.

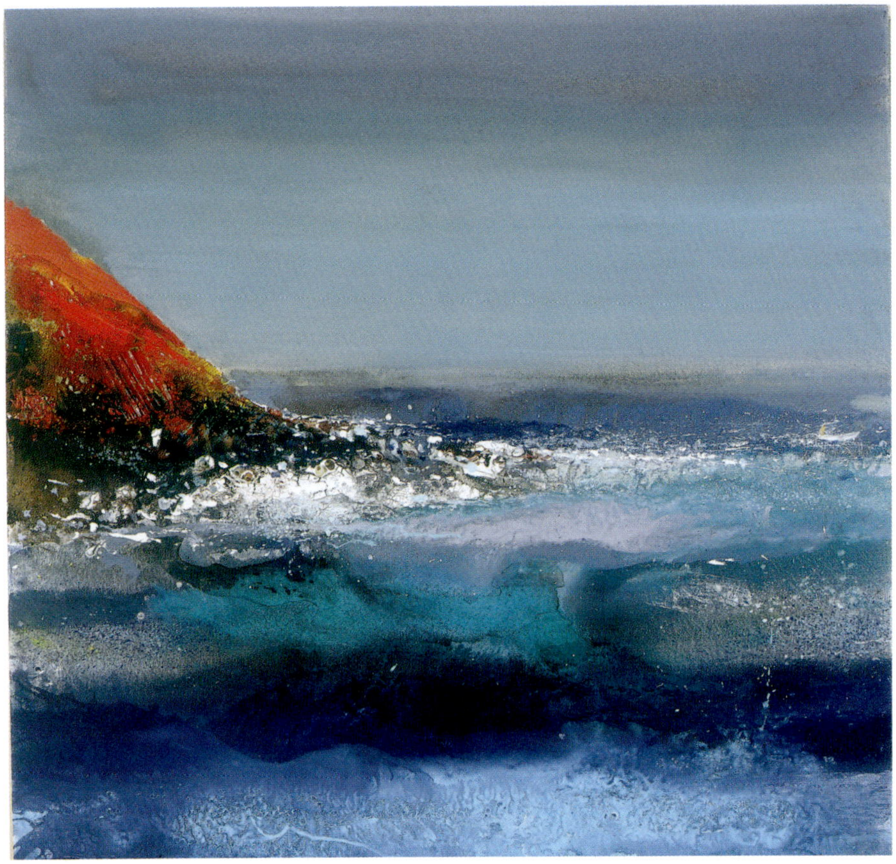

15
Store pot, 2005
Mixed media on canvas,
122 × 122 cm (48 × 48 in)

16
Botallack Cliff, 1998

Perhaps, I exaggerate the dangers of my work being swallowed up by the place. When I wrote about Boscastle, it was as an alien – someone who did not own the right clothes to walk to the cliffs, who could not work out why he was here and who knew he would soon be gone. However, Jackson was a West Country man, born, absorbed into the area, living in energetic harmony not only with the vegetarians and eco-warriors attracted to North Cornwall, but with the hedges and the herringbone walls, the valleys in which you could lose yourself and the icy little rivers that would one day become a flood. I observed the beauty; he was claimed by it. For a contemporary painter at least, there is this catch with beauty when you find it in a particular location and seek to re-create it: you are out of step with the prevalent aesthetic temper. The taboo on beauty long predates our age but has found renewed vigour in the embarrassed jokiness of Turner Prize Conceptualism, whereby you can deface or allude satirically to beauty, but must not be seen to be in collusion with it.

17
Treligga herringbone, 2005
Mixed media and collage on canvas,
47 × 84 cm (18.5 × 33 in)

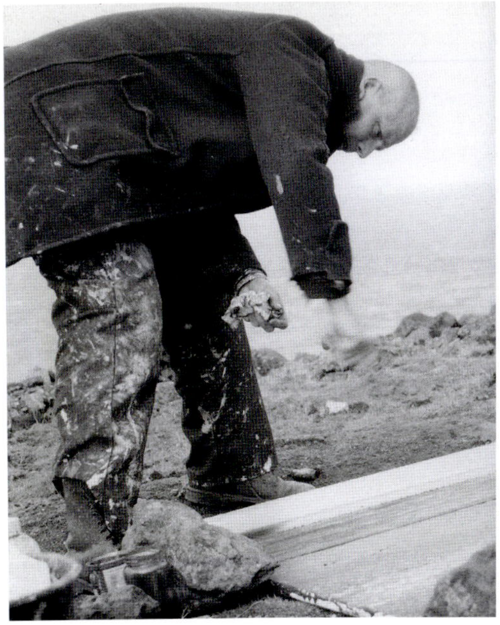

None of which seems to bother Jackson. Beauty is at the heart of his enterprise, that is the end of the matter. You can take it or leave it. Not the ivory tower, refined making of aloofly lovely things, but the engagement in a natural world whose beauty – the preservation of whose beauty – defines for him what being an artist is about. Yes, he accepts that had he stayed in Boscastle, the tag of being a local painter might have stuck to him (one of the village's paradoxes being that it is simultaneously austere and chocolate-boxy), but he now lives and works to the west of Cornwall, which has long attracted international artists at the cutting-edge of modernism. And should he ever be conscious, working there, of being on the margins, he will tell you that the margins are where life is.

The irony is that, in his processes, he could not be more tuned in to contemporary practice. When Simon Starling won the Turner Prize at Tate Britain in 2005, it was for the causes he espoused and the pilgrimages he made, for his 'thought processes' in the matter of ecology, commercial exploitation of natural resources, energy consumption, and so on, rather than for anything he produced.

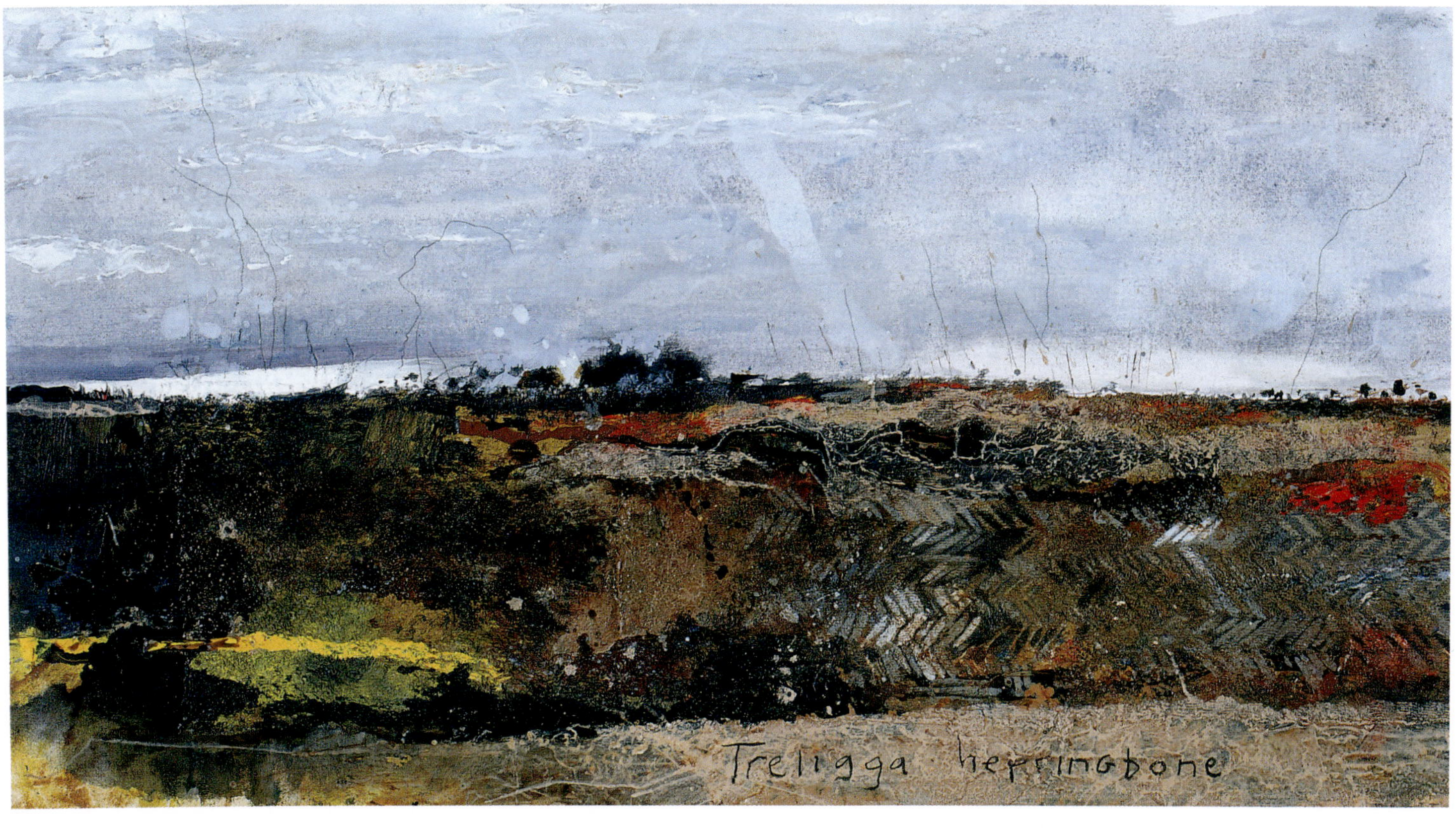

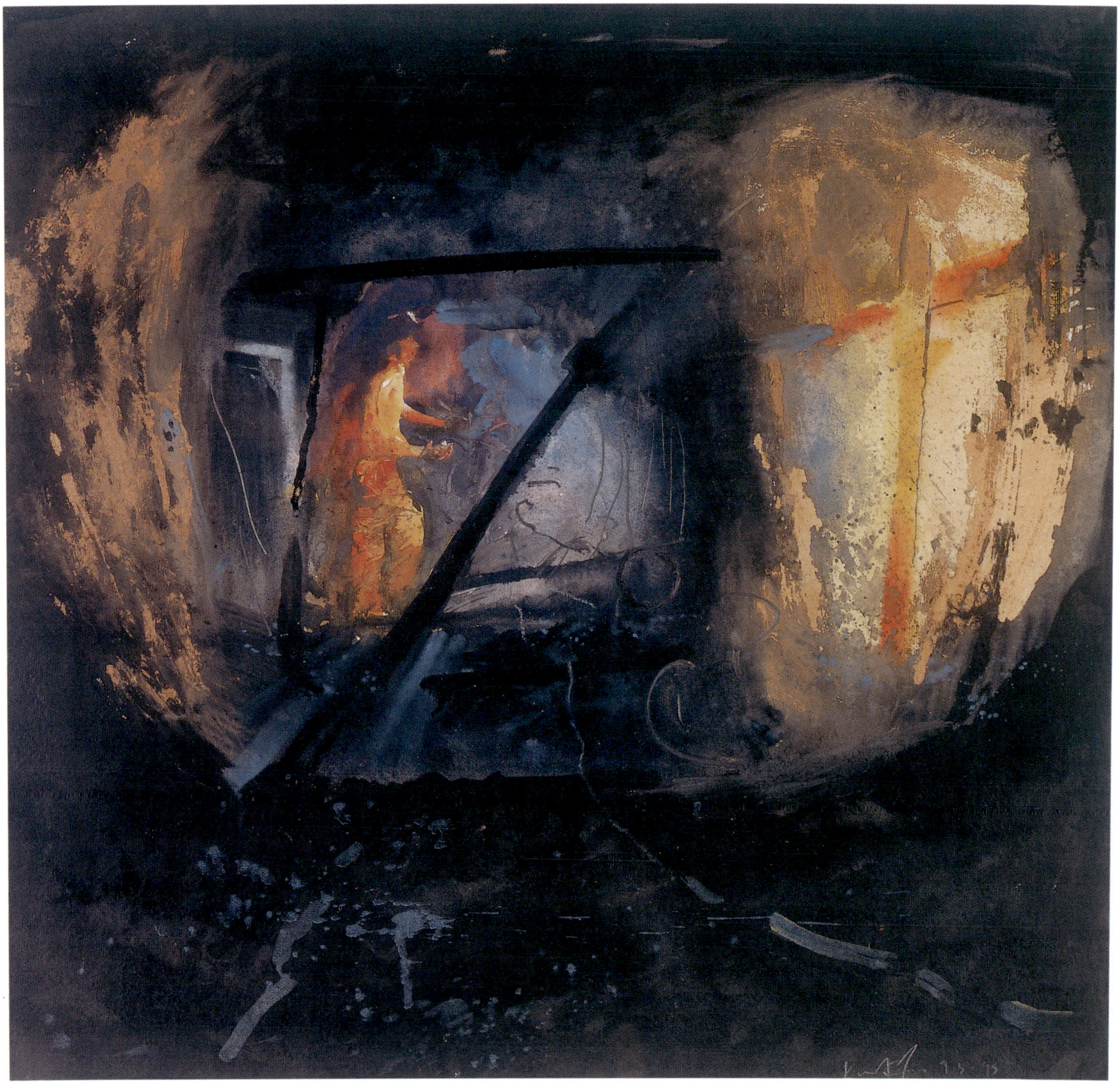

18
Jeff Tonkin operating the drill rig, Dolcoath South, South Crofty, 1995
Mixed media, 56.5 × 57.5 cm (22 × 22.5 in)

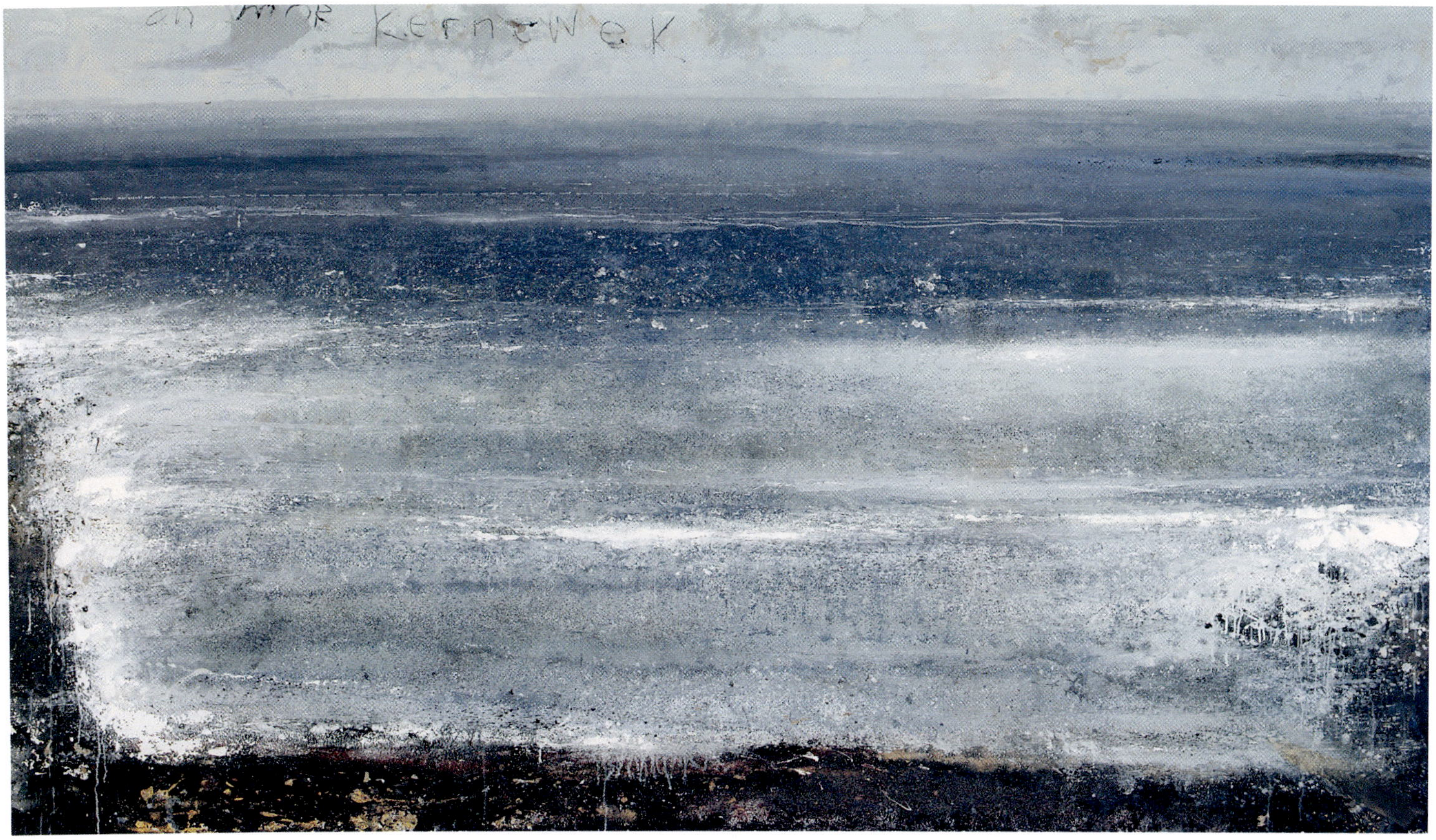

19
An Mor Kernewek, 2003
Mixed media on canvas,
199.5 × 325 cm (78.5 × 128 in)

Journeys and strategies are not a whit less central to Jackson's artistic practice. In the act of making one of his paintings, he is part activist, part environmentalist, part explorer, part travel writer: he cites Bruce Chatwin and Patrick Leigh Fermor as influences who are as important to him as other painters. Watching him paint, or sculpt, or make collages, you might take him to be a builder or a farm labourer, so physically does he absorb himself in his work. There is no separation in him, between the man who goes to sea with Greenpeace or descends into a tin mine, and the man who creates art. The one thing that disqualifies him from receiving fashionable Hoxton Square attention is that there is work to show for these processes afterwards. Just when he seems to be doing everything right as a Conceptual artist, he goes and spoils it by making a painting.

His parents were, and still are, abstract painters. He grew up with paintings all around him. The punky look that he cultivates, shaven-headed and multi-pierced, may well be a rejection of his middle-class Quaker associations. I picture him as a

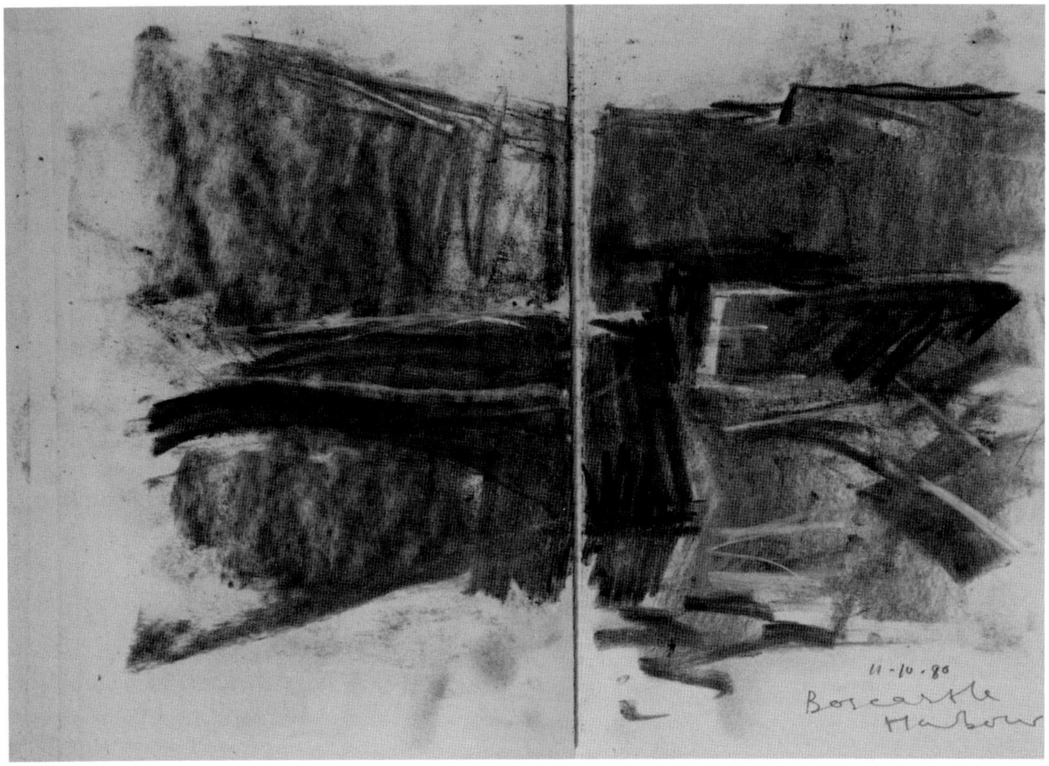

20
Boscastle Harbour*, *11/10/86
Charcoal, sketchbook size,
21.5 × 29.5 cm (8.5 × 11.5 in)

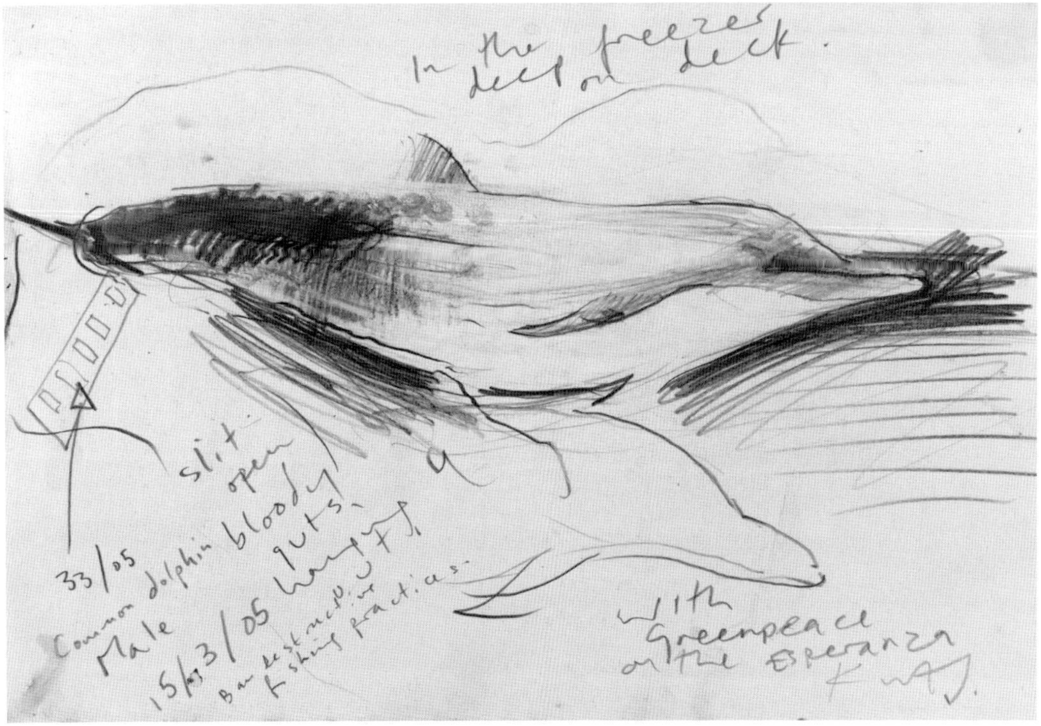

21
Dead dolphin found by Greenpeace*, *15/3/05
Pencil, 29 × 42 cm (11.5 × 16.5 in)

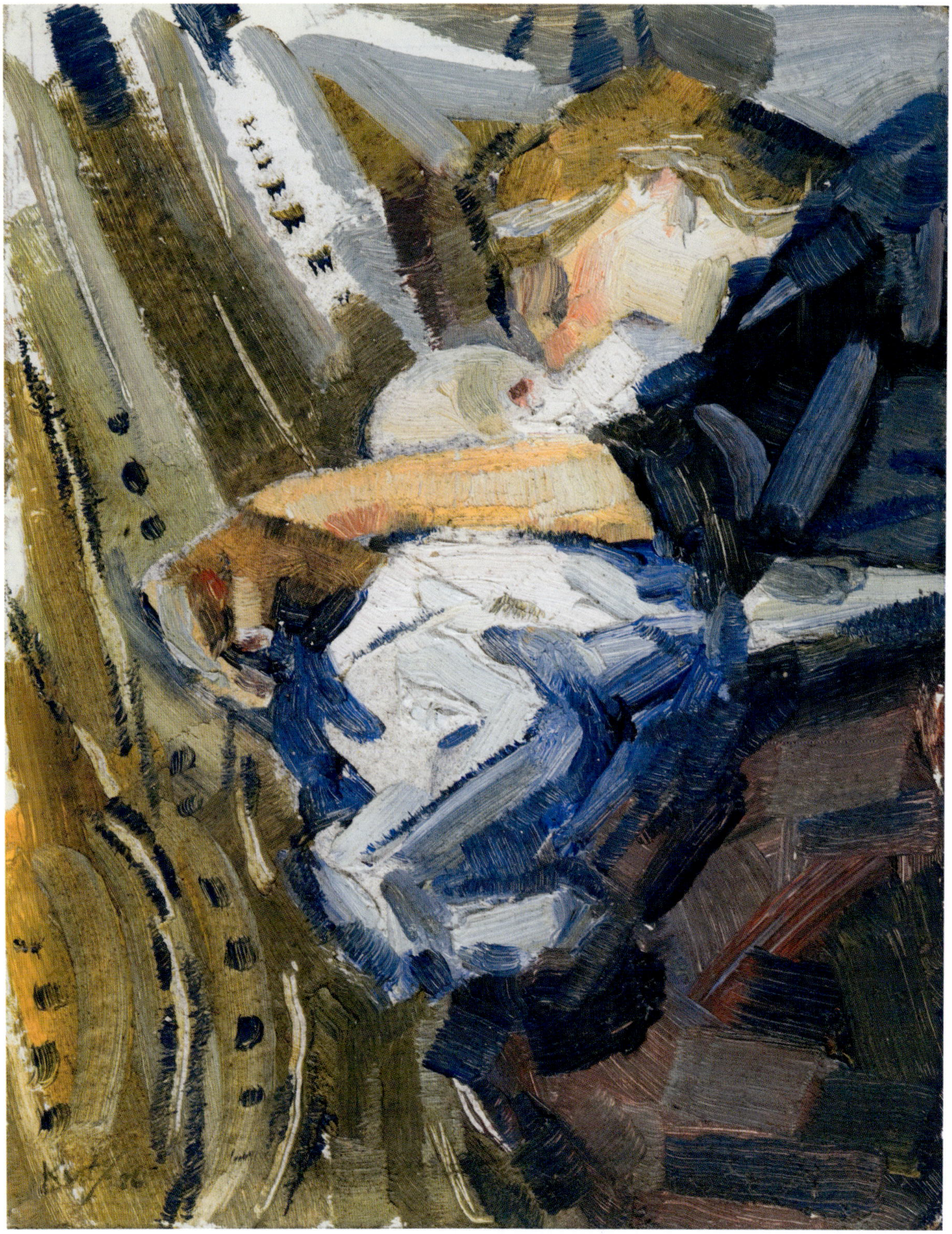

22
Caroline and Seth asleep, 1986
Oil on board, 20.5 × 16 cm
(8 × 6.5 in)

small boy roaming the country lanes of Dorset with his parents, learning the names of flowers. However, he tells me that his passion for natural history was self-induced: 'I came home from school, got into rough clothes and went looking in hedgerows, turning over stones, looking at birds.' I do not tell him that when I came home from school, I could not wait to get into a suit and go turning over the city, looking for birds in coffee bars. He knows. He catches me eyeing his spattered boots, the ink and paint and layers of earth that cake his fingernails, and laughs. The amazing thing to me is that out of his weather-beaten artisanal bulk should come work of such exquisite sensuousness. Perhaps the amazing thing to him is that I, in my unquiet urban cynicism, should like it as much as I do.

What I like in particular is the sense, in his paintings, that the view is never closed. You take a path, you discover the sea, you stumble on a fishing boat, but you never feel that your walk has, or ever will be, finished. There is always more to see: a dot on the horizon, further density of grass to penetrate, yet more saturation of light to yield to. It is as though he frees you from the tyranny of his vision of nature at the very moment that you choose to give yourself to it completely.

Flux is everything for Jackson, so he paints the same river again and again on different visits, explores the dangerous enticement of woods that are not today what they were yesterday, and scrawls diary-like entries on many of his works – 'Low tide, Priest Cove, hot and breezy', or 'Don't the cicadas ever want to be quiet?' – which establish that what we see is true only of that moment and will be different when we look again. There is no arrival point. Even when you reach the water's edge, you feel that your journey is only beginning. Everything flows and changes. Beauty, yes, but not beauty caught in an illusory eternity. Or form cheated of function. Precisely because they commemorate where men live, work, fish, mine, feed cattle, empty their boats, find and take their satisfactions, his landscapes are lovely and political all at once, gorgeous without being in the slightest degree softened or idealised. The only time he expresses anger in my presence is when we get on to the subject of the National Trust, which runs Cornwall like a fiefdom. 'They try to turn everything into a park', he says. After the floods, he returned to paint the Valency Valley and rejoiced in how much it had changed. Particularly, he loved the destruction of the Trust's dinky heritage signposts. 'It was as if Nature was saying, "F**k you!"'

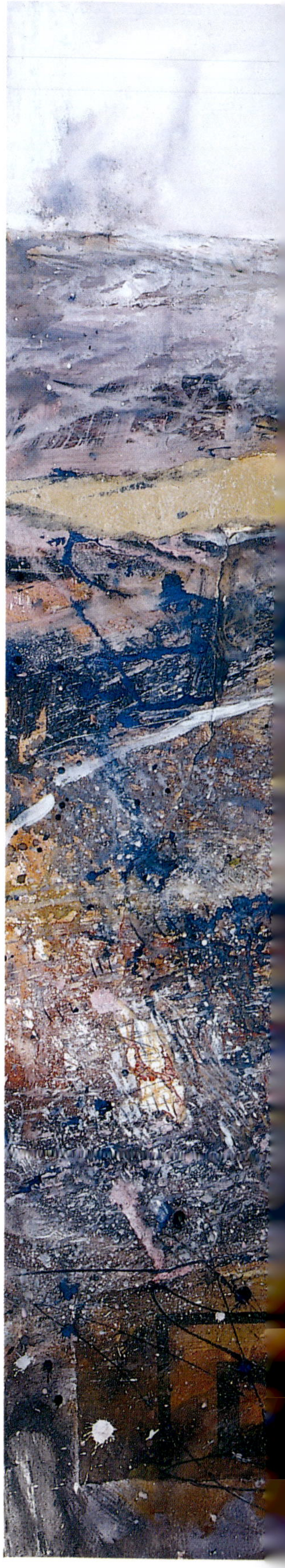

23
Windy dusk, October 2000
Mixed media and collage,
86 × 93 cm (34 × 37 in)

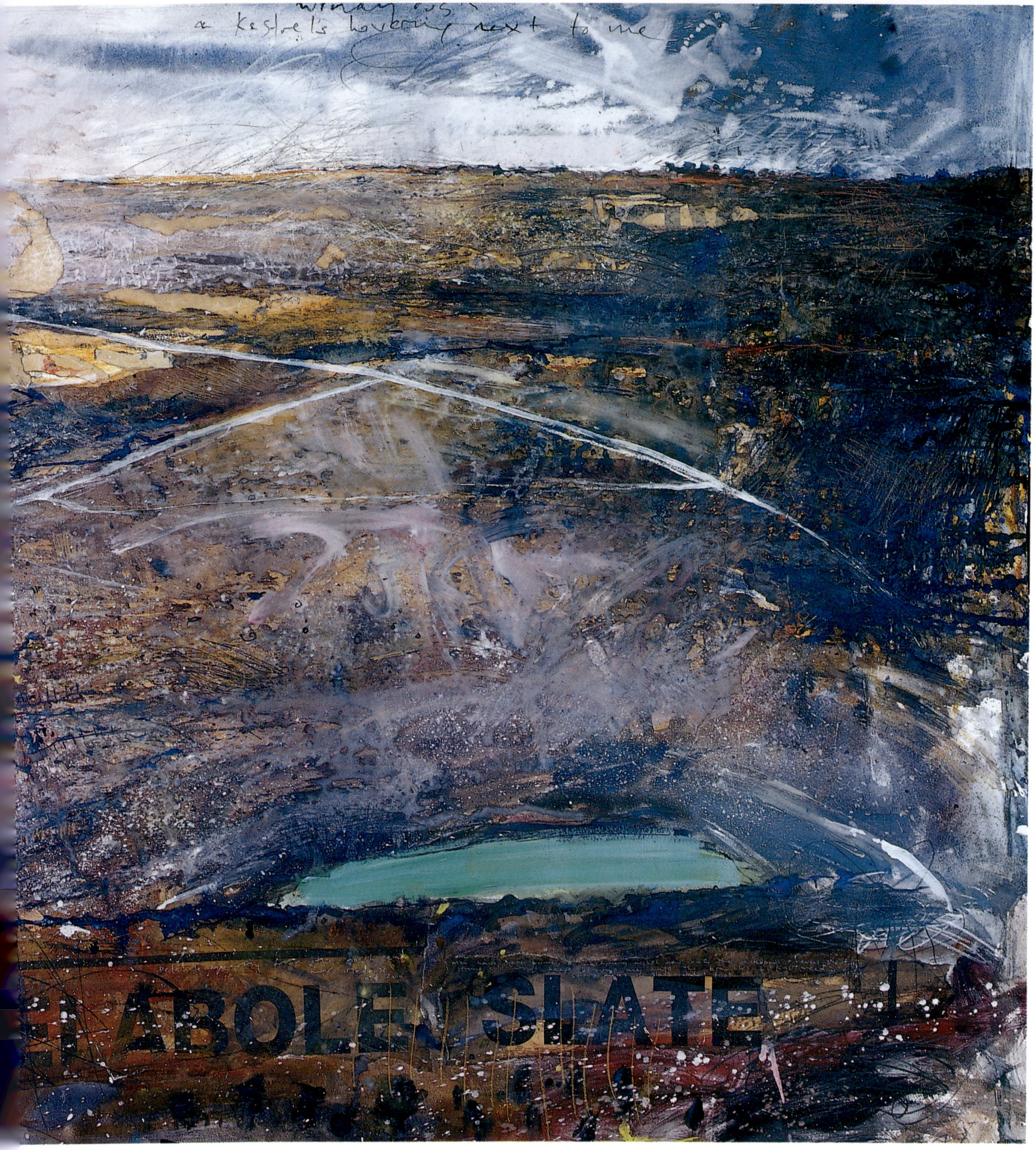
a kestrel's hovering next to me
ABOLE SLATE

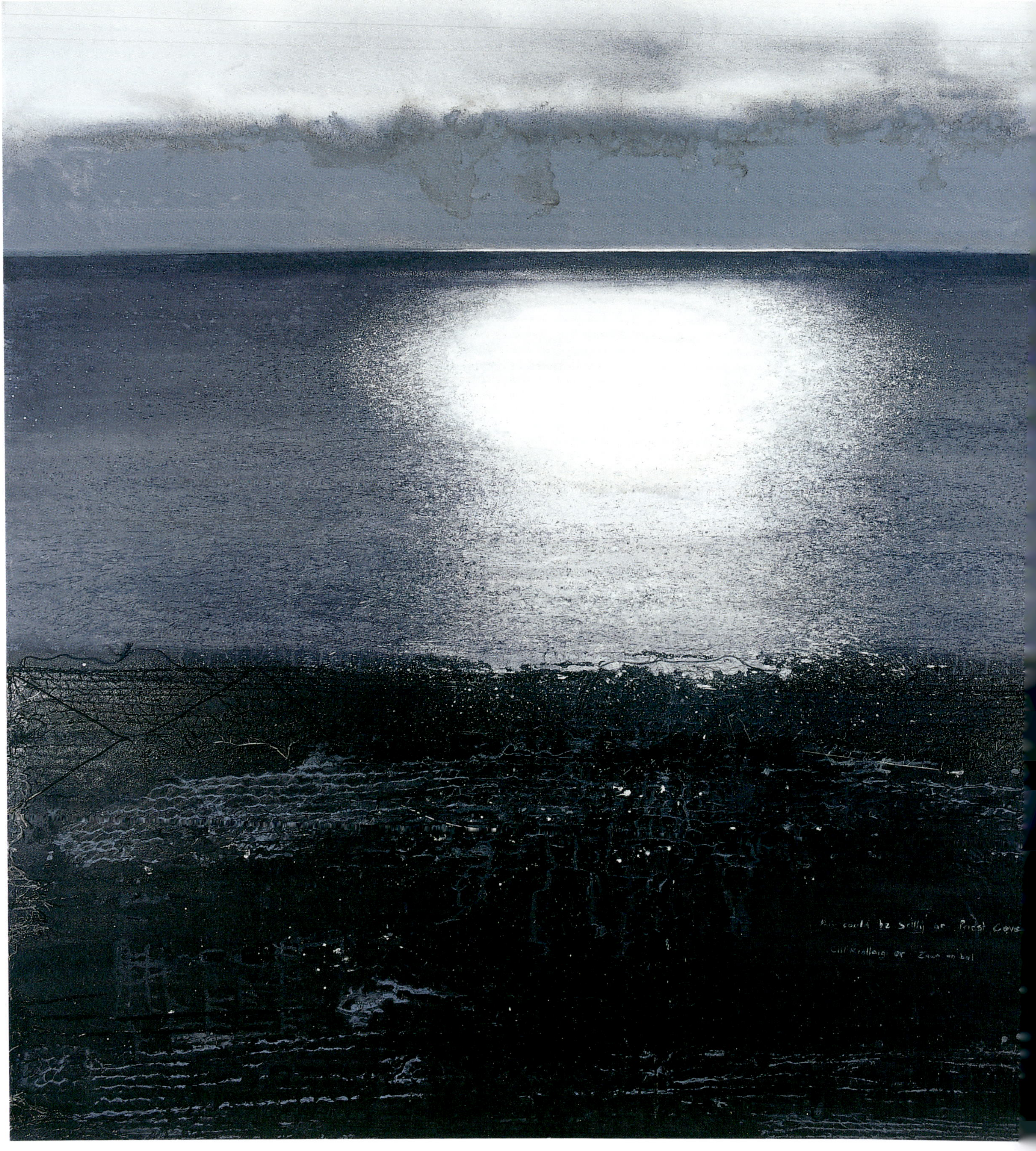
could be Scilly or Priest Cove
or Zawn an bal

24
This could be … 2000
Mixed media on canvas,
183 × 183 cm (72 × 72 in)

2 Look Closely

Mike Tooby

For many years, I have kept a postcard of a work by Kurt Jackson in an obvious spot in my house. It represents a small artwork on board. The painting concerned shows an open horizon, the sunlight flaring along the horizon and setting up an opposing rhythm of dark bands of foreground and sky. The effect is characteristic of much of Jackson's best-loved work. It evokes the light that is generally seen in Cornwall when looking west and south, rather than north, as seen in the title: *NW Winds, Storm Approaching, Raining, 8pm, 10/6/98, Botallack Cliff* (plate 25).

Jackson arrived to live in Cornwall in 1984. He spent five years in the place he first chose, Boscastle in North Cornwall, before moving to Penwith, also loosely referred to as West Cornwall. By settling above Botallack, he lives a long way from St Ives and Newlyn. The central points of his locality are St Just and the straggle of former mining villages running from the town to the north and east. The orientation described starts to map out a metaphor for Jackson's position in the artistic communities of the area. It conveys an effect that is impossible to see in St Ives, for example. There the viewer stands encircled by light, looking out to sea and along the coastline to the north and east, with the sun illuminating the gaze from over the shoulder, deepening the hues and sharpening the edges. This is distinct from the flickering white of the view beyond Cape Cornwall from above Botallack, looking into the sun, bleaching out colour, and turning deep blues in tones of green and grey.

Jackson respects the achievements of the generation of abstract artists who characterise the art tradition associated with St Ives, but rarely engages directly with the artistic debates that their work has generated, unless it is to look at specific pieces of work that he may admire on their own terms, such as the evocations of St Just by Peter Lanyon. His work references the nineteenth- and early twentieth-century artists who depicted the sea and the enclosed landscapes around Newlyn, but he is determined to avoid their sentimentality when illustrating the ways of life of the people living there. In terms of local artistic personalities, even though his work is utterly different from theirs, Jackson relates to Karl Weschke and Roger Hilton, who lived in the same locality as the artist and his family.

In Kurt and Caroline Jackson's family home, there are a few pieces by other artists, notably Roger Hilton and Michael Finn. Whereas Hilton's late work is characterised by a wiry explosion of colour, Finn's painting is assertively abstract. Bands of colour, which recall the same hues as the sea and sky depicted in the work on my postcard, are arranged in verticals, their soft edges creating a shifting sense of space and a delicate, quiet yet assured tone. There is also a dense painting by his father using a series of horizontal forms, with circular elements arranged in counterpoint. Peter Jackson was a successful painter in the 1960s. His art stands alongside his involvement in charitable projects, many associated with his Quaker faith; he worked internationally on reconciliation and conflict resolution, and at home on raising funds for social and political causes.

It has often been pointed out that Kurt Jackson lacks a formal art education, that he studied Zoology at university and took a particular interest in entomology and woodland habitats. His art tutor was, in effect, his father. It was alongside him that as a teenager on holiday he first painted the open sea, when they were both sketching on a clifftop in North Cornwall. For his father, watercolour was a recreational habit, distinct from his studio practice as a painter. It was, indeed, the association with those family holidays that prompted Jackson's move back to the region. Although he passed the mix of art-making and engagement in social and political causes to his son, the way in which Kurt has made them his own is striking. Rejecting Modernism, Kurt is committed to reinventing an alternative tradition of painting. He relates to figures of the radical Romantic tradition, such as the poet John Clare, and occasionally quotes the painters Caspar David Friedrich and John Constable in his imagery.

A work such as *NW Winds, Storm Approaching, Raining, 8pm, 10/6/98, Botallack Cliff* is, however, underpinned by the language of modern abstract art. The bands of colour that form the essentials of the composition recede and swell in a shallow pictorial space. The play of dense blue and the flecks of white create the illusion that we are gazing at the distant horizon. Its emptiness gives the opportunity to express the weather and light of Cornwall, which is so characteristic of Jackson's work. Furthermore, two key things that require consideration are affirmed by this picture: the physical scale, and the vital lower quartile of the image. The scale is deceptive in the reproduction. Although this work has a great sense of space, created by the juxtaposition of the far horizon and near foreground, the actual

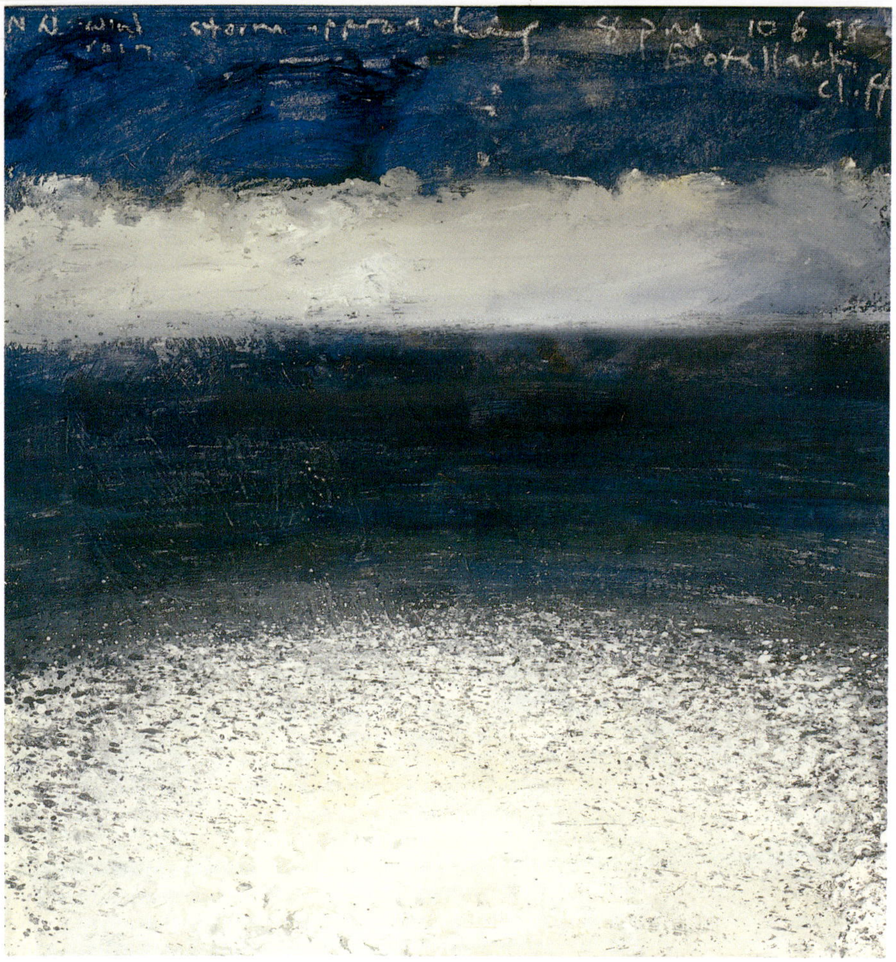

25
NW Winds, Storm Approaching, Raining, 8pm, 10/6/98, Botallack Cliff
Acrylic on board, 21.5 × 20 cm (8.5 × 8 in)

dimensions are just 21.5 × 20 cm (8.5 × 8 in). The writing across the top, a device that emerged in Jackson's work during the late 1990s, draws our attention back to the surface and reminds us of the small size of the image. The marks in the lower quartile, the touches and gestures of the artist's hand, fall away as if following the turn of the wrist. They have loosened the base of the image from the edge of the sheet of paper. This passage of the picture, being nearest to the viewer, falls out of focus as we look up and beyond at the horizon.

The foreground of *NW Winds, Storm Approaching, Raining, 8pm, 10/6/98, Botallack Cliff* is telling. One might speculate that it is in the near at hand, the detailed, the closely observed, that the zoologist operates. It comes as no surprise that entomology was the particular branch of study in which Jackson specialised – in Northwest Europe, entomology is, by definition, the study of some of the tiniest, most miniature phenomena of the natural world. At the point at which he was defining and refining the continuing study of the open horizon out to sea, Jackson turned inland. He had already produced small-scale paintings and studies of the interior of North Cornwall, which may be described as more Ruskinian in their approach than his work after his move to Penwith, the surface of the image

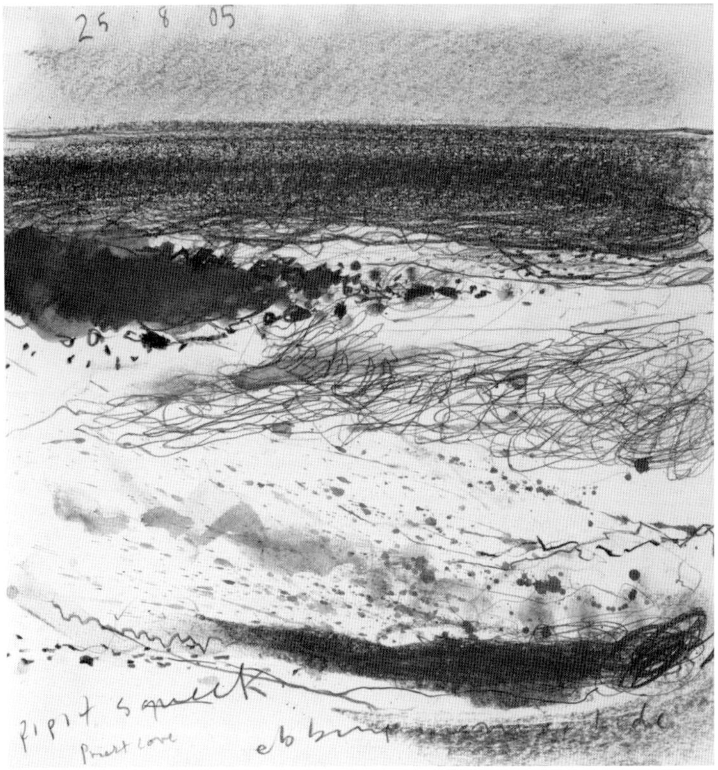

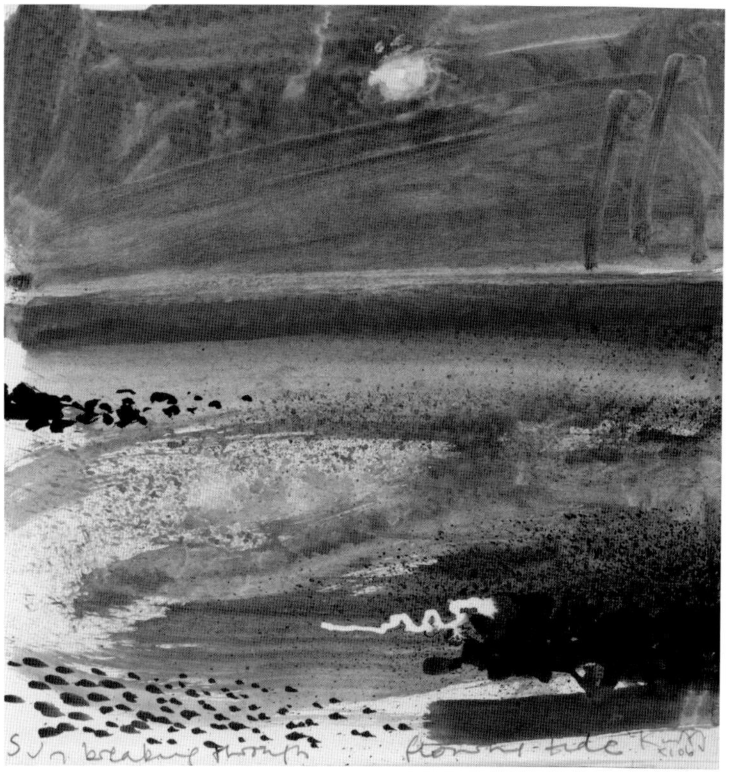

being enclosed by dense detail, with only glimpses of the space beyond the near-at-hand subject.

Later on, he began to turn inland from the coast between Botallack and St Just, in what was now a recognised part of his journey. *A3071. The Road to St Just, 2000,* initially became the best known of his works here, with the road from St Just to Penzance turning into a route for discovering details about the physical landscape around him. Chapels and road signs, hedges and wind-stunted trees occupied a pictorial middle ground that was distinct from the views out to sea. Jackson had created an alternative vocabulary to the seascape, through which to explore his locality.

Meanwhile, perhaps to round off the stock of imagery he had developed during the second half of the 1990s, Jackson created a number of series about individual places. The most important of these is 'Porth', a sequence of paintings made in and around Priest Cove. These continuing series of works used the open horizon as a key motif, but framed it with details at the edges of compositions, particularly in the foreground space that falls below the focal point. Occasionally fragments

26 (above left)
Pipit squeak, Priest Cove, 25/8/05
Pencil, 25 × 25 cm (10 × 10 in)

27 (above right)
Sun breaking through. Flowing tide, November 2006
Mixed media, 25 × 25 cm (10 × 10 in)

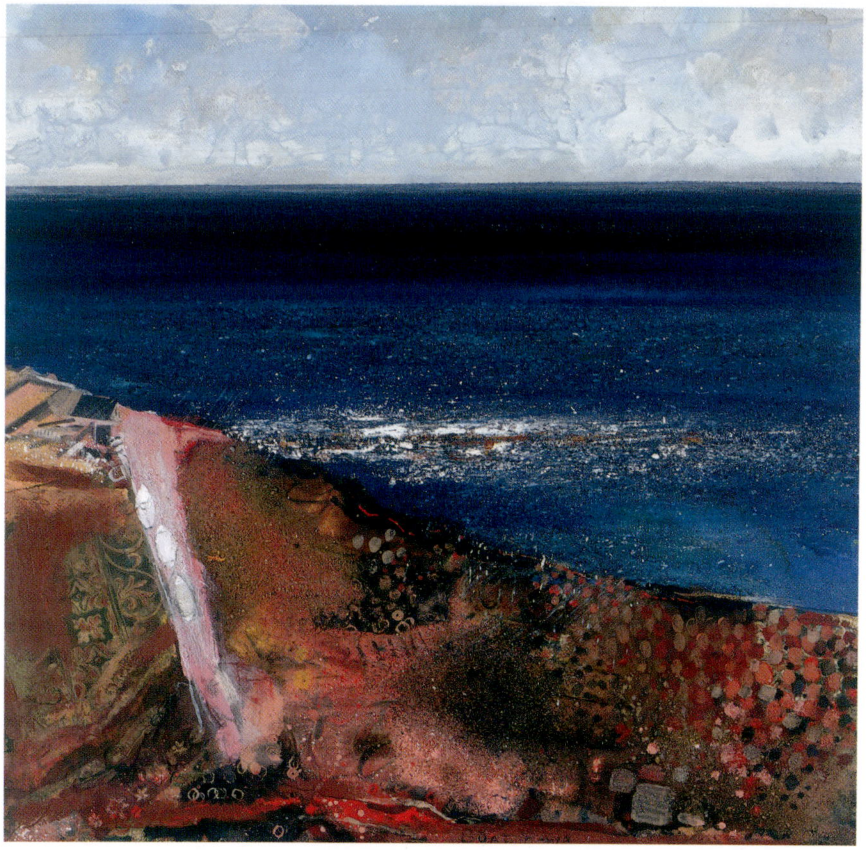

28
Boat Cove, 2005
Mixed media on canvas,
100 × 100 cm (39 × 39 in)

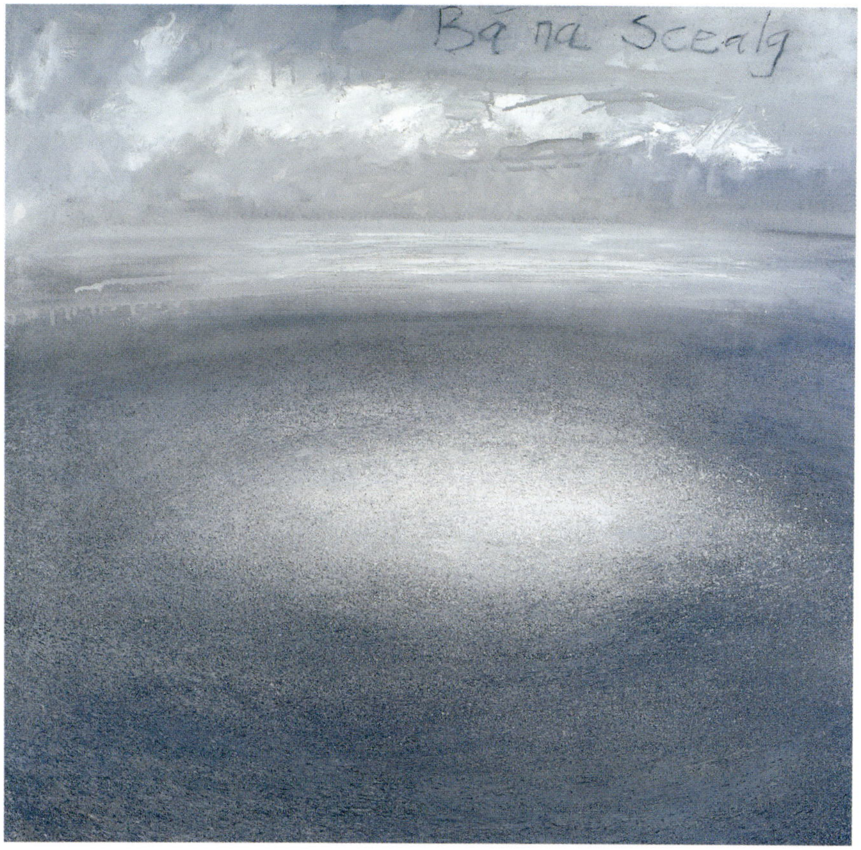

29
Bá na Skealg, August 1999
Oil on canvas, 91.5 × 91.5 cm
(36 × 36 in)

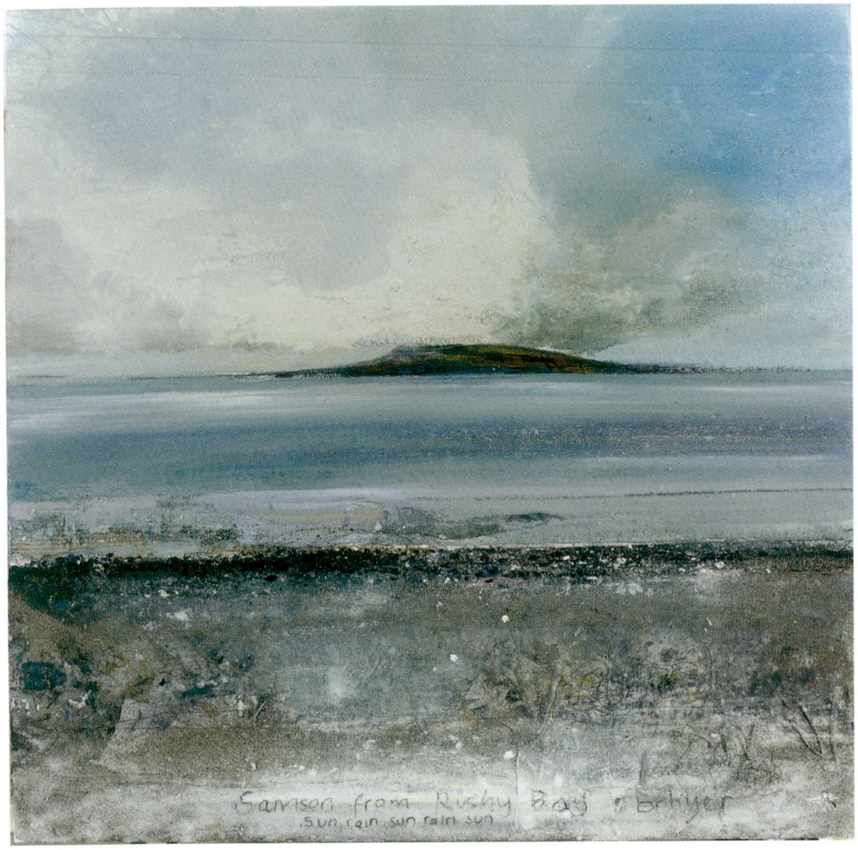

30
Samson from Rushy Bay, Bryher, 2003
Mixed media and collage on canvas,
122 × 122 cm (48 × 48 in)

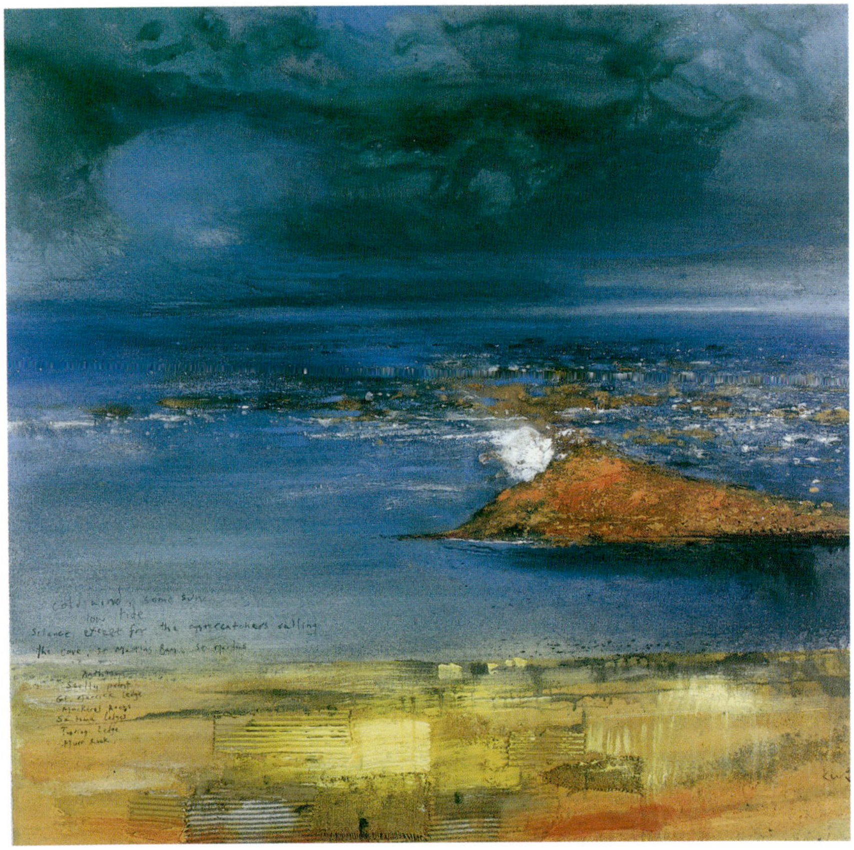

31
Cold wind, some sun, St Martin's Bay, 2002
Oil on canvas, 122 × 122 cm (48 × 48 in)

of material found at the site are added. These shift between studies of the near-at-hand – beach detritus, a shed, the steep sides of the cove itself – which usually appear in juxtaposition with the glimpses of sea and sky beyond.

The focal point is specific, transforming the recording of the passing circumstances as they emerge, shift and decay into an account of the moment of the artist's attempt to situate them in the continuing sense of the wider world. This enables us to understand how he finds a sense of place most clearly delineated by those unknown people who defined in stone the prehistoric sites near his home, and the continuity of craft production in the communities in which he lives.

The fishing people and miners, the makers of the derelict machinery and the straggling habitations that scatter the once industrial coast between St Just and Pendeen are evidenced by their dwellings, the detritus of their work, cheek by jowl with the makers of circles, tombs, paths and levelled settlements of the ancient past. By observing closely the traces of human presence in the landscape, we find a sense of endurance and flux in each particular moment of his work. As Jackson's work has evolved since the turn of the twenty-first century, some things have remained constant, whereas others have changed. He has pursued his exploration of the same places for the last two decades, such as Botallack Moor and Priest Cove. He has gone further in looking at the industrial aspects of the landscape, working underground at Geevor Mine and in other quarries, and he has developed the concept of the journey as the basis for a body of projects by travelling along rivers.

In each project he has used texts sparingly, and descriptions made to writers to emphasise the direct physical relationship of humanity to the places depicted, whether through swimming, lying on the ground or other activities in which the body forms part of the landscape. In many cases, he has emphasised how he has often spent time in the place depicted with his wife Caroline. Each work is pinned to a personal experience of a moment in each specific location. When visiting his studio, however, he is keen to describe how his work is not necessarily best understood as plein air painting, or made in the manner of site-specific painting. Instead, his notebooks and sketchbooks, or studies and foundations of paintings, are principally worked up in the studio.

One must note an irony about the creative tensions between close looking, the personal experience of place and the formalism of the construction of his images. It is that part of the success of his work, in common with modernist landscape painters, is its potential for reproduction. This is different from, yet comparable to his rich experiments in printmaking. In this sense, he calls to mind the artist Graham Sutherland, who also produced works at Geevor Mine, which were for many years best known through reproduction. He moved between closely observed notes and sketches, working them up in the studio as paintings, also intended for print and mural-scale reproduction.

In generating an 'idea' of Cornwall, Jackson has gained recognition and familiarity in recent years, as a result of the rapid growth in museums and commercial galleries showing and presenting art in and from this region. For many people who have no idea who he is, he is nevertheless familiar for the way in which he has created images for unique reproduction – most notably in the mural-scale series devised for the temporary walls on the north side of Paddington Station. He used his skill in organising telling imagery within a consistent design structure to transform what was essentially a promotional device into a strong work in its own right.

His work responds to the concepts of light, place and time through a pictorial language opposite to that used in the extended metaphors deployed by the great abstract artists who have been associated with Cornwall from the 1930s to the 1990s, such as Terry Frost, Patrick Heron or Bryan Wynter. They saw painting as being parallel to the abstract emotion that is experienced in nature. By removing detailed information concerning places, particularly that associated with certain incidents or human interventions, they sought to make universal the feeling of being in the landscape.

The straight open horizon in *NW Winds, Storm Approaching, Raining, 8pm, 10/6/98, Botallack Cliff* directs us towards the Romantic and Modernist tradition of using such a motif to connote infinity. The open horizon has become a kind of shorthand – and not quite a metaphor in the Modernist sense. In Jackson's 'after modern' rather than 'postmodern' outlook, he plays with our familiarity with the precise way in which artists acknowledge the signifier that the horizon line connotes the infinite.

Throughout his working process, however, Jackson seeks to retain an explicit connection between that initial epiphany in the landscape and the finished work. But we must not think that his conjoining the work with the specific experience of time and place is a mode of presenting information. Jackson operates in a language where the sense of colour, light and surface evokes the experience of precise moments and places. In this way he is not informing a painting tradition with technical innovation so much as imbuing an artistic practice with the fresh insights of someone with an eye and mind

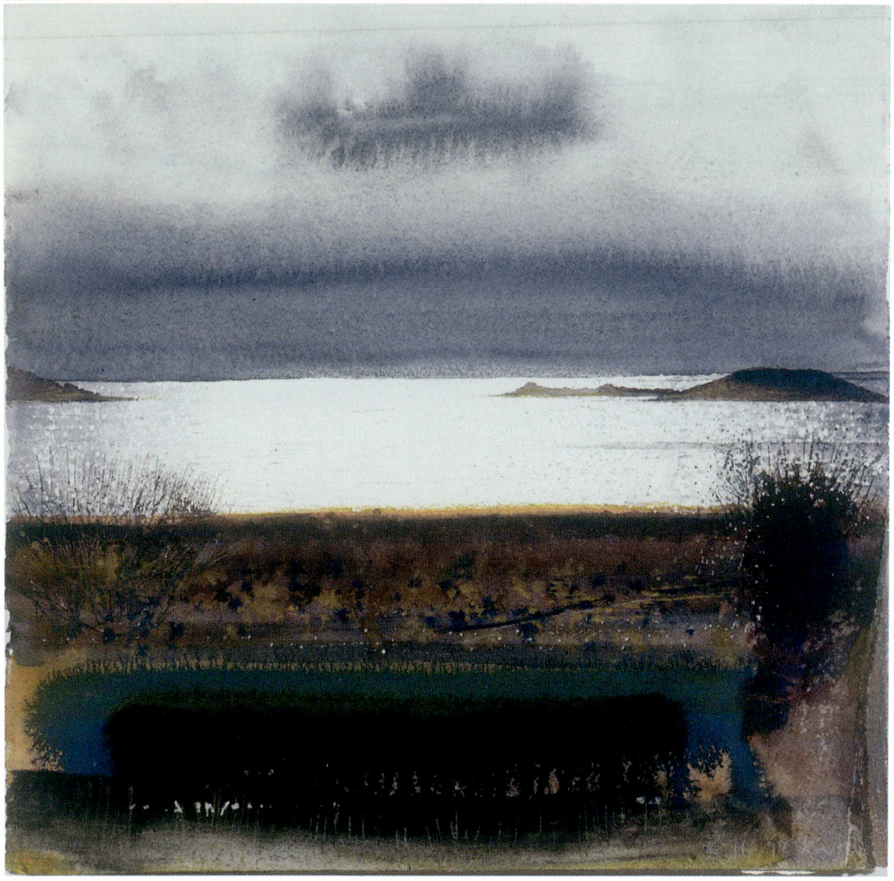

32
Eastern Isles from St Martin's, Scilly, 2/11/98
Mixed media, 28.5 × 28 cm (11 × 11 in)

developed in an utterly different, scientific tradition of observation and analysis. It is the entomologist's eye for the specific, in all its intense detail, transformed through the artist's feel for material and visual expression that we see in Jackson's best work.

Although it is intriguing to speculate on the relationship between his painting language and the abstraction that his father espoused, it would be wrong to project a specific metaphor of light drawn from his father's faith and practice on to his work. Nevertheless, in seeking out the light, and emphasising how it surrounds and pierces the ancient landscapes, modified as they are by continuous inhabitation, we are constantly reminded of the ways in which we live 'in the light'. By retaining illustrative detail and scripts of specific locations in his works, Jackson emphasises the ways in which visual experience operates in the memory of specific moments that precipitate epiphanies, as well as through the understanding of the universality of the experience.

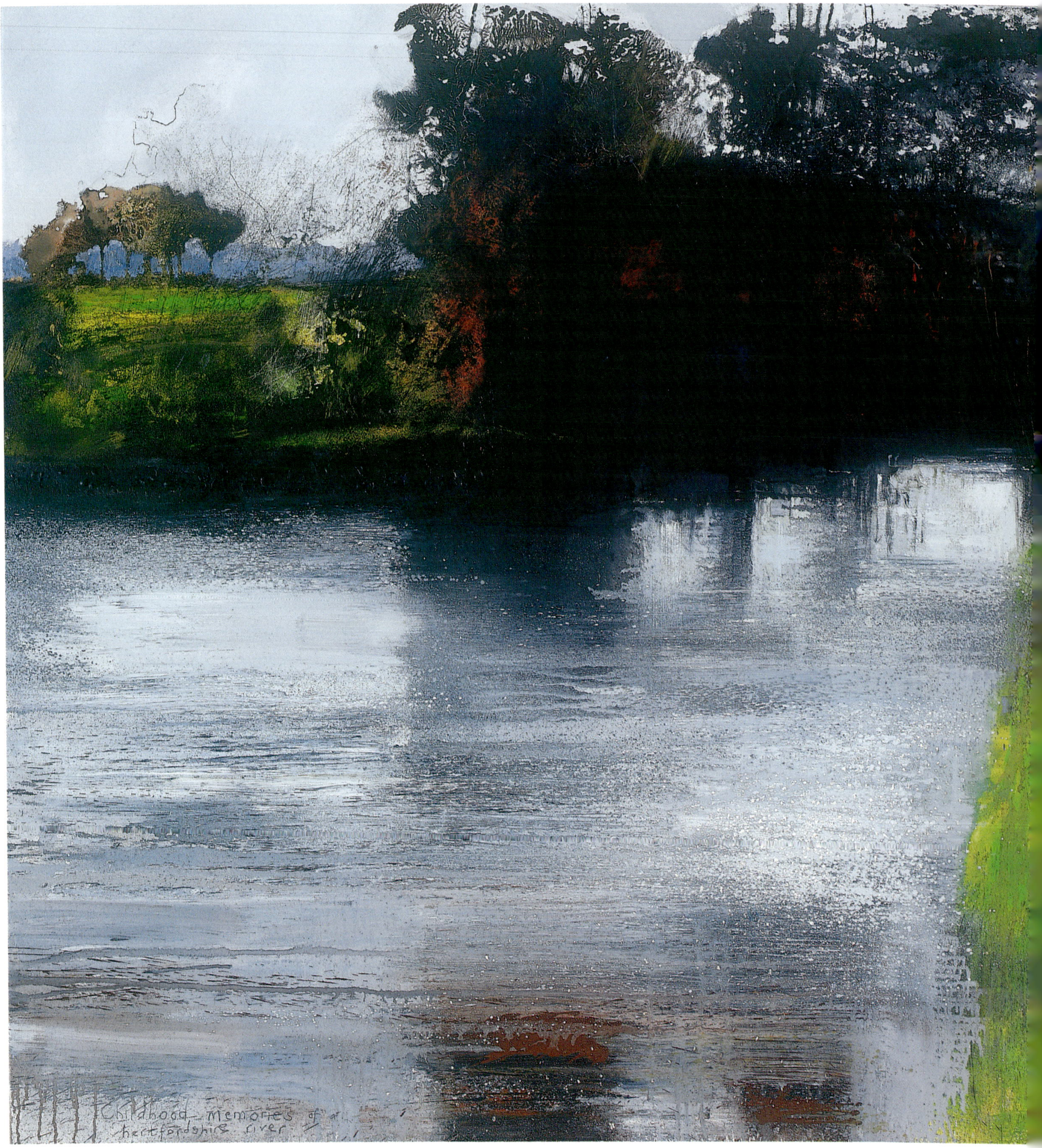
Childhood memories of a
hertfordshire river

3 From the Source to the Sea

Helen Dunmore

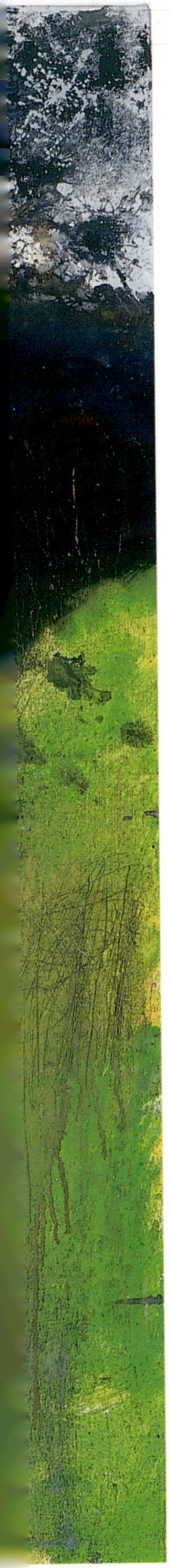

33
Childhood memories of a Hertfordshire river, 2004
Oil on canvas, 122 × 122 cm
(48 × 48 in)

The first river in Kurt Jackson's life was the River Ver, which he describes as being 'as small as a river can be before it becomes a stream'. The Ver, which was ten minutes across the fields from his Hertfordshire home, had dwindled as a result of upriver water extraction. During Jackson's childhood in the 1960s, it was a place of muddy meanders, minnows, sticklebacks, pondweed and gudgeon. Its disused watermills and watercress beds remained, suggesting a more impressive industrial and agricultural past. The young Jackson spent hours there, exploring, wading, building dams, watching fish jump for flies and above all drawing and painting, recording what he saw and what his imagination made of his observations. At times, he would use felt-tip pens, crayons or drawing pencils; at others he sellotaped a leaf or a feather to the page, and used words and images to fix his impressions.

This catholic approach to materials has persisted, and is a hallmark of Jackson's work. His plein air technique allows him to situate himself in the landscape to which he is responding, and the written notations he makes on the paintings are not only records but also a form of calligraphy that extends the action of the painted surface. He will incorporate found objects in a painting, as he does when a scurf of litter washed up on the banks of the River Avon becomes the foreground in *Shirehampton sandpipers, stillness, 2008*. The litter is part of the river's story, and it becomes part of its telling, just as a feather or a leaf reveal not only the beauty of their own structure but also the local ecology of the river.

In Jackson's view, the pictorial and aesthetic form one layer, whereas the drawing and the painting are informed by a deep crossover between natural history, culture, politics, local gossip, myths, legends and personal experience of place. The artist's fascination with the social, industrial and political history of landscape was also kindled in those early days living by the Ver. In its heyday, the river flowed deep and strong. Roman galleys rowed up the Ver, which gave its name to the city of Verulamium (St Albans). In medieval times there were

11 watermills along its 20km (12 mile) length, and a child who had fallen into the millrace was miraculously brought back to life by his mother's prayer to St Alban. It seems likely that early intimacy with the Ver's silt of history has influenced Jackson in his search for what lies within and beneath the appearance of the natural world.

At the same time as Jackson was growing up by the Ver, he was spending long summer holidays in the slate-mining village of Delabole in Cornwall, where his family had a cottage. This was the start of a relationship with the Cornish landscape that has been a deepening, sustaining force throughout Jackson's life. In the valley below Delabole a very different stream ran, rural, pristine, with banks of pure yellow marsh marigolds and ragged robin. There were dragonflies and kingfishers, and when he turned a piece of slate over there would be caddis fly larvae. Down at Port Quin, streams were full of eels.

These early experiences are described as solitary. The child is alone with the water, and with everything that lives below the surface or nearby. As a teenager Jackson travelled alone, hitchhiking and exploring in Britain and abroad. It was when he met his wife Caroline at Oxford that he began to understand the richness of travel and work with someone else there as a companion, witness and sharer of the journey. Caroline's role is vital; her presence feeds into what the painter is doing and why he is doing it. This presence maintains his confidence and sustains the dynamic of his work.

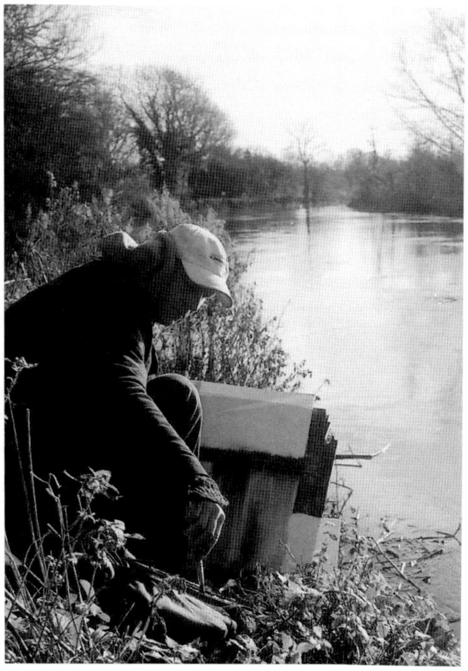

34
Thames, 2004

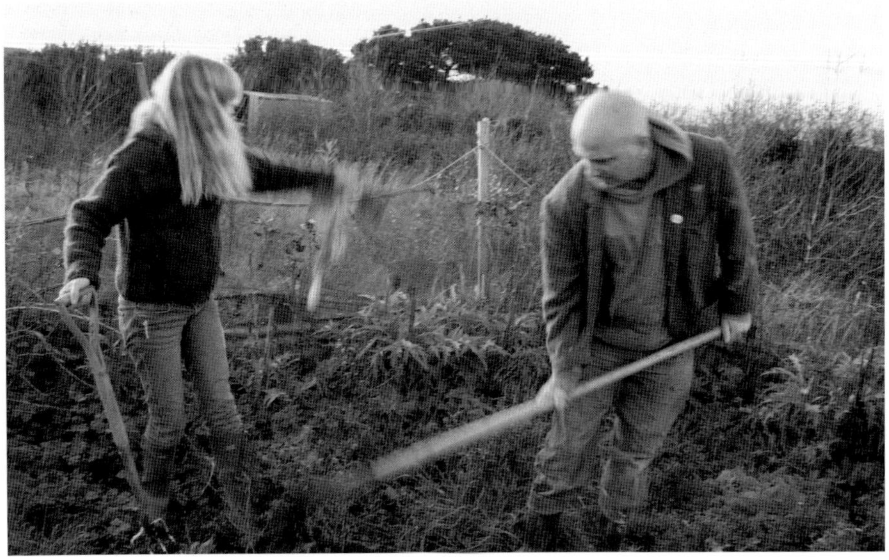

35
Caroline and Kurt, 2007

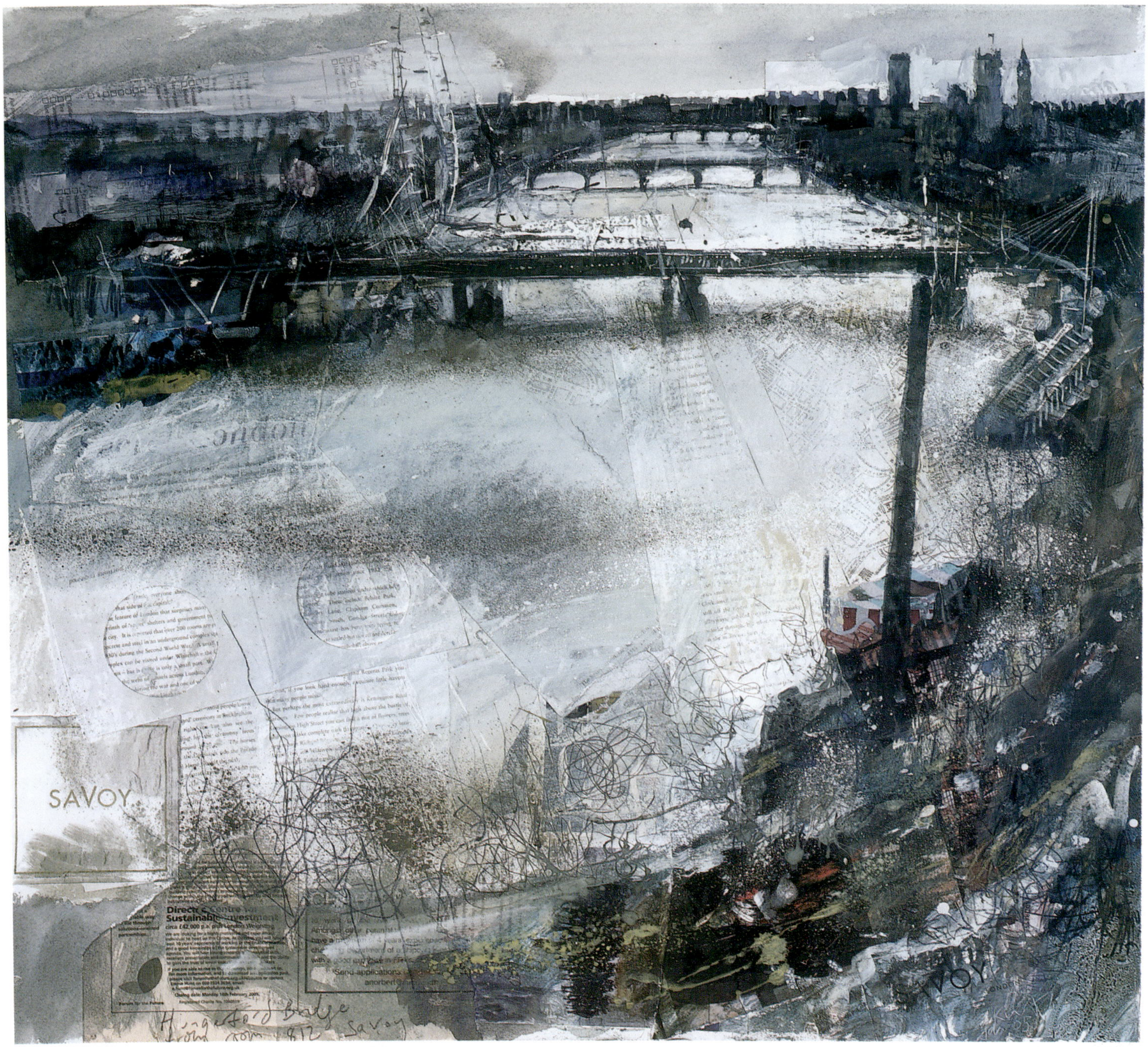

36
Hungerford Bridge from room 812, Savoy Hotel, January 2005
Mixed media, 57 × 62 cm (22.5 × 24.5 in)

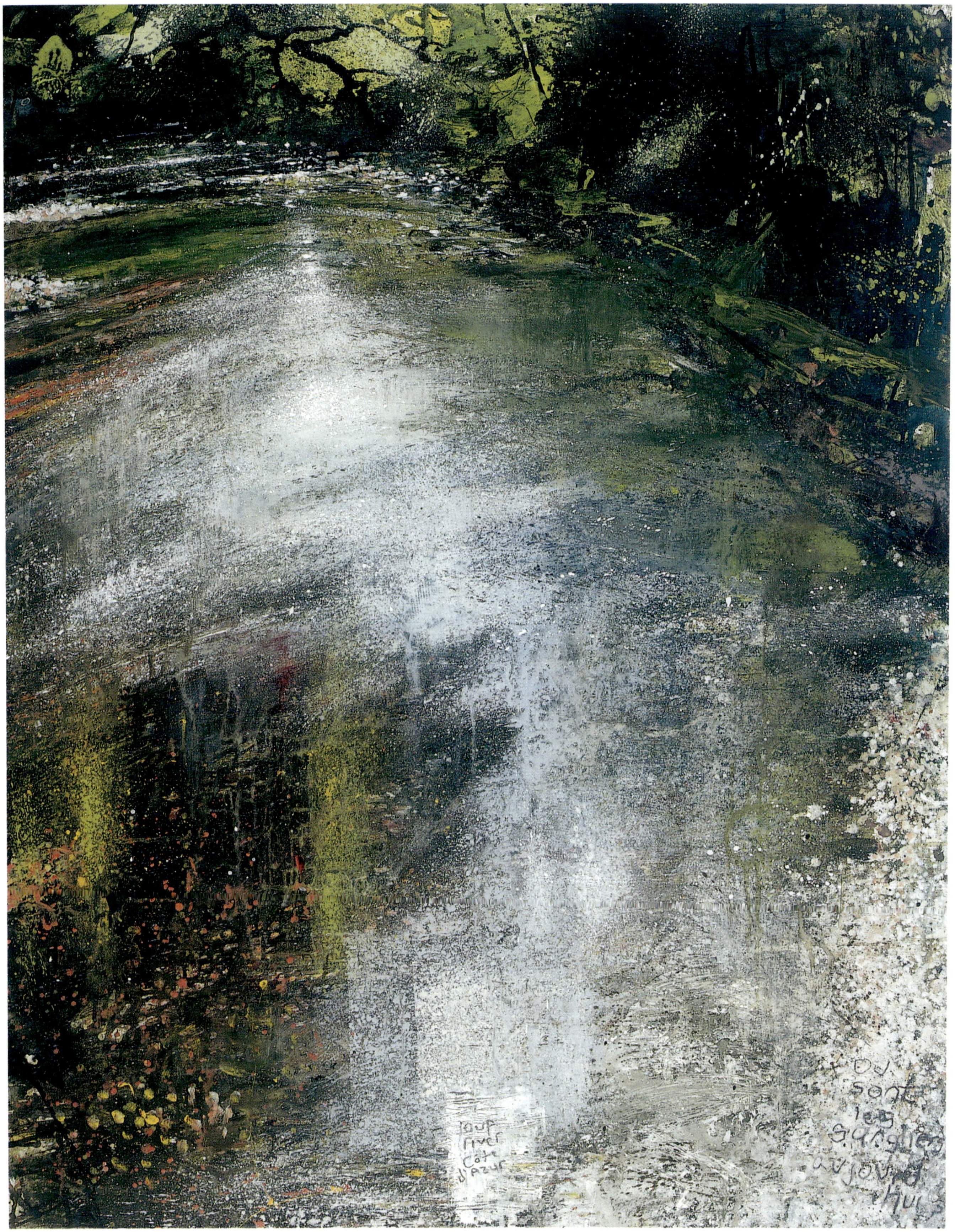

37
Loup River, Côte d'Azur, 2003
Mixed media on linen, 127 × 96 cm (50 × 38 in)

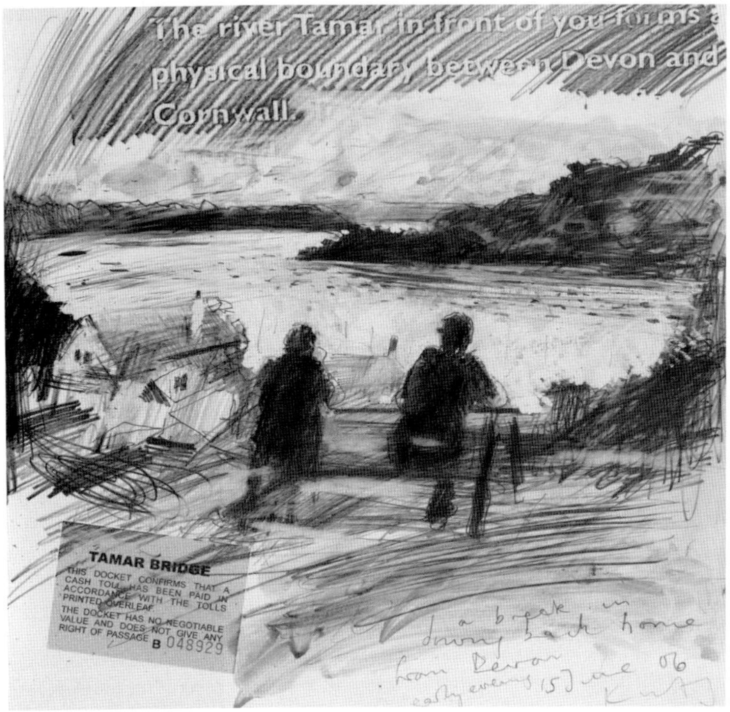

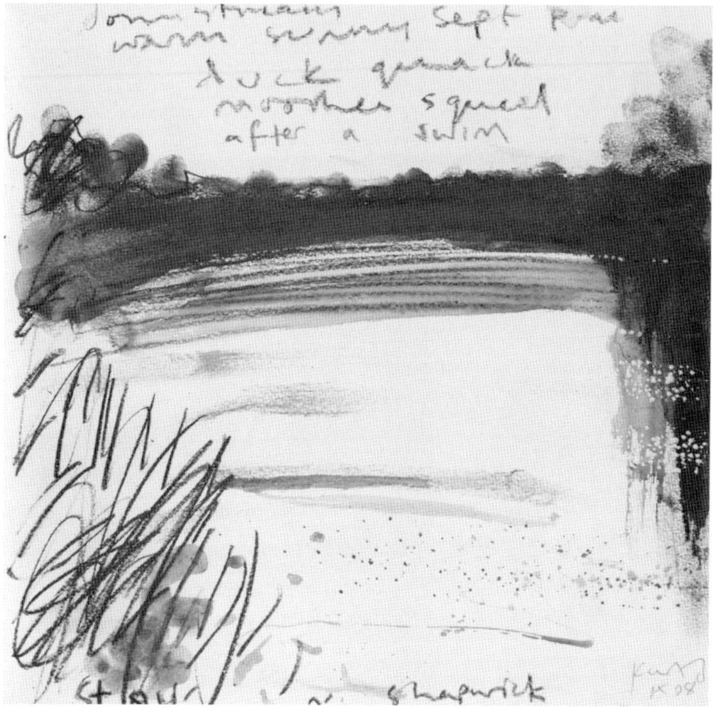

38 (this page, left)
The Tamar, Plymouth, 15/6/06
Pencil and collage, 30 × 29 cm (12 × 11.5 in)

39
The Stour near Shapwick, November 2008
Pencil, 25 × 25 cm (10 × 10 in)

The large river projects that the artist has undertaken reflect months and even years of exploration, drawing, painting and sculpting. Kurt and Caroline have walked along the riverbanks of the Aude, Aveyron, Avon, Liffey, Tamar and Thames. They have canoed, waded and swum through the waters, and camped beside them. They have talked to farmers, water bailiffs, travellers and fishermen. This intimate, organic approach to exploring the landscape is very much something which they share. Certain paintings, such as *Caroline in Pinkney Wood, Sherston. Raindrops and fox smell, January, 2006,* beautifully express the power of Caroline in Kurt Jackson's landscape.

One of Jackson's sketchbooks records a journey down the River Hayle, by canoe, with Caroline. Free, vigorous drawing captures the impetuous and slightly uncertain quality of their passage. The strokes are rapid; there is little time or energy to spare as the two force their way through an overgrown waterway, lug their canoe over obstacles, or paddle hard as the waters widen and become tidal. There is no mistaking the zest and engagement they show. Jackson speaks of 'early Edens': the Ver, the Delabole stream and also the many French rivers where he would camp with his parents as a child. The family avoided campsites, preferring

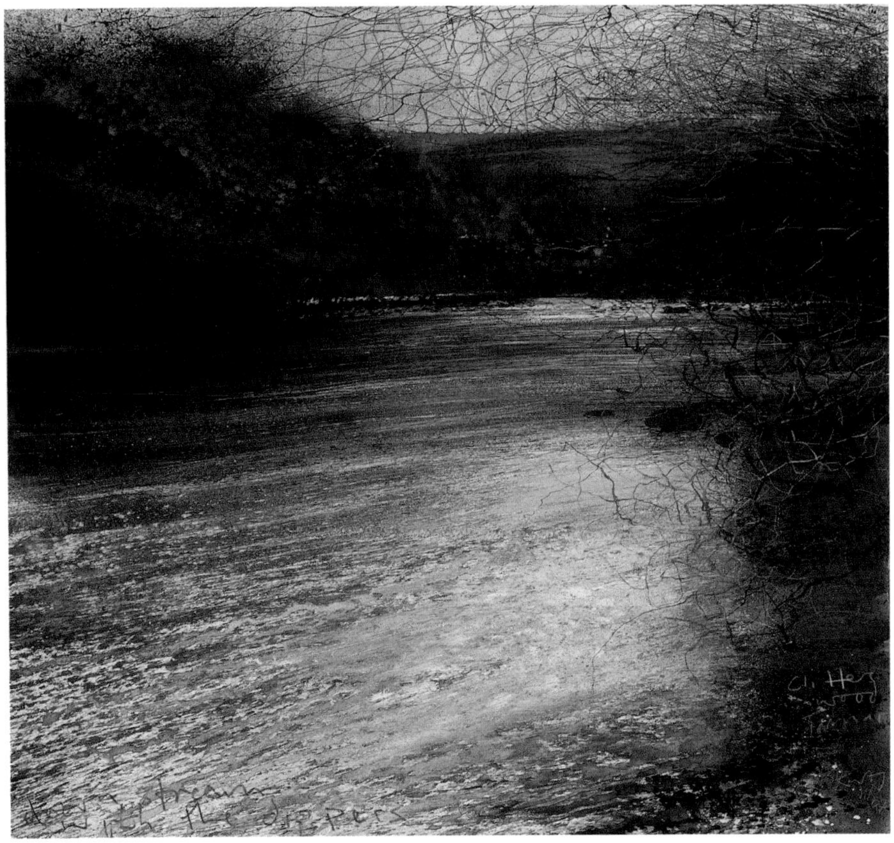

40
Downstream with the dippers, Clitters Wood, Tamar, March 2007
Mixed media, 57 × 59.5 cm (22.5 × 23.5 in)

instead to pitch their tent in a field or on a riverbank, swimming, canoeing and making coracles. Jackson returned to these rivers with his own children, to rediscover and re-explore the Aude, Aveyron, Lot, Rhône and Viaur. Rivers, Jackson says, are landscapes of memory, and in his work the intensely personal memory overlaps with the collective social or historical memory.

Rivers carry water, but they also carry information. They bear soil and mineral traces that colour them, cloud them and change the way they absorb the light. A red stain of soil after a torrential downpour, chemical run-off, driftwood, boats, people, stories, language, history, are all borne downstream by the current. Rivers form boundaries, but they also unite. Their banks are seedbeds for human settlement, because where a river runs, people move. Long before nature was tamed by roads, goods, people and stories travelled by water.

All this riverine information seizes Jackson's imagination, and flows into his work. He remarks of 'The Avon Project' that his paintings reflect the entire life of the river: its growth and development from source to sea. The same is true of his work on 'The Tamar – Dowr Tamer'. This river is Cornwall's natural northern boundary, which makes the county an 'almost island'. The geography of the river also marks linguistic, cultural and historical boundaries. Like everyone living in Cornwall and travelling out of it, Jackson knows the Tamar well, and in time his awareness has sharpened into a desire to explore the river from source to mouth, and to make paintings, drawings and sculpture out of this exploration.

The Tamar paintings trace the marks of abandoned industries, of disused railways and deserted quays where barges no longer dock. They show a landscape where the wild and the industrial have become interconnected. An oak thicket hides a disused mine-shaft. Places may be misinterpreted, unless the beholder knows their history. Jackson learned about the vanishing heavy industry on the riverbanks that now appear remote and rural. The area of Clitters Wood by the Tamar was once a tin and copper centre of European importance; there was tin-streaming here from medieval times, and by the eighteenth century there was booming manufacturing of tin, copper, arsenic, sulphides and wolfram. The long-gone tumult of metal on metal and the snaky criss-cross of railway lines find their visual echo in Jackson's painting *Downstream with the dippers, Clitters Wood, Tamar, March, 2007* (plate 40), where the surface of the water looks like beaten metal.

Such echoes and allusions are very much part of Jackson's layered approach to his material. He stresses the importance of 'reading about the lives that had been lived there – the inventiveness of people making the landscape work for them'. There is the paradox that these workers' lives may be lost to record, but their impression on the land endures for centuries. In *Wet Sunday, Tamar meanders. Old Man's Beard, Halton Quay, December, 2007*, the disused stone quays where once barges trafficked upstream with Plymouth's night soil are now covered in fantastic wreaths of wild clematis. Shivers of wind and light break up the water surface, but no boat moves.

Both the Tamar and the Avon series are concerned with the effects of flooding and erosion, with weather systems and industrial activity. As Jackson observes, a mass of indestructible plastic rubbish on a river's curve is a reminder that what cannot be recycled degrades only in part. But this rubbish has to be in the picture. It cannot be edited out, to make a more seemly world. The glistening, secret waters of *Joyce's Pool, the source, December, 2005* reveal the Avon's birthplace, but they are no more authentic than the muddied tidal reaches at Avonmouth, with their scum of litter. Jackson's paintings and drawings trace the multiple identities of the river

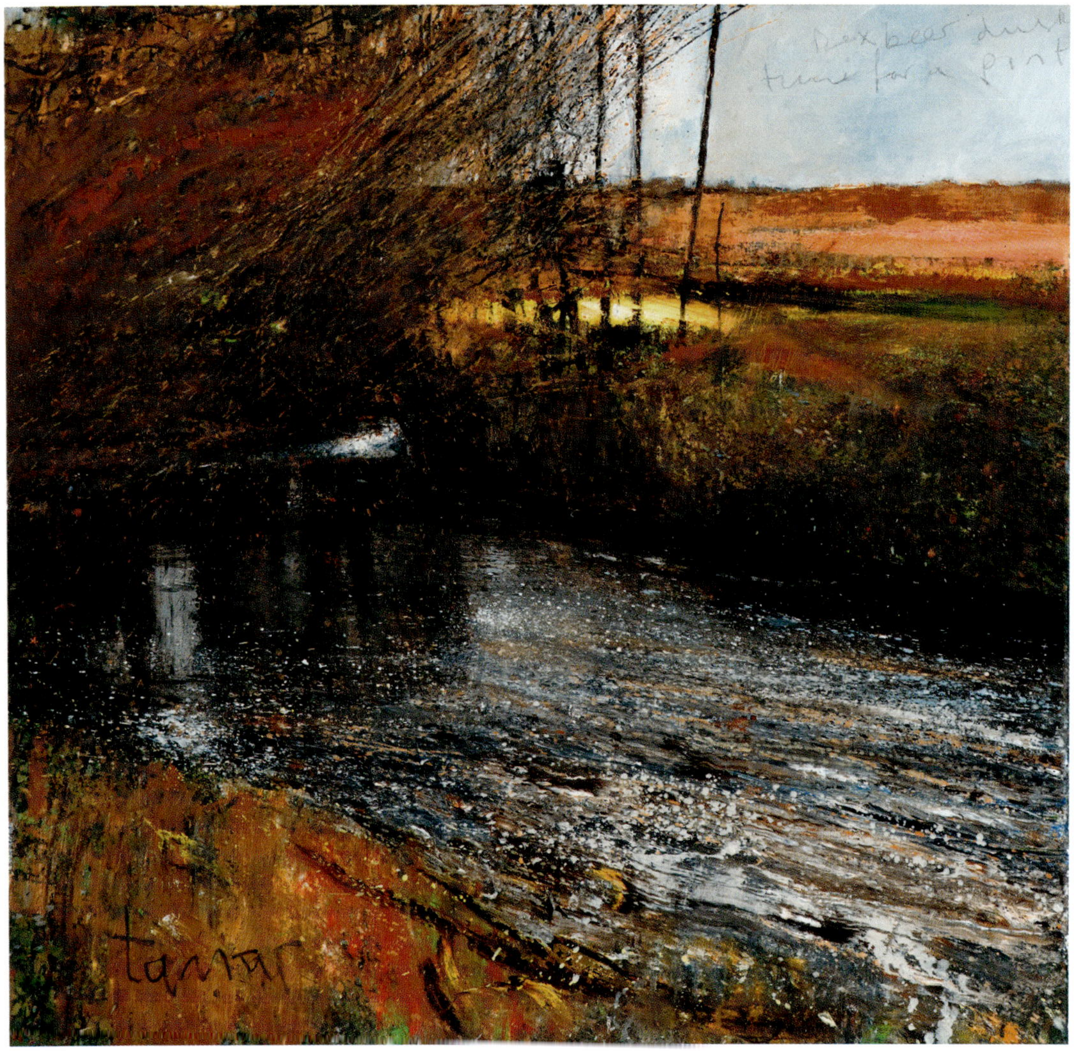

41
Dexbeer, dusk, time for a pint, 2008
Oil on canvas, 91.5 × 91.5 cm
(36 × 36 in)

through a fluid process, as the river becomes, from moment to moment, a new thing.

No matter how immediately the drawing or painting is made, *en plein air,* there is an intense, subtle interplay between what Jackson sees, and what will be seen on the page or the canvas. He asks the question, 'Am I recording what I find, or my joy in what I find?' A recent film made by his daughter Zinzi (*The Avon Project, Part 2: Bath to Avonmouth, 2009*) provides an extraordinary record of Jackson at work on the 'Avon Project'. In the last part of the film, Jackson appears at work on *Shirehampton sandpipers, stillness, 2008*. It is a cold day. The camera watches the painter, who seems almost to seize upon the landscape as he spreads out his

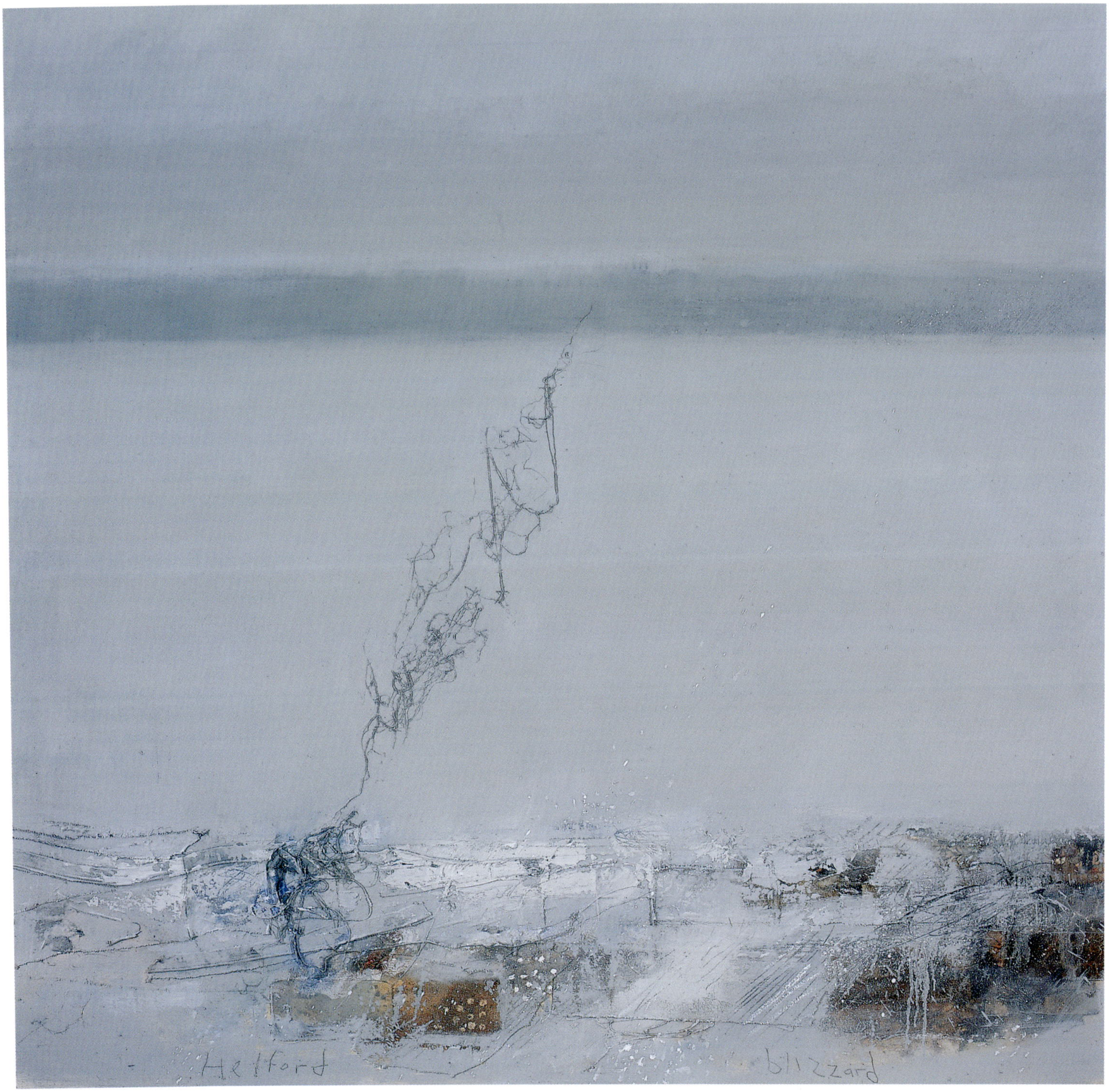

42
***Helford blizzard*, 2004**
Oil on canvas and collage, 152.5 × 152.5 cm (60 × 60 in)

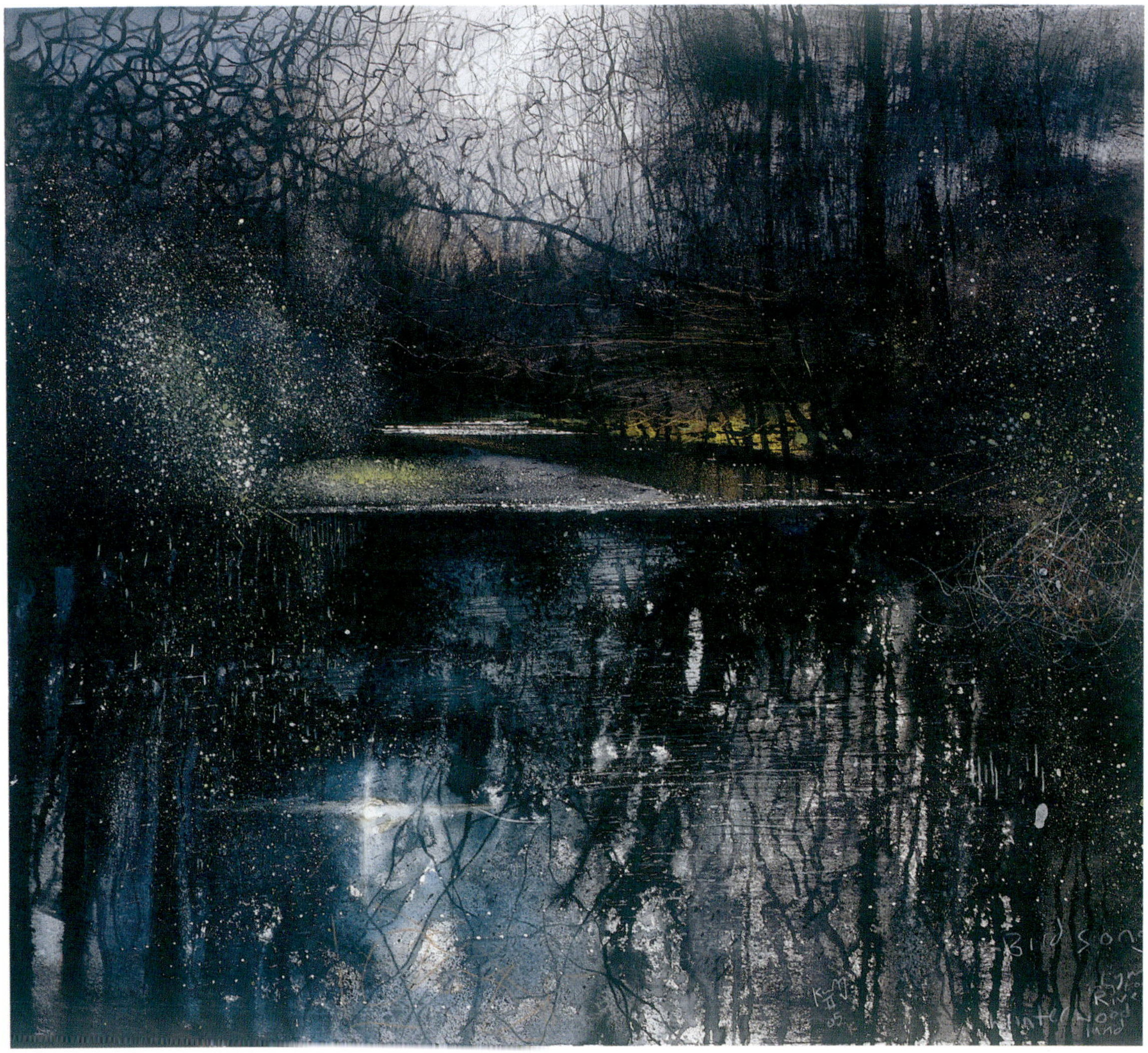

43
Bird song, Lymington River, winter woodland, February 2005
Mixed media, 57 × 62 cm
(22.5 × 24.5 in)

canvas on the ground. It is a remarkable portrait of an artist at work, made by someone whose familiarity and insight allowed Jackson to forget the film process and to pounce like a hawk on his own subject. There is a strong sense of the physical effort involved in working on this scale, in the open air. The canvas is unwieldy. Breath smokes and fingers chill. Quick, sharp-witted decisions need to be made in every moment of the work, both on a conscious level and from fragments of those deep layers of consciousness, that rise to the surface to inform the painting process. The figure develops a rhythm as it steps backwards, forwards, freezes into attention and then reaches to lay down the paint with sudden,

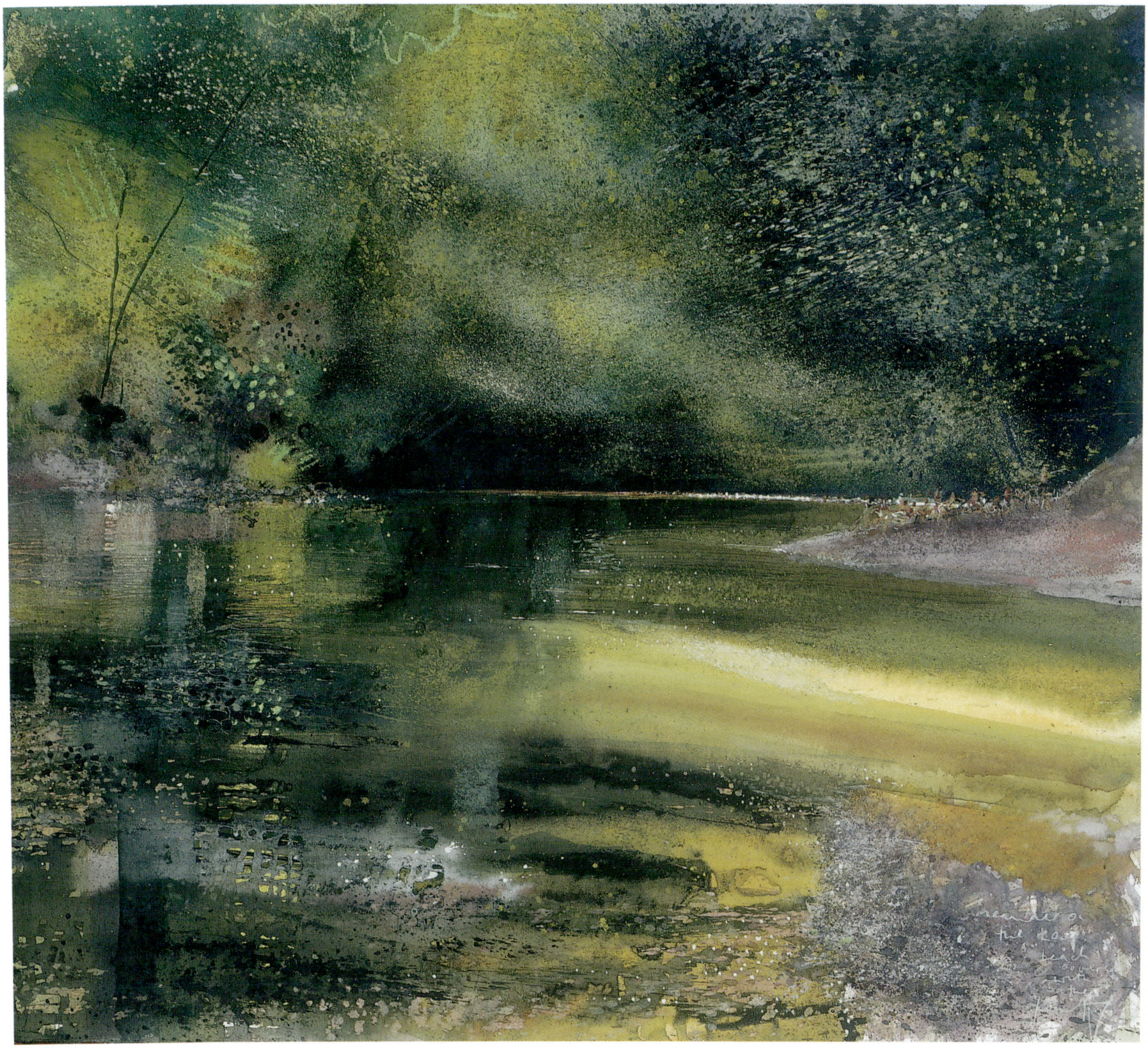

44
Meander on the Loup, beach covered with bathers, 2003
Mixed media, 56.5 × 62 cm (22 × 24.5 in)

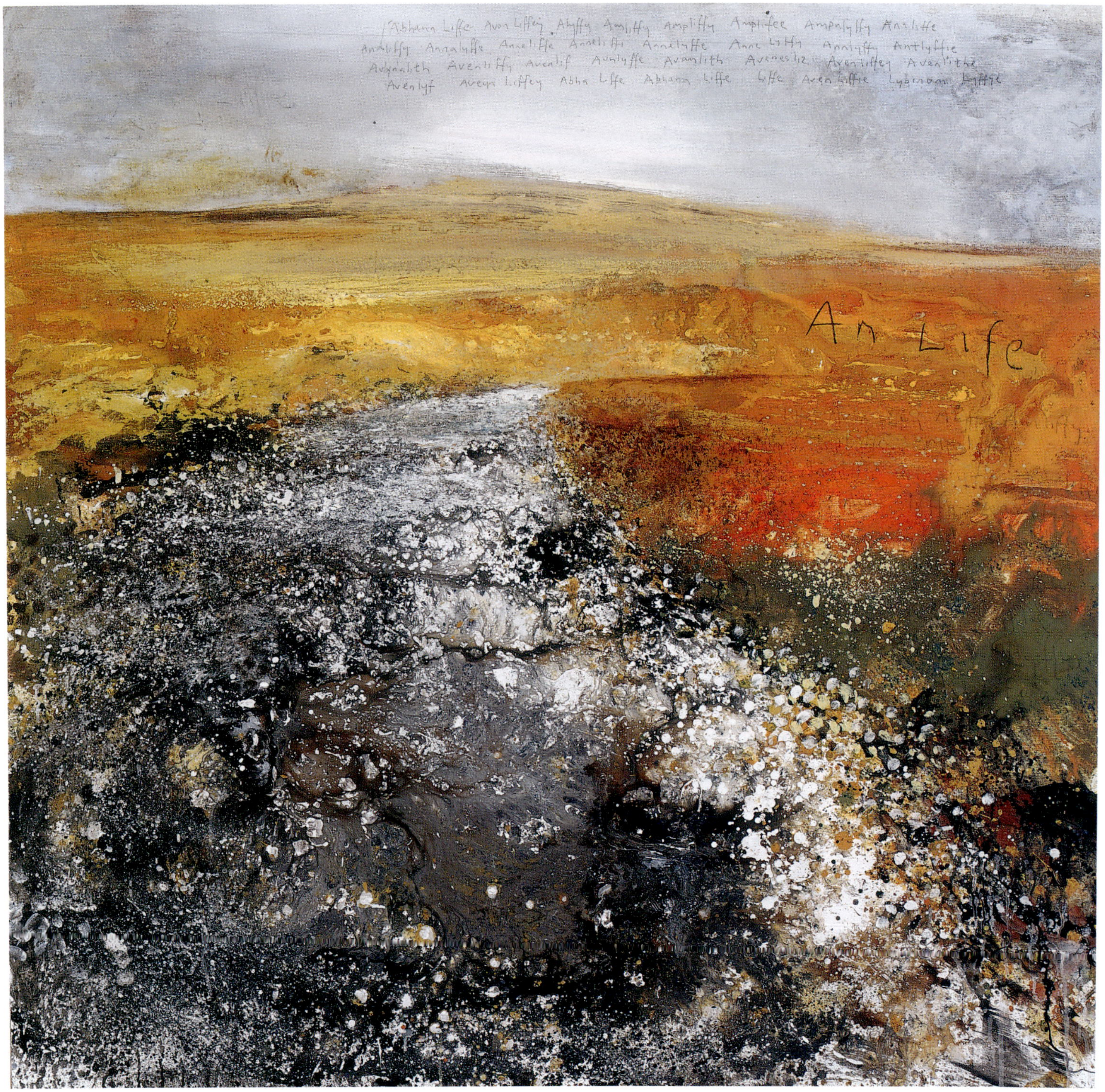

45
An Life/The Liffey, 2006
Mixed media on canvas, 140 × 140 cm (55 × 55 in)

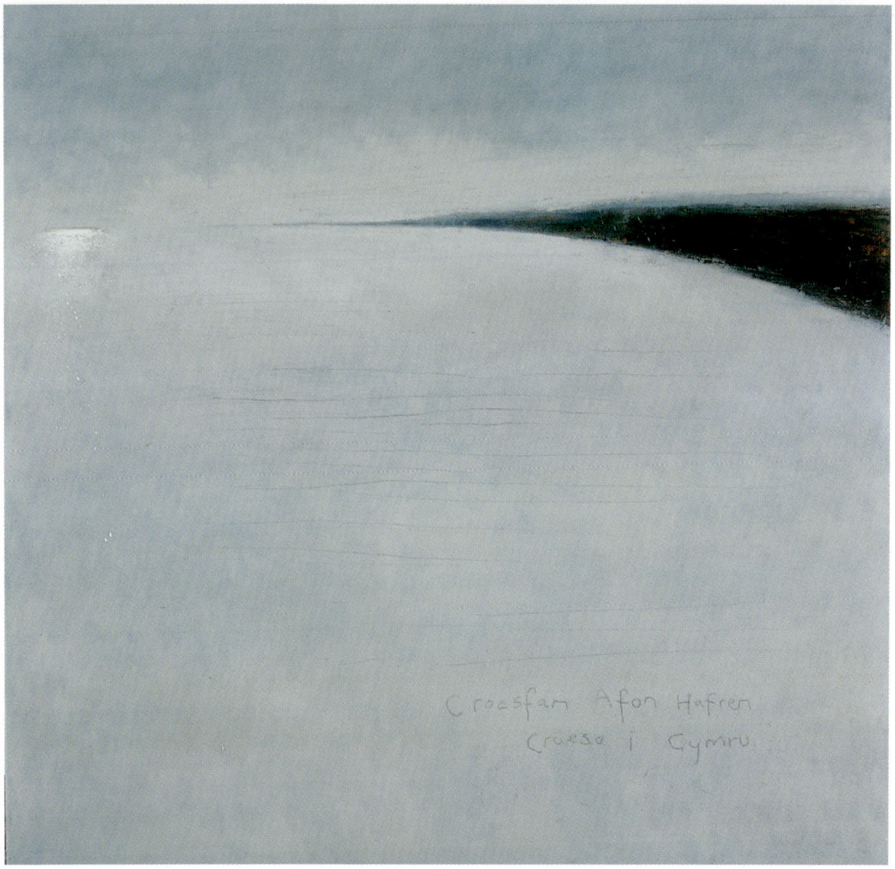

46
Crossing the Severn into Wales, 2004
Oil and collage on canvas, 152.5 × 152.5 cm (60 × 60 in)

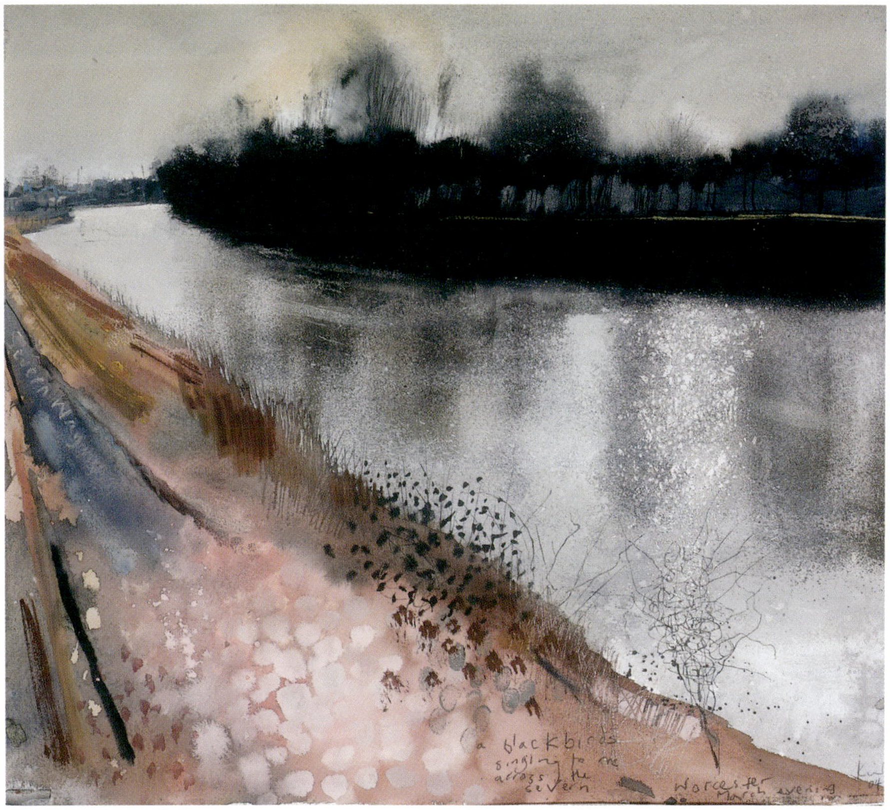

47
A blackbird is singing to me across the Severn. Worcester, March evening, 2004
Mixed media, 56 × 62.5 cm (22 × 24.5 in)

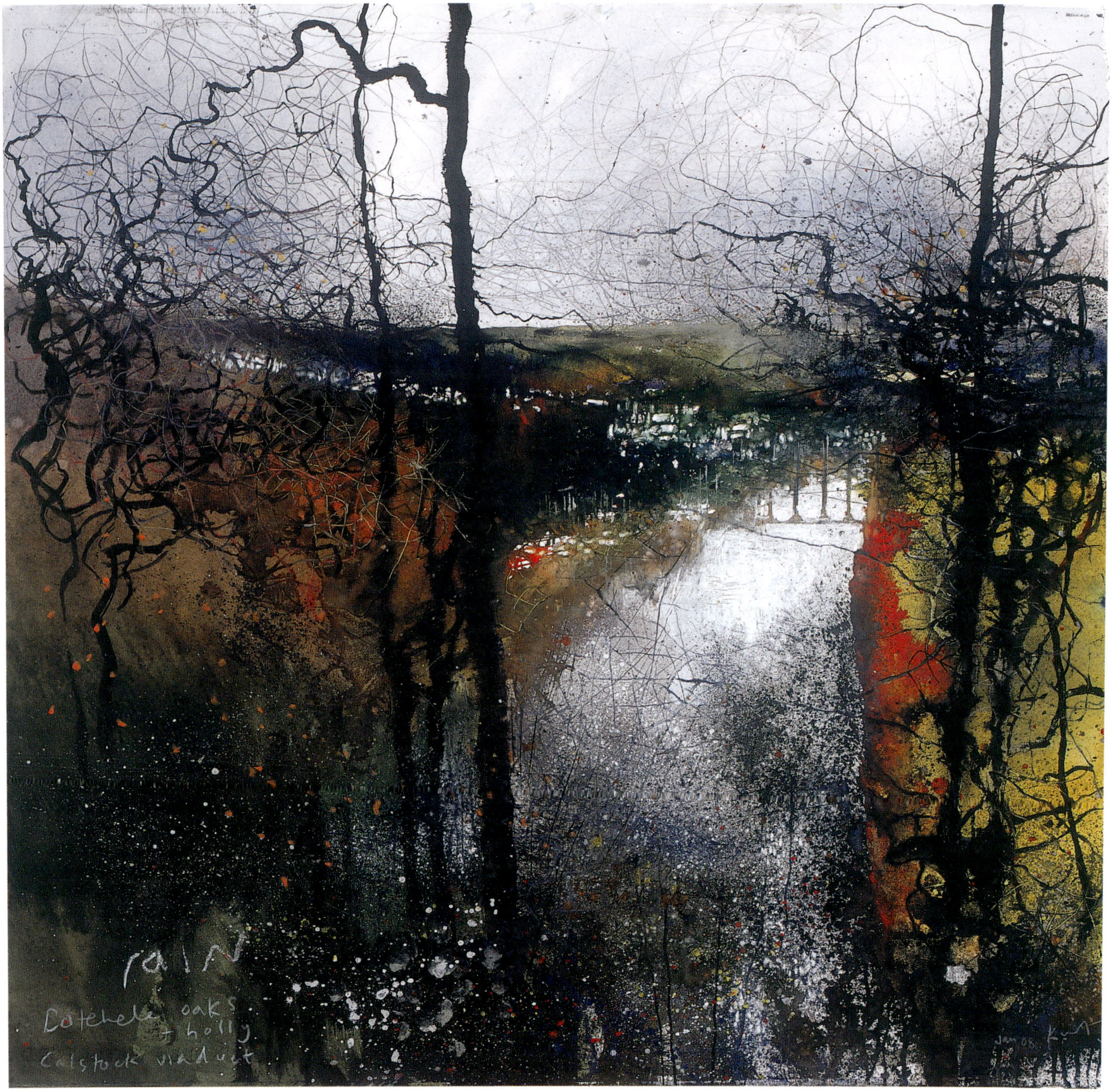

48
Rain. Cotehele oaks and holly, Calstock Viaduct, January 2008
Mixed media, 57 × 57.5 cm (22.5 × 22.5 in)

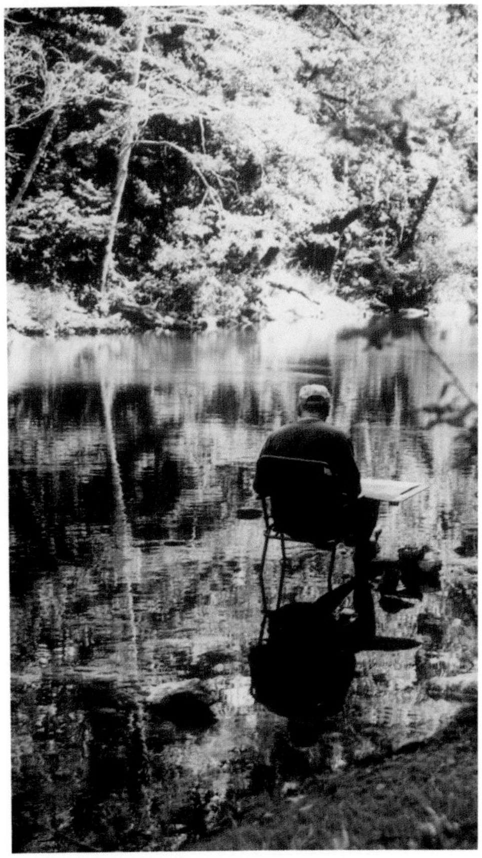

49
On the Viaur, France, 2000

complete confidence, rubbing, scrubbing, minutely dotting, flicking with balletic precision as the sheen of mud and water begins to develop on the canvas.

From the earliest stages of his career, Jackson has been a watcher and an inhabitant of wild places, whose familiarity with a landscape grows as he experiences it through all moods and weathers. Close to home, he can engage with a place over a long period of time, not months but years, and perhaps for a lifetime. Time becomes another character in his paintings, as a tree or a hedge or a stretch of water is visited and revisited. Although there are no rivers in West Penwith, where Jackson lives, he has engaged with the Tregeseal stream through a closely studied series of 145 works. This sequence of paintings, one for every ten paces along the stream's banks, reflects something on which Jackson places immense value: 'intimate knowledge of the place I live in, and the people who live here'. The Cot stream, which runs close to Jackson's home, has been a frequent subject, explored in such paintings as *Cot stream under a sallow, 2004*. These two streams are near enough for the artist to revisit frequently to make occasional paintings and drawings, which inform the growth of a deeply personal, creative relationship over time.

Time is a presence in this body of work on many days. Often Jackson notes the hour, and it becomes clear that these paintings were made at all times of day, in each of the seasons and in many weather conditions. To paint like this calls for a slow tuning in to the subtle rhythms of a day lived by light, and it also requires the knowledge that no matter how fast the painter's hand moves to express what he sees, it is always capturing the past rather than the present. This is particularly poignant when the subject is a river. The river that flows past Jackson when he begins his day's work is not the same one as that which he sees by nightfall, even if he has not moved from the spot. The river is now a different creature, bringing different information to all the senses. Perhaps Jackson's paintings gain some of their aesthetic power from this tension between what is recorded and what is lost forever. Their fascination is akin to that which we feel when standing on a bridge, watching the endless flow of a current that never eddies in exactly the same way twice. These paintings remind us of the limitations of our own days, as well as the intensity of their pleasures. We will die; but first we will see all this.

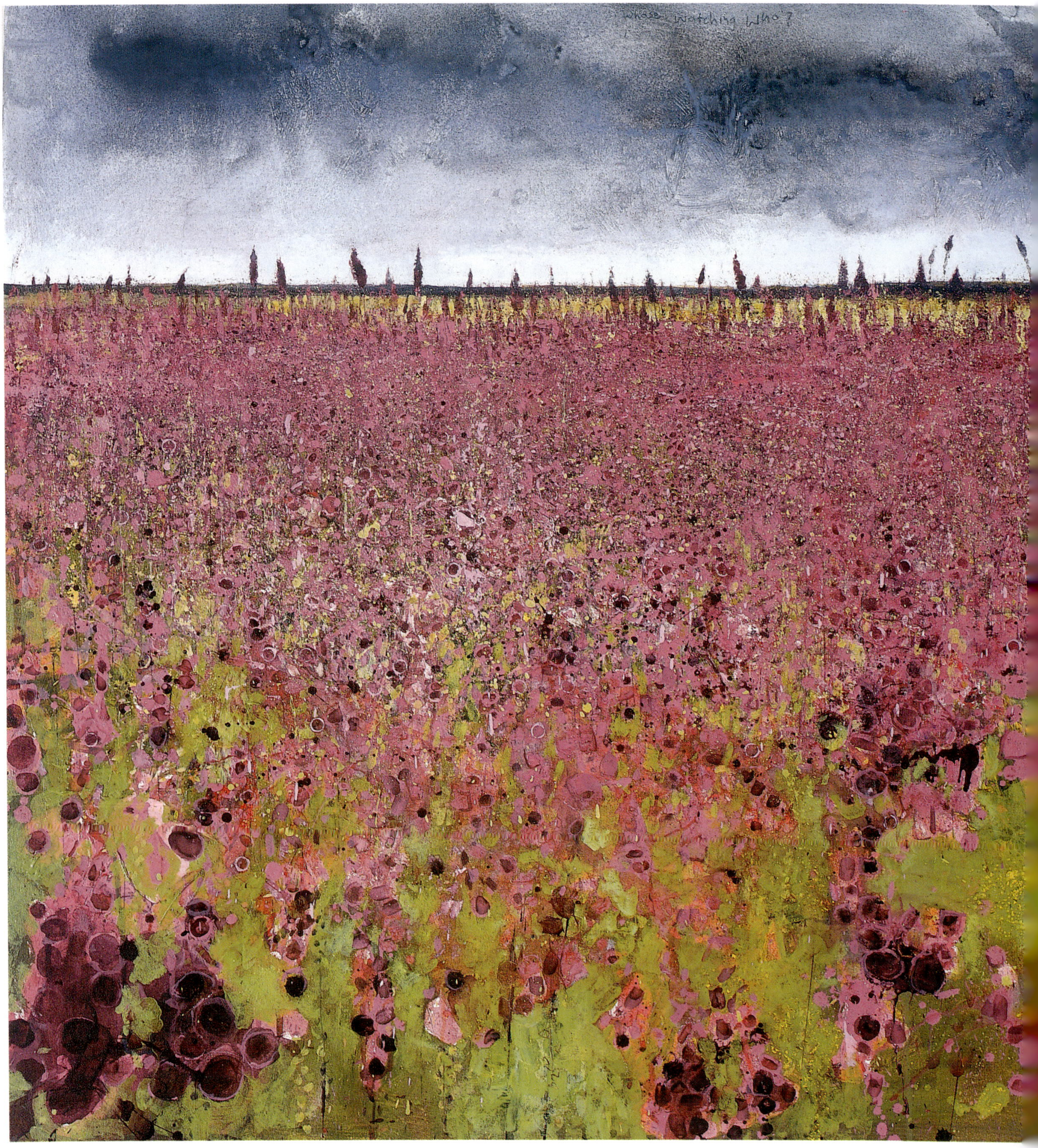
Whose watching Who?

4 A Day with Kurt Jackson

Philip Marsden

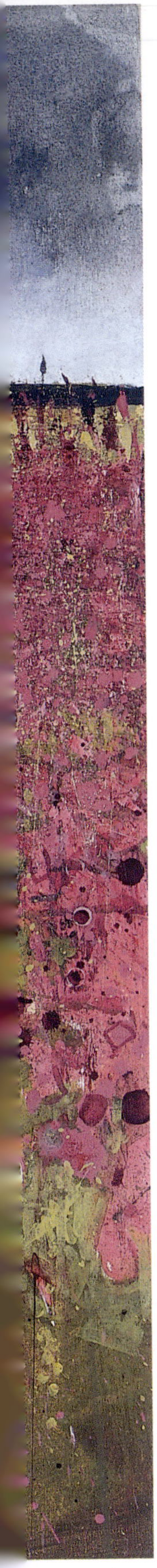

50
Who's watching who? 2001
Acrylic on canvas, 91.5 × 91.5 cm (36 × 36 in)

The Atlantic swells are breaking, folding into green-glass humps and shattering into spray. It is early morning at Cape Cornwall and low cloud is driving in over the water. I pull down my hat and head inland. Away from the sea sound, the Tregeseal Valley is filled with gorse and bluebells, mine detritus, old dammings and shorings, fenced-off shafts and ruined works.

Take the lane to the right. Not really a right, more straight on. Up between head-high hedges, bright with stitchwort and campion, past a barn with a whitewash message on its door – *Congratulations Clive and Linda* – and out on top with the wind fierce and the sea far off. To the north, on the skyline, are the cane clusters of four tepees, more hedges and no trees, a herd of Friesian cows and above them, a wind turbine. *You can't miss our wind turbine.* Go over a gate and through a field and another gate to reach it.

Kurt Jackson is with his wife, Caroline, in the studio. He crosses the granite-flag yard and we greet each other warmly. He is larger in life, with a sense of solidity, a firmness on the earth. He collects sandwiches, a sketching backpack and we are soon both out in the lane. He is talking as we walk, gently pointing out his new walled vegetable garden (the lintel a granite off-cast from Brunel's Viaduct at Hayle) and his own set-aside fields, until suddenly we reach the hedgeless expanse of the moor and are brought to a standstill by the hugeness of it all, by the great sea of gorse and heather spreading north and east, by the distant reef-profile of Carn Kenidjack and, at our feet, by the furry coil of a caterpillar. 'Woolly Bear', Jackson bends to place it in the gorse, 'either a Fox Moth, or a Grass Eggar'.

In places, in little lanes rutted deep from centuries of use, pond-sized puddles stretch from hedge to hedge. We slip and scramble along the banks. This is a route of great age, crossing the moor from Cape Cornwall in the west to the quiet harbour at St Ives and now signposted as a hiking path – 'Tinners Way' – a name that came into use as the last tin mine closed ten years ago. At Chun Quoit, we stand before the remains of the Bronze Age tomb. The granite capstone gives it the appearance

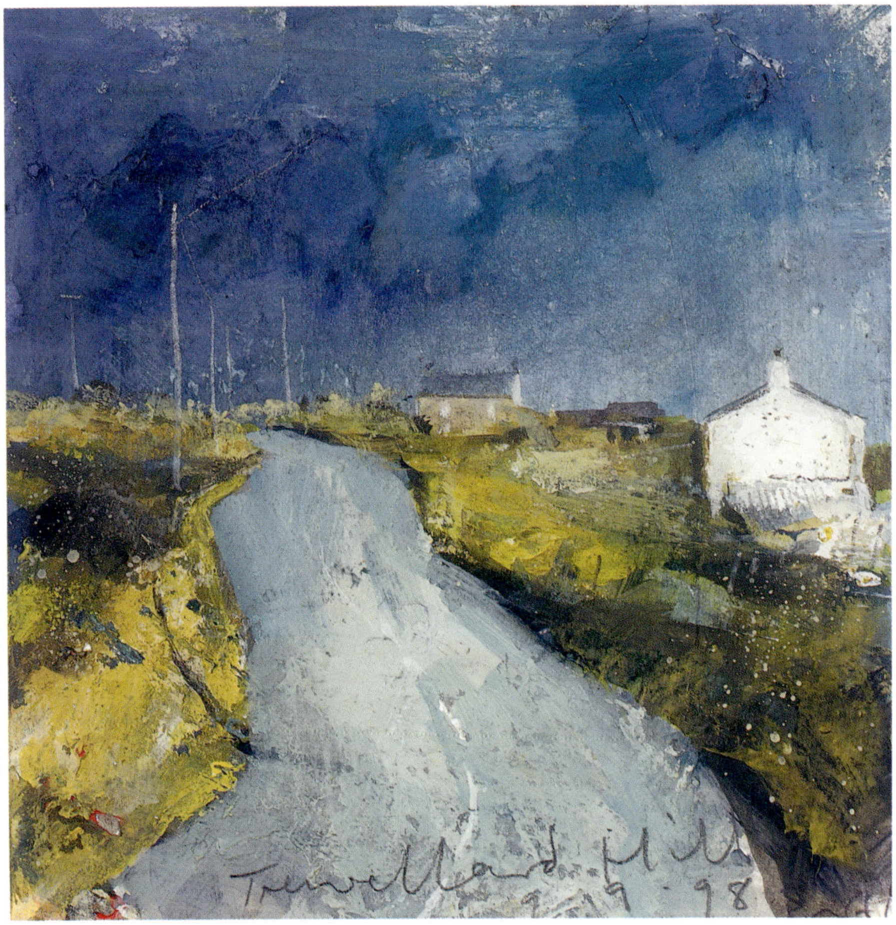

51
Trewellard Hill, 1998
Acrylic, 24 × 21 cm (9.5 × 8 in)

of a giant mushroom. The moors of Penwith are dotted with burial mounds, ancient hut footings, cromlechs and stone circles. They leave the landscape with the suggestion of some eternal, unanswered puzzle. Jackson runs his hand over the pitted feldspar of the tomb: 'The people I have met up here. Poets, painters, New Age travellers, amateur archaeologists, the lot.' There is no one here today.

We speak of the layers of speculation that lie over these sites. I tell him about a theory that the megalithic builders of this area were themselves trying to interpret the landscape with their burial chambers, that each generation lays its own theories over the moors and the relics it finds from previous generations. 'But I suppose that is only another theory', I reflect. 'Yeah, maybe they were just burying their dead', Jackson smiles. 'Look, I'll show you something interesting.'

We reach Chun Castle, a few hundred square metres of low hilltop, ringed by an Iron Age wall. Running down the centre of the fortress is a dividing line: on one side the ground is covered in thigh-high bracken, early foxgloves and campion. On the other, it is smooth, trimmed and raked to a mossy sward. Jackson stands astride the border, his arms open, explaining that by some quirk of stewardship the site is now managed by the Cornwall Wildlife Trust and a local farmer:

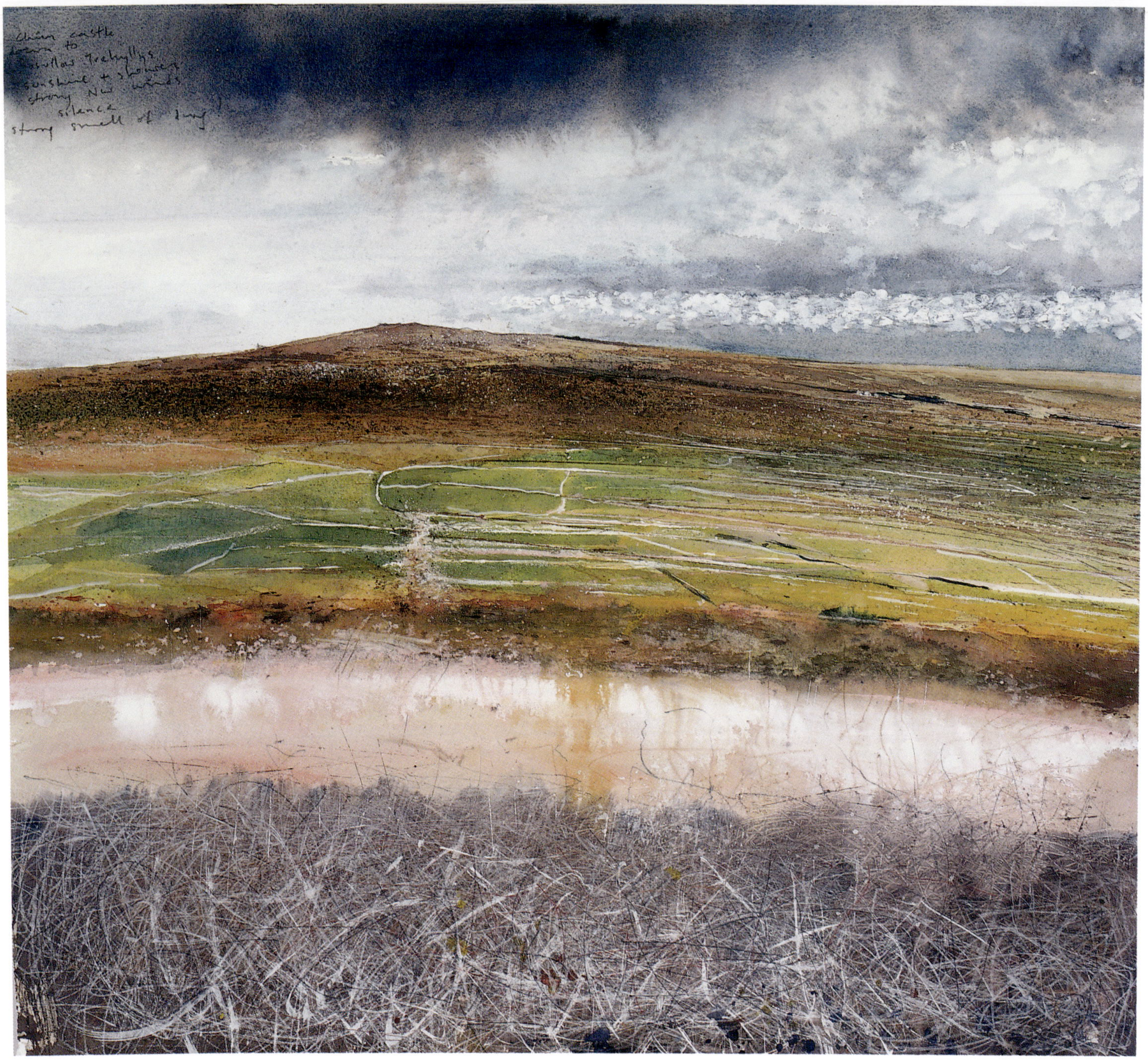

52
From Chun Castle down to Bosullow Trehyllys, sunshine and showers, strong northwest winds, silence, April 2001
Mixed media, 57 × 60.5 cm (22.5 × 24 in)

'One lot, here, believes in cutting the fern and the other does not. Imagine an aerial photograph of that after 20 years. What weird religious practice will they read into that?' The clouds are thinning. Between them, the distant blue is dotted with islands of cirrus. Jackson pulls a sun-faded baseball cap over his bare scalp and starts sketching for the first time. He is standing before the rock-cut well, inside the perimeter wall. Rapidly he draws the granite blocks, filling in the shadows and fissures and the ring of water beneath them. He balances on a rock mound.

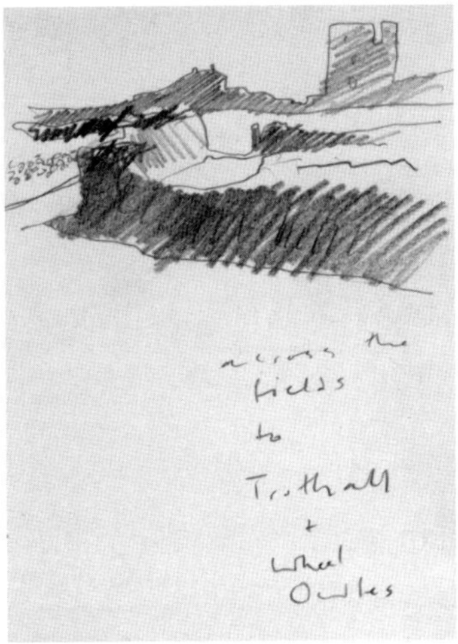
across the fields to Truthall + Wheal Owles

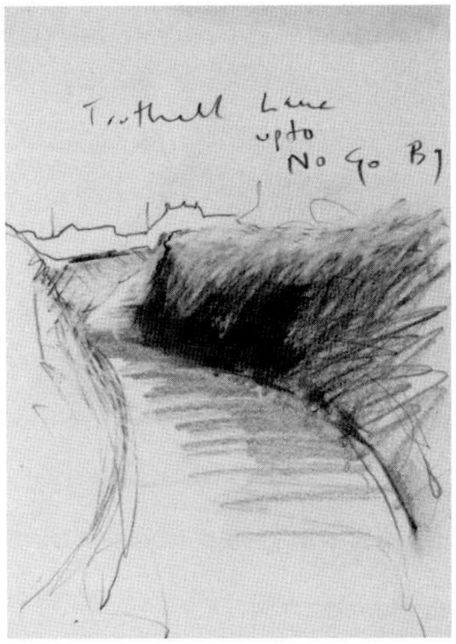
Truthall Lane upto No Go By

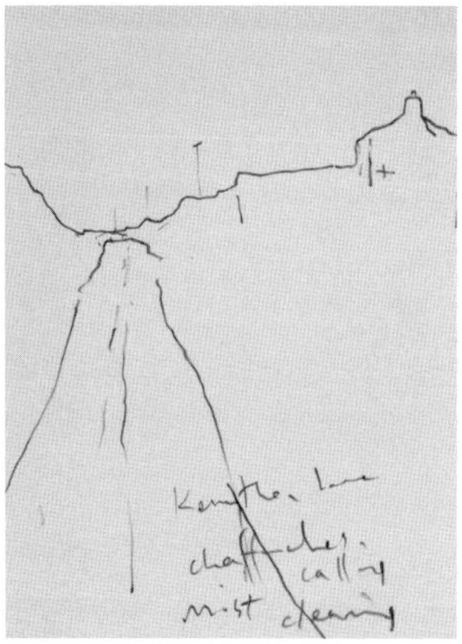
chaffinches calling
mist clearing

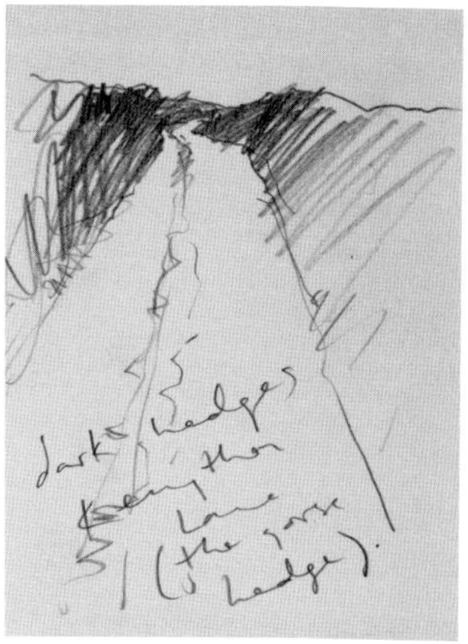
dark hedges
lane
(the gorse hedge).

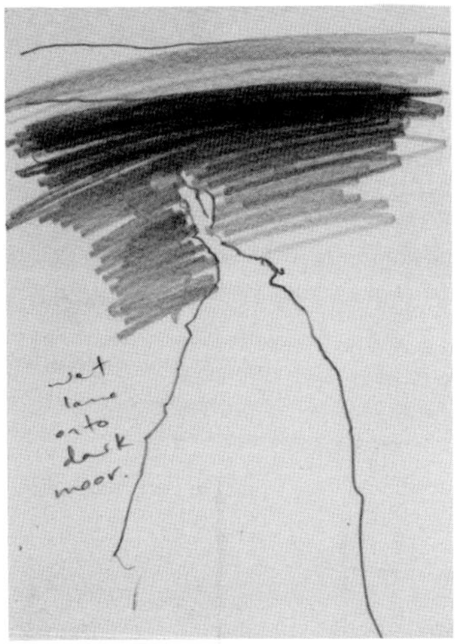
wet lane onto dark moor.

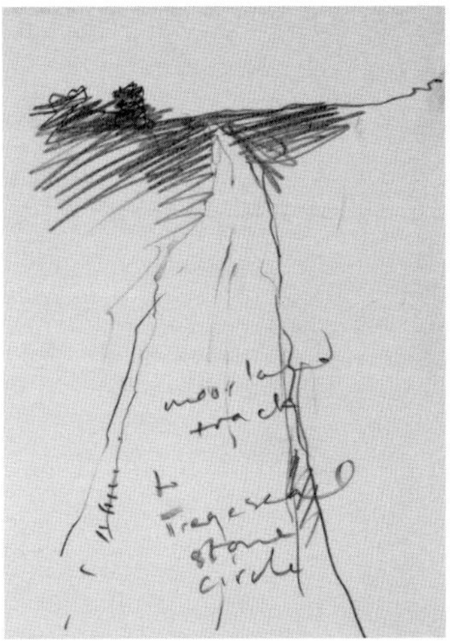
moorland track
to Tregeseal stone circle

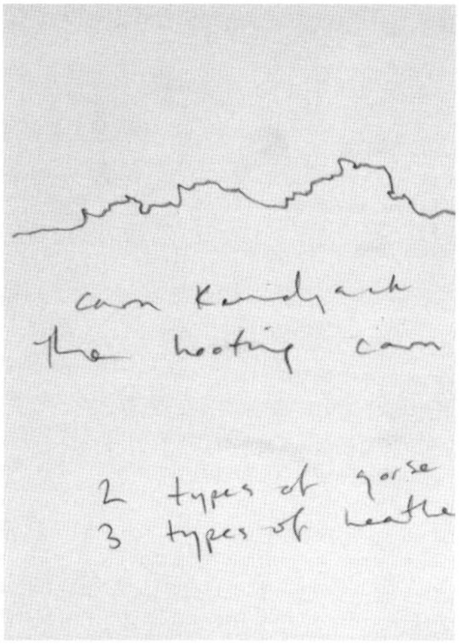
carn Kenidjack
the hooting carn
2 types of gorse
3 types of heathe

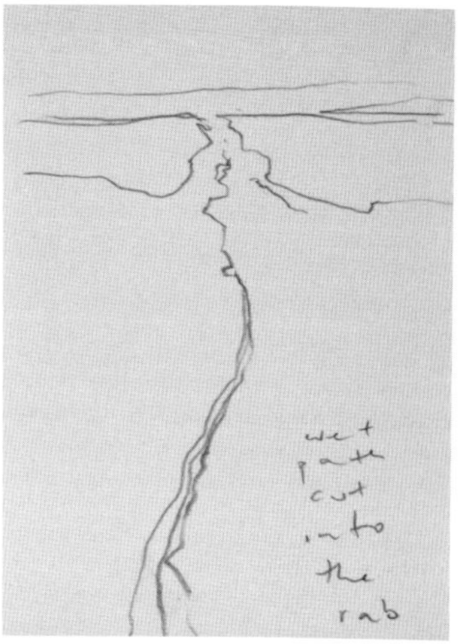
wet path cut into the rab

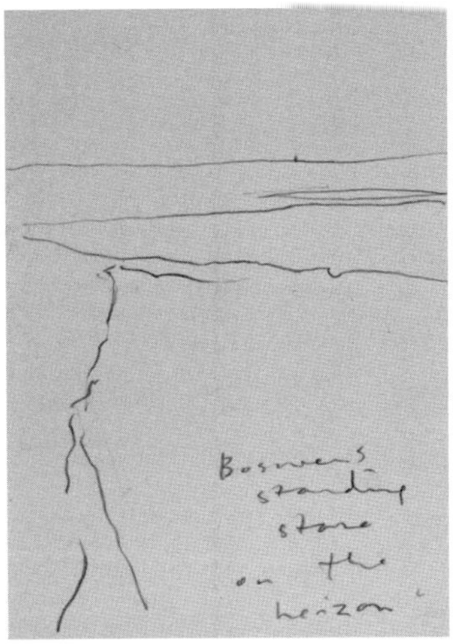
Boswens standing stone on the horizon

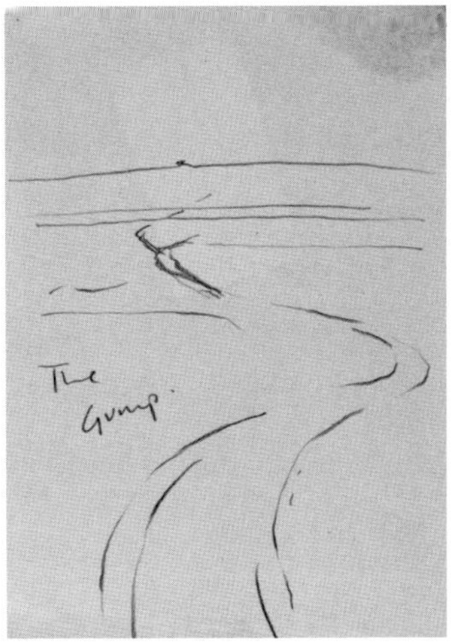
The Gump.

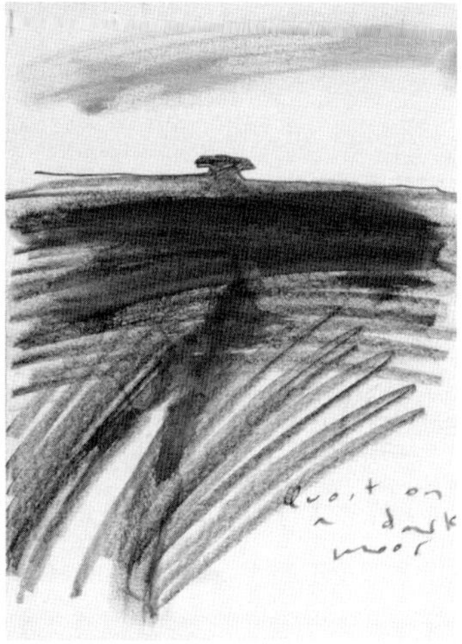
Quoit on a dark moor

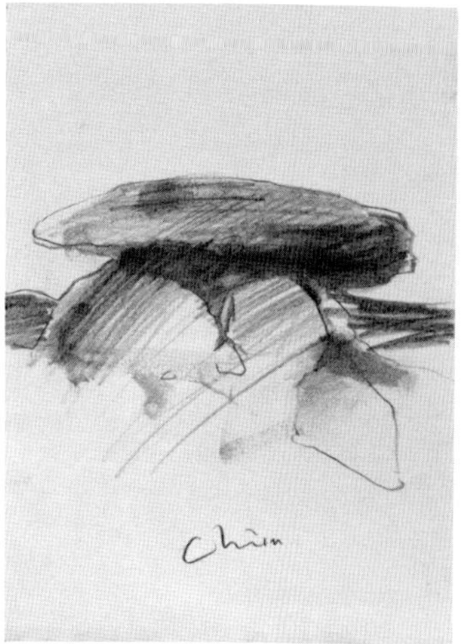
Chun

53
The Tinners' Way, Forth an Stenoryon, 2001
12 of 234 drawings produced on a day's walk from Cape Cornwall to St Ives. Pencil, each measures 20.5 × 14.5 cm (8 × 5.5 in)

'They were lucky', he says as he looks up and down from the page, 'to find water all the way up here'.

At the ruined settlement of Bosullow Trehyllys, Jackson again stands drawing. When the pencil has done its job, he plucks a bluebell and scrubs its pigment on to the page. Then he dips his thumb in mud and rubs that in another corner. I wander out over the wall, overwhelmed by the strangeness of the site, by its fossil-stillness. Suddenly I'm brought up short. Crouching against a rock, breathing quickly, motionless but for fearful darting eyes, sits a herring gull. Its shoulder is spattered with blood, and its beak is red from pecking at the wound. Jackson comes up, packing away his sketchbook. 'Maybe shot – or flew into the cables'. The gull rises to its feet as we approach, flapping its one wing and hopping away. We cannot get close. 'Fox dinner', he says. We scramble up out of the settlement and back on to the track.

In 2001 Jackson showed his series the 'Tinners Way, Forth An Stenoryon'. For nine months, through autumn, winter, spring, he came up here and worked for hours in the rain, sun and fog, sketching the ancient sites, the bald skylines, and

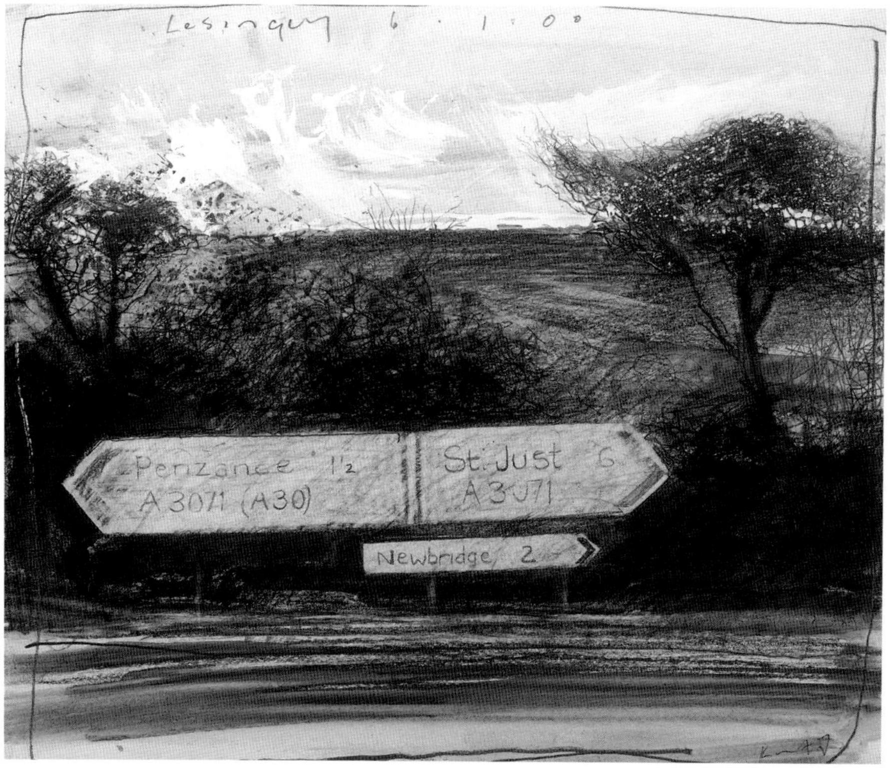

54
Lesingey drawing, 6/1/2000
Graphite and ink, 30 × 30 cm (12 × 12 in)

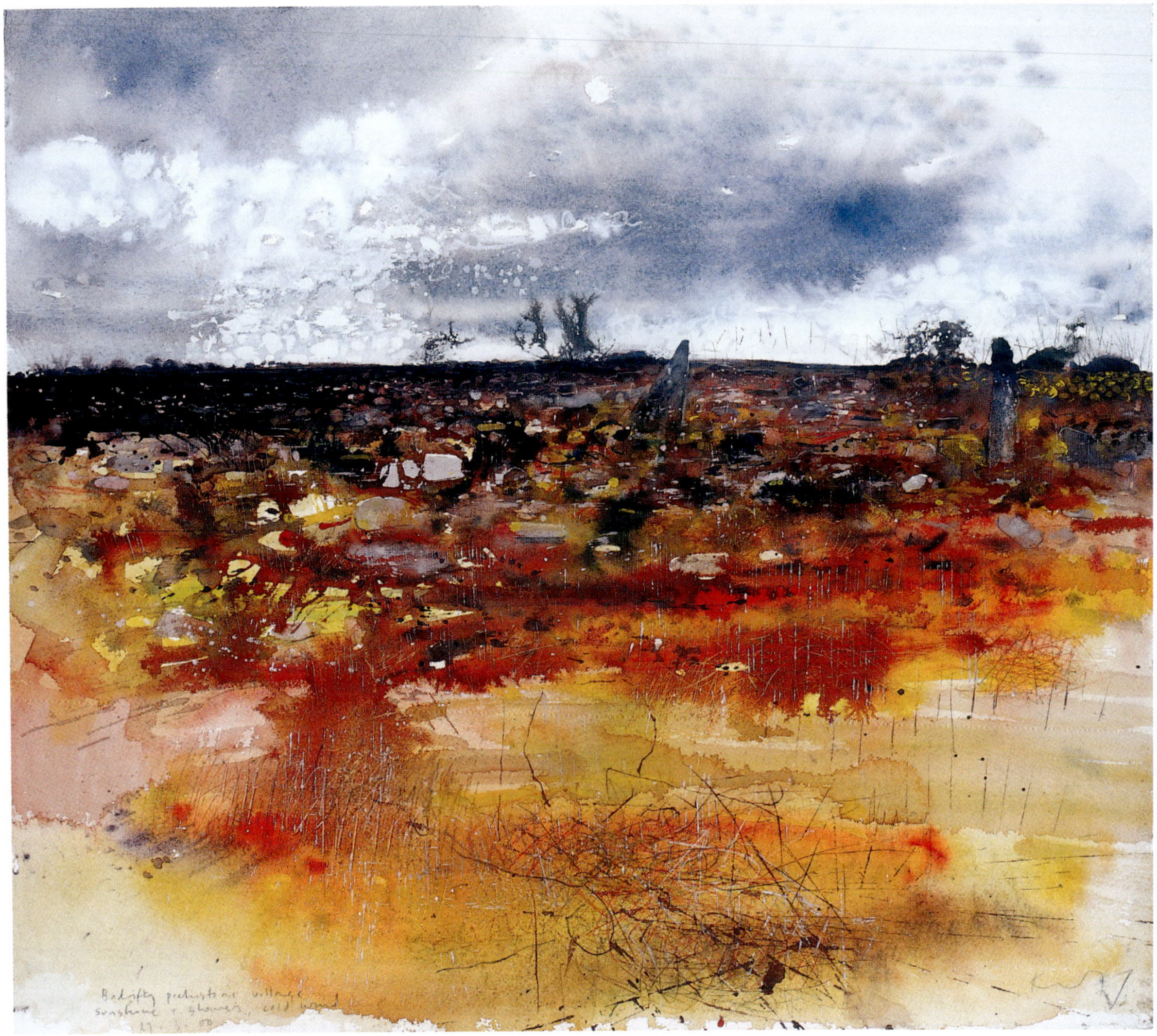

55
Bodrifty prehistoric village, sunshine and showers, cold wind, 29/3/00
Mixed media, 57 × 63 cm
(22.5 × 25 in)

the track itself with the hedges converging into the distance. It was the time of the outbreak of foot-and-mouth disease. The moors were more empty than usual. Every foray had to be cleared with the landowners, so his intimacy with the area now extends beyond its studied forms and colours, its companion mammals and bird-life, its beetles and wildflowers, to the wind-hardened human inhabitants. Each farm we pass brings out an anecdote from Jackson. 'Only one of those people was anything other than completely welcoming', he concludes.

'Dakota farm, burnt gorse, dry grass, winter sun, winter rain. Carn Galva and hedges, bumble bee buzzing past my head. Bosullow Common, lane to Garden Mine Cottage, a weasel runs past me'. The marginal titles of Jackson's paintings are always brief and specific; those of the 'Tinners Way, Forth An Stenoryon' series are no different. There is a haiku-like quality about them, combining classical elements of *sabi* or 'solitariness', engagement with nature, and *karumi*, 'lightness of touch'. When I ask Jackson whom he places in his neighbourhood of artists, expecting

him to nod to J.M.W. Turner or Richard Long, he appears uncomfortable. He pauses, before citing the seventeenth-century Zen monk and master of haiku: 'Basho'.

After several hours up here, the horizon begins to etch itself on the retina. We are climbing up towards the hilltop stone circle of the Nine Maidens (Boskednan). One of Jackson's paintings records this landmark. Beneath a charcoal sky, a strip of brightness glows above the land. The stones themselves are so small against it that they appear as tiny serrations on the horizon. Yet the eye is drawn straight to them. Many of his works have the same single feature of absolute precision surrounded by looseness. And so it is with the moor – a vast expanse of undulating land, raw nature, yellow gorse, burnt-blond grass – and then the deliberate placing of a hut circle or a ring of standing stones.

We are sitting outside the pound in another Iron Age settlement, at Bodrifty. The sun flashes on spears of sedge grass. The building stones are half-buried in vegetation. We are perched on waterproof trousers, eating sandwiches, surrounded by lark song, the smell of gorse and the flitting of goldfinches. Jackson was a passionate collector from an early age – not only of butterflies and moths, but of beetles and flies. He pinned rows and rows of them to corkboard. The hunter's acquisitiveness does not square now with his eco-principles, but the deep immersion in the natural world does: 'My parents had to put on an extension to house them all. I gave the collection to the St Albans Museum.'

We pack up, and Jackson fingers the buds of a foxglove as we leave. 'The Cornish name is *manegow an spyrysyon*, meaning "gloves of the ghosts"', he says.

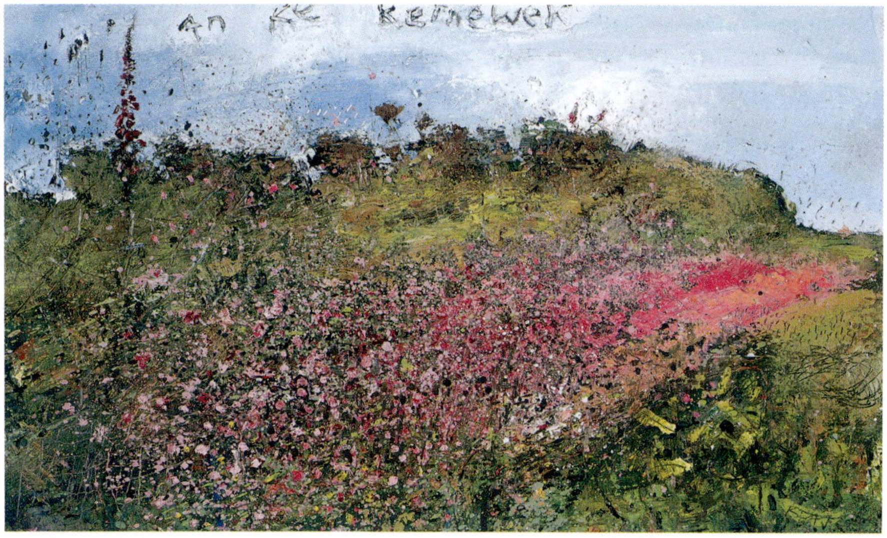

56
***An Ke Kernewek*, 2005**
Oil on board, 28 × 44 cm
(11 × 17.5 in)

The sun has grown bright. Its glare presses heavily on the brow. At Mulfra Quoit, the far-off sheen of Mount's Bay appears to the south. We speak of mutual friends, of places we know in the Hebrides, and of the year that Jackson spent in Africa.

In Lady Downs Lane, he points out where he has stood and worked. But painting does not feature highly in his conversation. In fact, he hardly mentions it. Even when he does stop to sketch the detail of a stone hedge, he speaks of other things – the remoteness of the lane, the house at the end that has no water, where they collect water by bicycle. The concentration is somewhere deep-down, leaving the mind free to talk about the people who live there, about the man in an old Cornish longhouse who is developing his own designs to harness wind energy, and about another, here on the right, whose legendary parties punctuate a life dedicated to developing a new patented fuel for cars.

We carry on up Lady Downs Lane, passing an abandoned vehicle and a closed-up cottage and, in the roofless ruins of a byre, a string of washing – red trousers, red T-shirt, white trousers. But for the whole length of that lane, we see no people. We reach the moor again. The land here drains to the north. Through the 'V' shape of a valley we glimpse the tower of St Senara Church and the village at Zennor. The triangle of sea beyond is flecked with white tops. Just two weeks ago, a storm dumped several inches of rain over this hill in a matter of hours. It took out the stone bridge at Zennor and a car that was on it at the time. One body was found near the wreckage, another was washed out to sea. The third, the body of a young woman, has not been found.

A hawthorn stands alone above the spring. We glance at it. Then we find ourselves pausing, drawn in by its isolation and its wind-skewed shape. The more we look at it, the more expressive it becomes. On the branchless upwind side, the bark is polished, sheep-rubbed, the hairs still stuck in it. There is something animal-like in the shape of the boughs. They are not round in section but oblong, as if muscled. From the downwind side streams a great scarf of foliage, the fresh green leaves with the tinge of red still on them, and the white blooms, and the loose-hair strands of new growth waving above them. Jackson ducks in beneath the canopy. 'Odd... you would expect at least one nest, being the only tree around. There's none', he reflects.

He stands back. Yet we remain there, caught by the spell of the tree, by the afternoon light on its boughs, by the twisted course of every branch that leads up from the bole until it is lost in the labyrinth. Now Jackson is clutching his sketchbook, scribbling the growth-tangle out across the page, talking: 'There is an

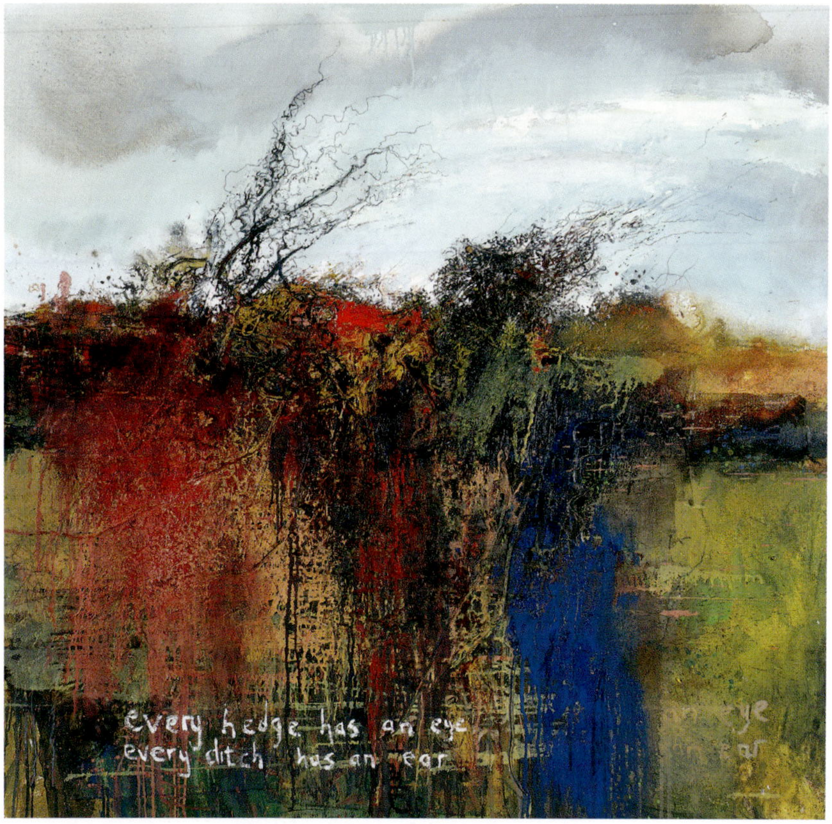

57
Every hedge has an eye, every ditch has an ear, 2004
Mixed media on canvas,
122 × 122 cm (48 × 48 in)

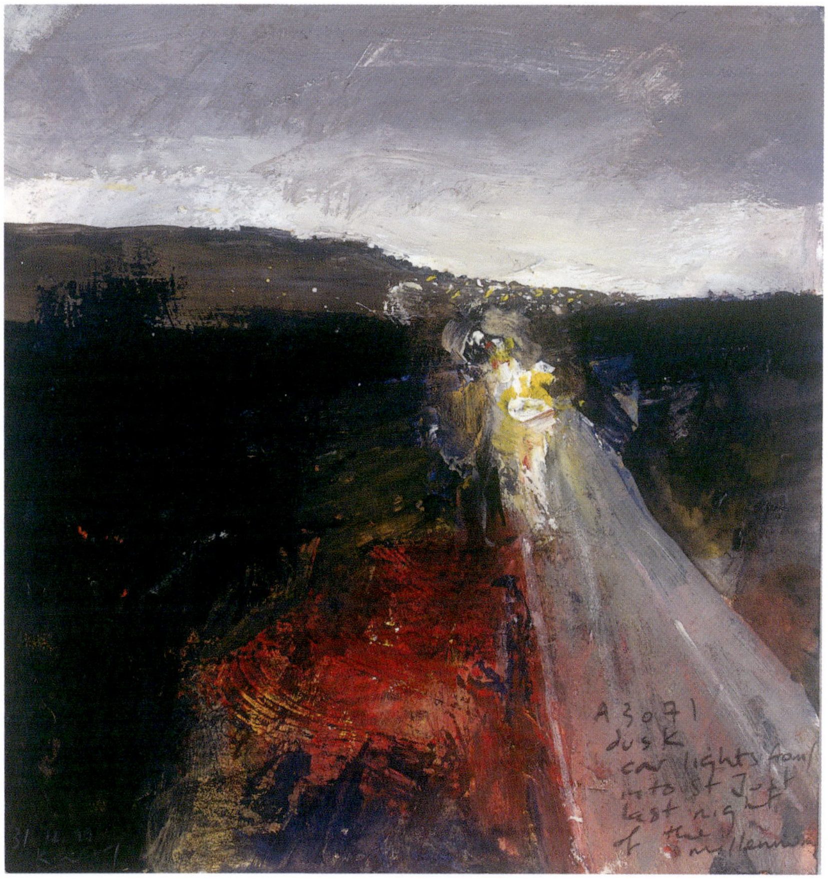

58
A3071, dusk. Car lights from/into St Just, last night of the Millennium
Acrylic, 19.5 × 18 cm (7.5 × 7 in)

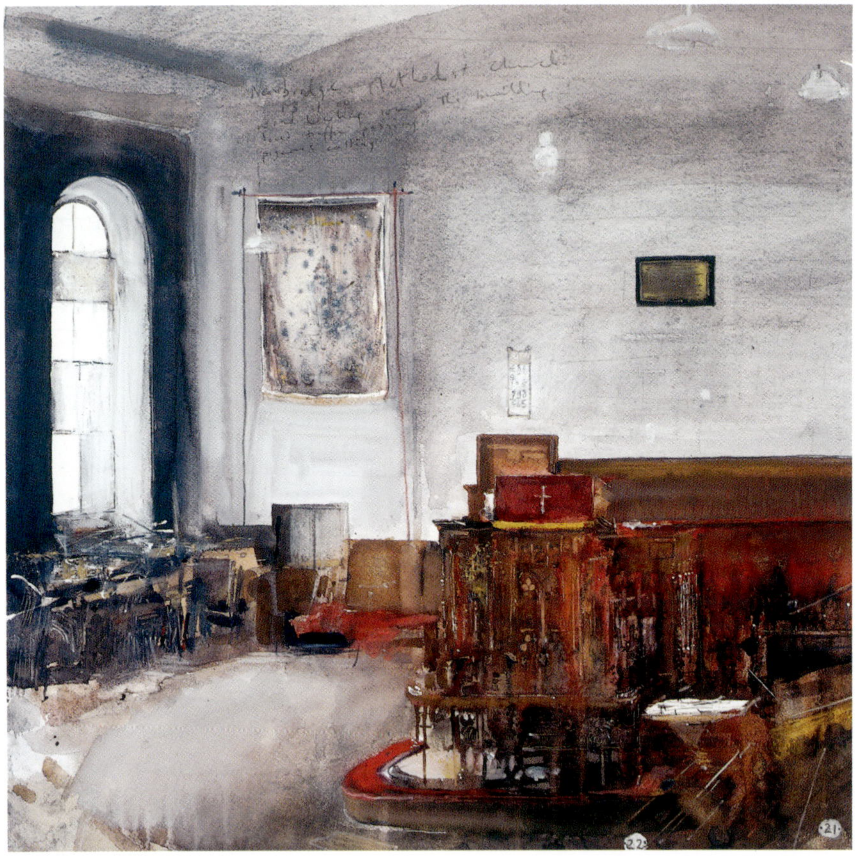

59
Newbridge Methodist Church. Wind howling around the building. Traffic passing, pigeons calling, 13/1/2000
Mixed media, 57 × 55 cm (22.5 × 21.5 in)

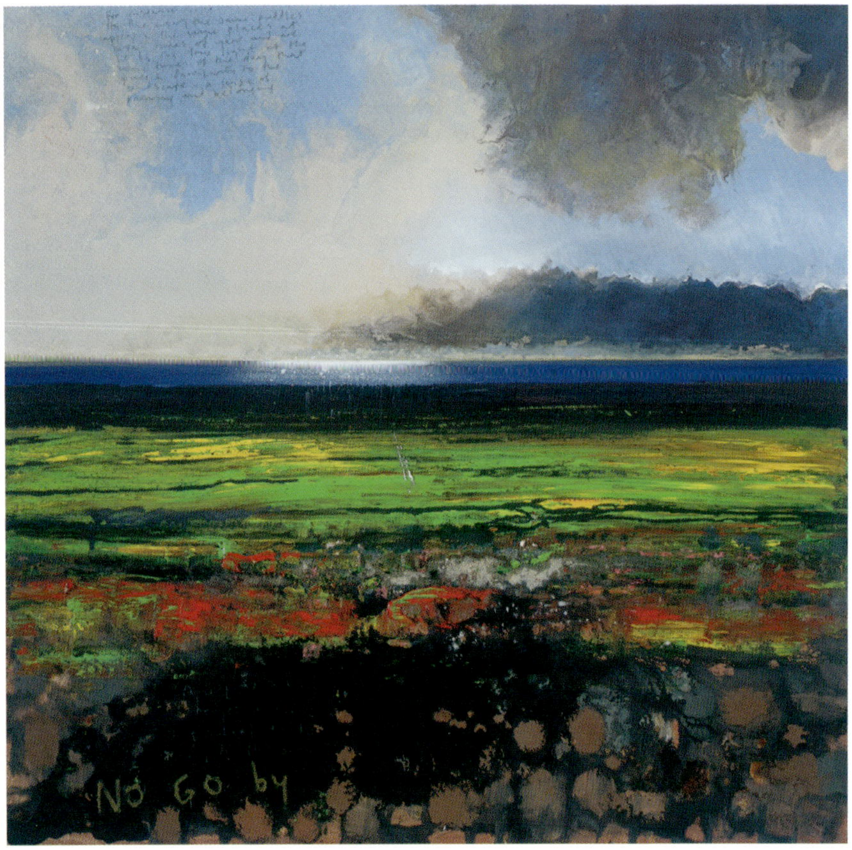

60
No Go By. Autumn hedges and fields, wet wheel tracks down to the sea, 2006
Oil and collage on canvas, 91.5 × 91.5 cm (36 × 36 in)

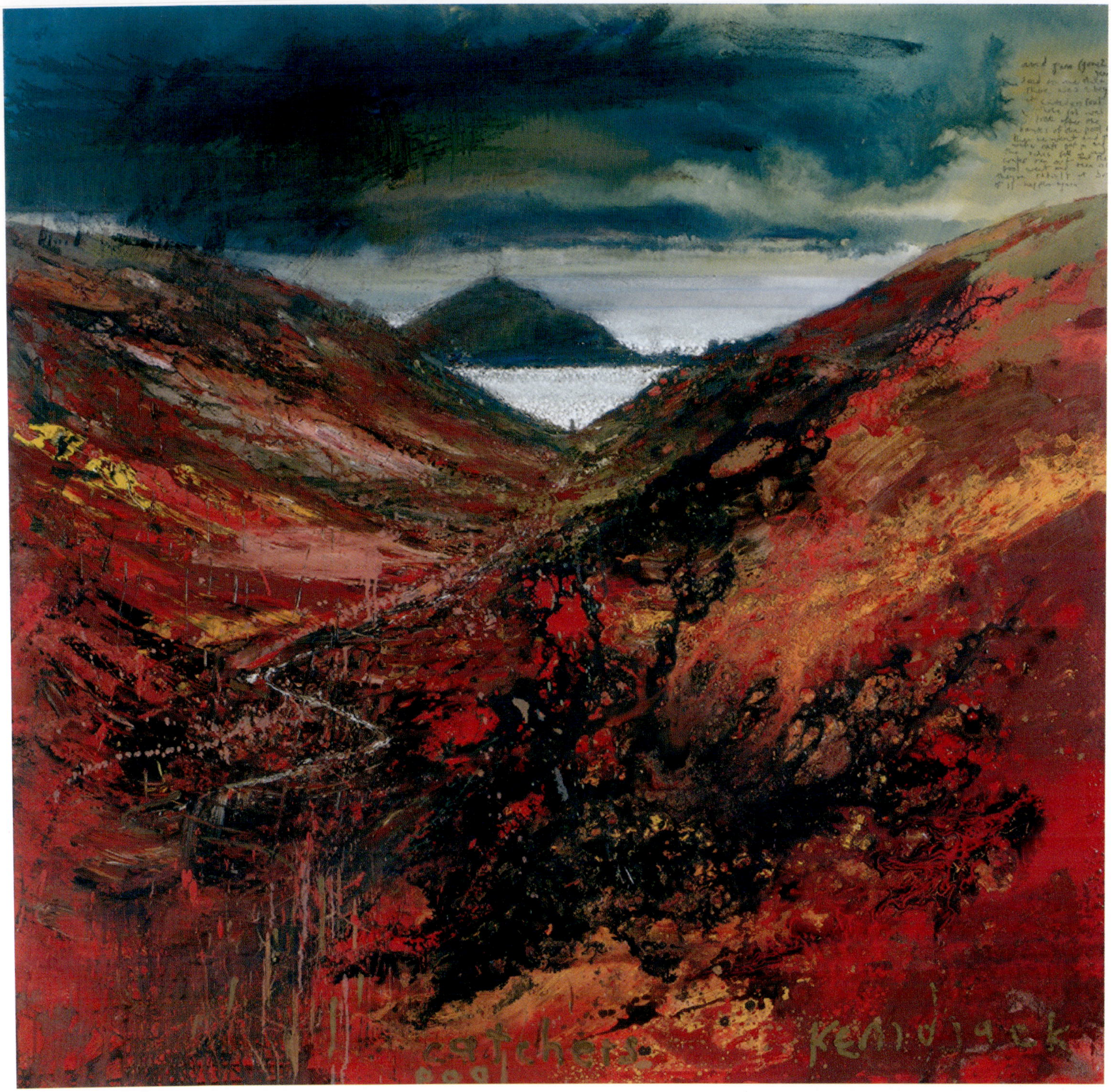

61
Catchers Pool, Kenidjack, 2006
Mixed media on canvas, 152 × 152 cm (60 × 60 in)

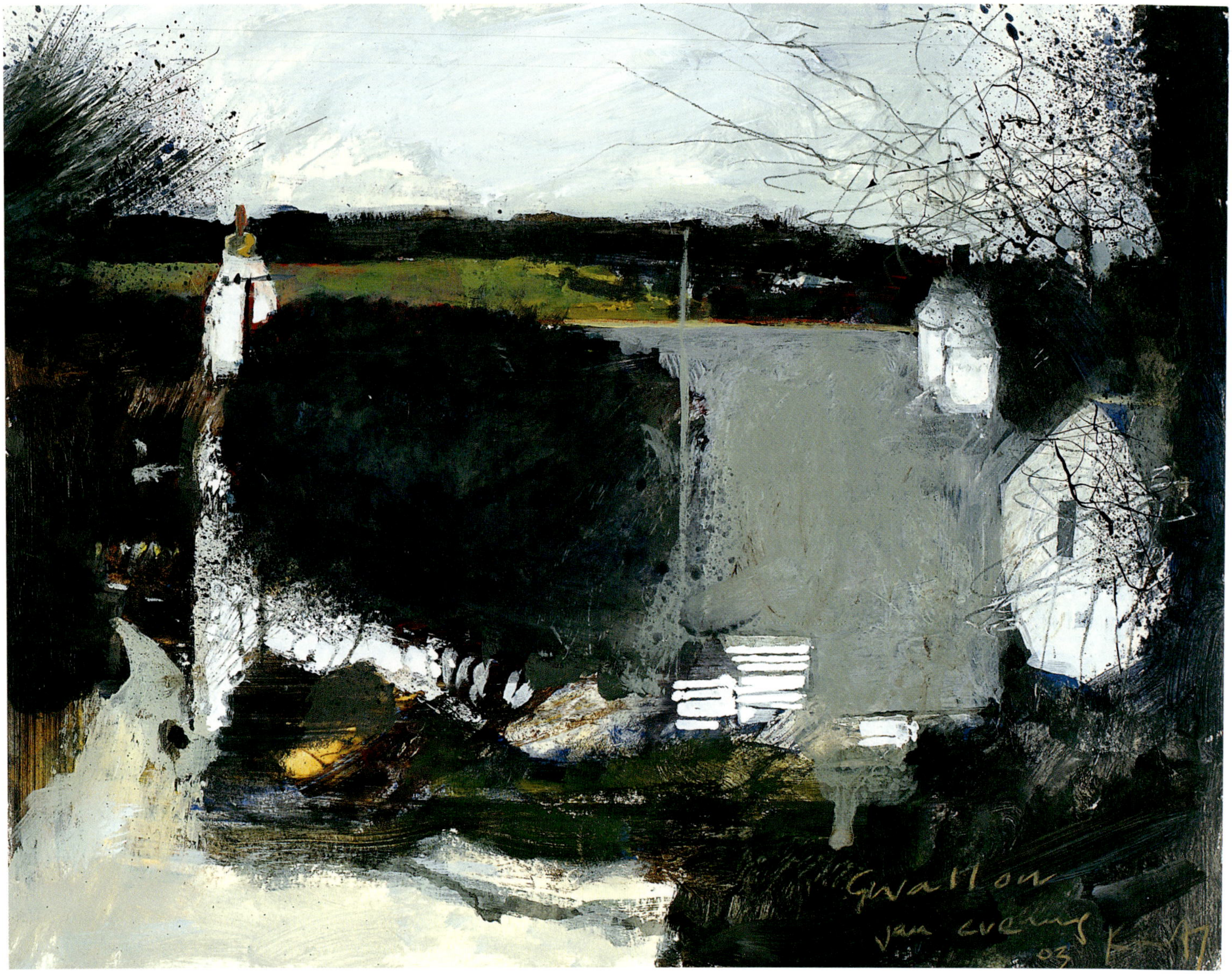

62
Gwallon, January evening, 2003
Acrylic, 23 × 28 cm (9 × 11 in)

old hawthorn near Morvah. Over the hill there.' He gestures with his chin to the south. 'A few years back, I went there every week. I have still got those sketches, 52 images of the same tree. It's like a flip book or something. The tree is getting its clothes on, its flowers and fruit, then losing them again.'

He steps up and tears off a leaf and rubs it on the page: 'I met a forestry man the other day.' He is still drawing. 'He said that some of these hawthorns have been around for five thousand years. They die back, spring up, die again and come back, but it's all from the same root. Five thousand years!'

The last we see of the moor is a great burn scar. The heat-stripped stumps of the gorse rise from pools of ash, like the ribs of an old ship. Jackson stops to sketch them. Not happy, he turns the book upside down and rasps it over the charcoal tops.

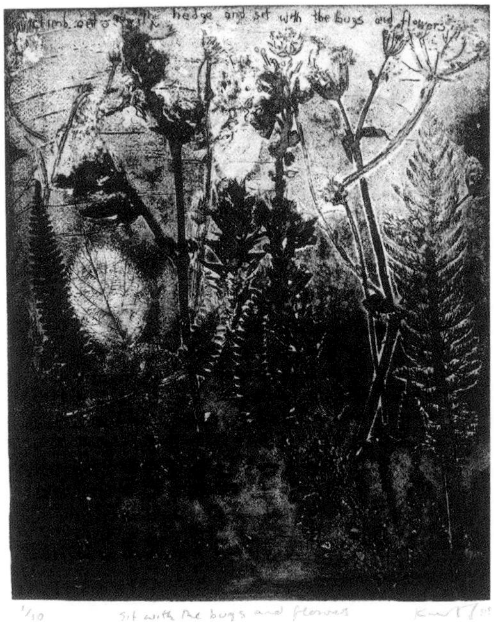

63
***Sit with the bugs and flowers*, 2005**
Etching and drypoint, 25 × 19.5 cm (10 × 7.5 in).
Edition of 10

'Hey!' He sounds surprised. He holds up the book for me to look at and the random shapes somehow capture the wild pattern of that fire field. He is constantly experimenting, playing with whatever comes to hand. It is a way of engaging, and because he does it ceaselessly, many of the experiments pay off.

The day slides towards evening. We leave the moor, walking down a path torn to bedrock by the recent flood. The land levels out. We pass trout ponds and driveways, carports and buzzing lawnmowers. We reach the main Penzance road and walk in single file down a narrow pavement. For the first time all day, we fall silent. Passing the pottery of Bernard Leach, we reach St Ives itself. St Ives! The great Cornish outpost of twentieth-century art! Where Ben Nicholson sliced up the view into Cubist blocks, where Terry Frost transcribed the light as solid sweeps of colour, where Barbara Hepworth brought the moor-shapes down from the moor and chiselled and polished them until they looked like nothing so much as themselves, and where the Tate has now honoured their work in a much-visited museum.

'Do you come to St Ives much?' I ask.

He shrugs, 'Not that much'.

We head towards the harbour. Kurt Jackson suddenly chuckles. 'I was in a taxi the other day, up in London, and the driver says to me – *Just been down your way on holiday. St Ives. Lovely place*. I ask him – *Did you go to the Tate?* He looks at me in the mirror – *What? You mean there's a Tate Gallery there as well? I had no idea.'*

Jackson smiles. He gazes out over the rooftops to the ten-mile sweep of the bay, to the distant headland of Godrevy and its ivory lighthouse, and beyond that, to the lines of Atlantic swells pressing on towards the coast.

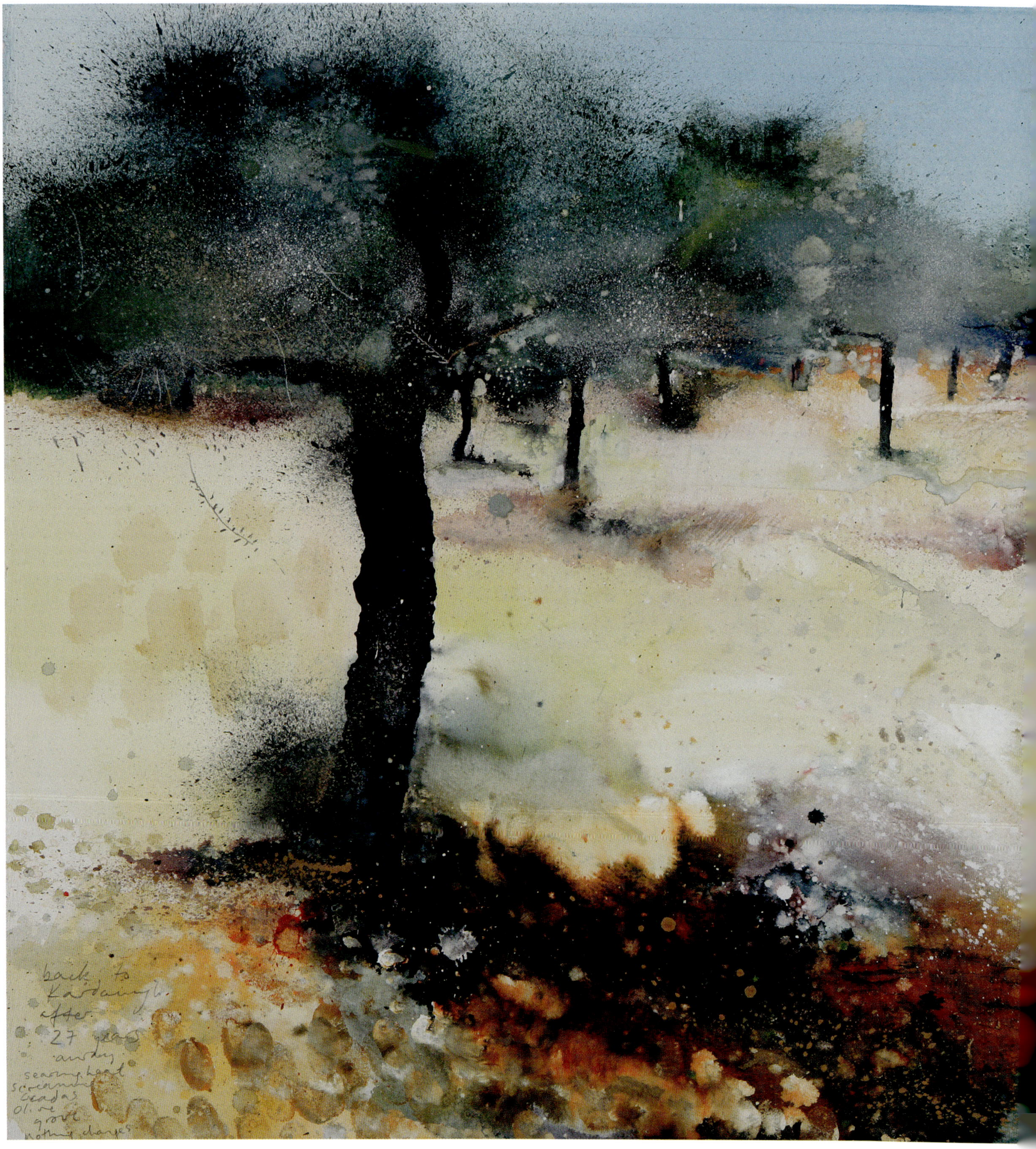
back to
Kardamyli
after
27 years
away
searing heat
screaming
cicadas
olive
grove
nothing changes

5 Two Trees/Five Senses/ A World

Bel Mooney

A precious Kurt Jackson painting hangs above my home-made work surface on a white-painted stone wall in what was once a rough storeroom and is now my study. The small acrylic landscape, measuring 21 × 21 cm (8 × 8 in) is brooding in the depths of its greens, and shows two trees, one behind the other, wearing the sky like a halo fringed by the bird-like leaves of fig. With the intense simplicity of a haiku, the artist's words offer up the moment: 'nightfall | fig behind olive | cicadas have gone quiet | crickets are singing now'. In the centre of the picture is the twisted black trunk and main branch of the olive tree and a mist of grey-green leaves set against the darkness of the fig tree behind. In the distance beyond the two trees is a line of tiny trunks shimmering in the pale evening light, which lead you to reflect on the continuity of ancient flora and its interdependency with human life in that place.

The date scrawled in the lower right-hand corner adds dimensions to the story set within the white frame: 8/05. This painting is from Jackson's 'Kardamili' series, created in a small village on the coast of the Mani Peninsula in Greece, which is almost the most southerly part of mainland Europe. You realise how punishing the August heat must have been, how welcome the respite of evening, when the harsh, relentless din of the cicadas is replaced by the gentler chirrup of crickets and the painter can pack up for the day.

Jackson's 'Kardamili' paintings hold a deep personal significance for the artist and, equally importantly, connect to his global preoccupations. This is not being fanciful, as if to invest one small tree painting with a weight of political significance as arid as Greek soil on an August day. No, it is to suggest that behind Jackson's love of this one remote area is a profound awareness of the cultural and environmental history of the genius loci. The spirit of place is carried in the sap of fig and olive trees and in the atoms of every minute organism that inhabits their ancient wood.

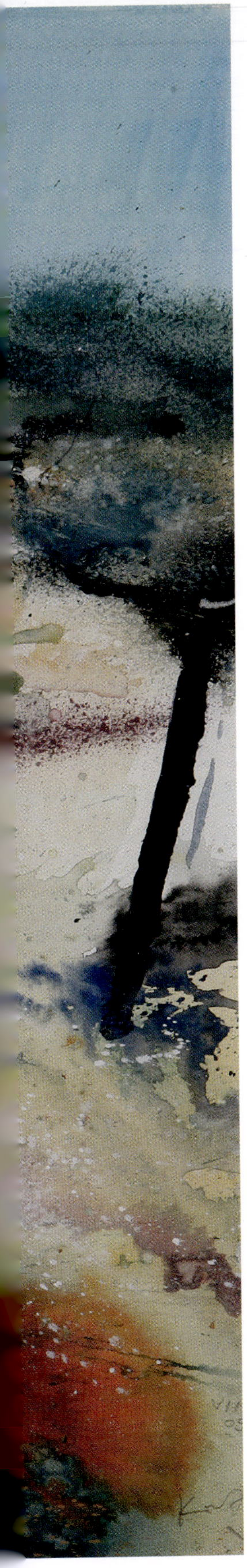

64
Back to Kardamili after 27 years away, searing heat, screaming cicadas, olive grove, July 2005
Mixed media on paper,
56 × 60 cm (22 × 23.5 in)

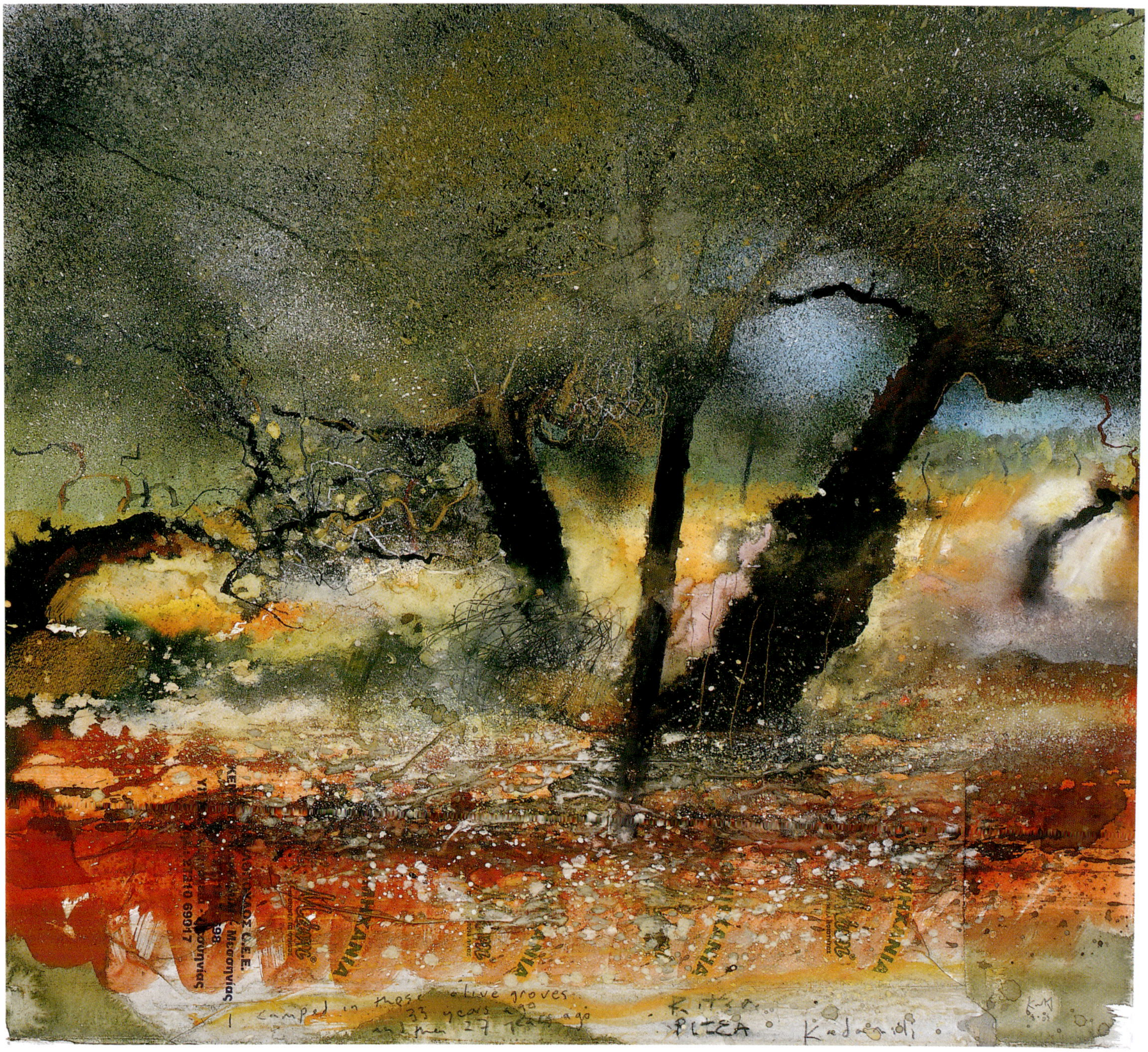

65
I camped in these olive groves 32 years ago and then 27 years ago. Ritsa, Kardamili, August 2005
Mixed media and collage, 56 × 59 cm (22 × 23 in)

66
Church of Agios Nikolaos: 'Bruce Chatwin's Church', Chora above Kardimili, August 2005
Mixed media, 25 × 25 cm (10 × 10 in)

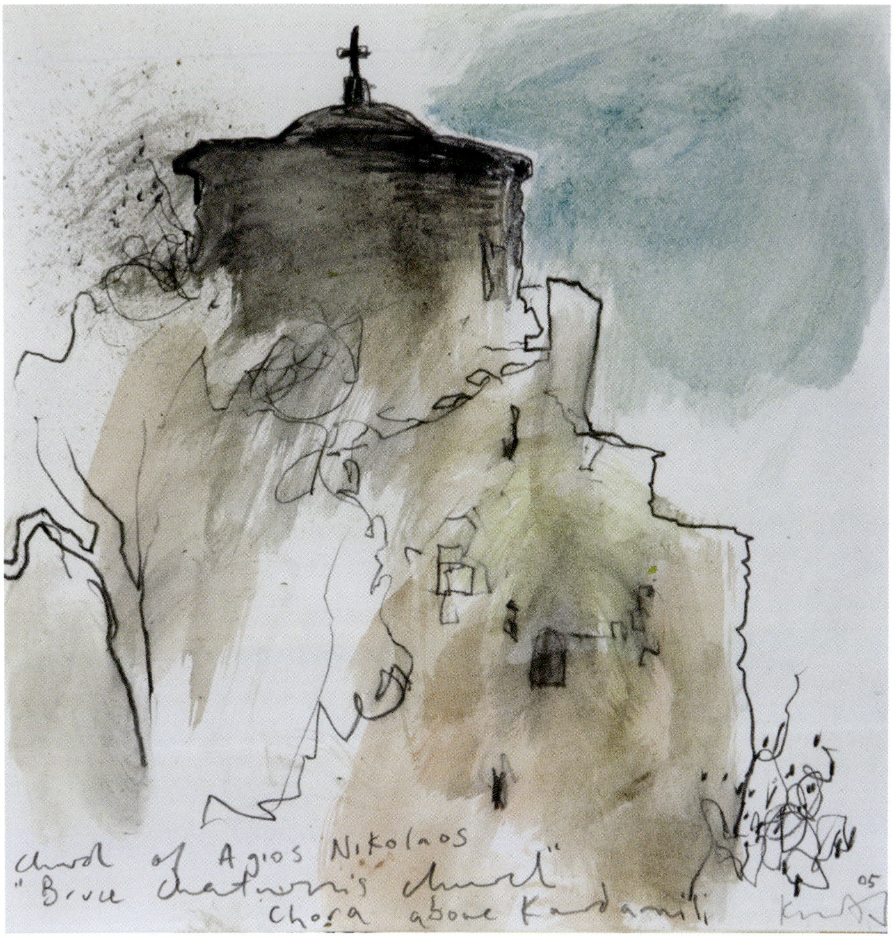

So there are many layers of meaning in the painting I glance up at while writing this essay. The autobiographical fragments lead backwards into the nostalgia of the past. Then the painter's characteristic use of descriptive words captures the moment, the sensuality of the present. Beyond that, you cannot look at a Kurt Jackson painting without being aware of wider concerns, which lead inexorably towards debates over the future of this planet. The journey takes us from the artist's robust childhood towards a spiritual meditation on our fragile destiny.

To begin with the past, Jackson first visited Kardamili in Greece in 1973 when he was twelve years old. He was blessed with an artist father so imaginative that, inspired by reading Patrick Leigh Fermor's classic book on the Mani Peninsula, he loaded his family into an old Land Rover and drove to see this Eden. They slept on the beach or in the olive groves for the whole summer, and Jackson immersed himself in the natural world. He never forgot those olive groves: the red earth, the ancient black trunks, the lapping of what Homer called 'the wine-dark sea' in the *Iliad*.

Then, at seventeen years old, he hitchhiked back to Kardamili from Athens with a girlfriend, to find that the place was the same but the rules had changed: the police would not let them camp freely in the open. No Eden can remain untouched by the modern world. Fatefully, it was on that same visit, in another part of Greece, that he had a life-changing encounter with two men who had just finished reading Zoology at Oxford. As a somewhat recalcitrant comprehensive lad who had never heard of the dreaming spires, Jackson became consumed with the desire to study at the university. It was an unlikely career choice, but he got in, met his future wife Caroline and, in time, began his career as an artist. His work would always be driven by his passion for the natural world he had studied with careless rapture as a child, and with forensic insight as a student.

It is no wonder that he wanted to share his vision of that particular Eden with the life partner who is one of the guiding spirits of his work, as well as its ballast. So in 2005 he took Caroline and their three children to live simply in a small stone hut at the top of the olive groves in his determination 'to paint it properly'. This time the place was given deeper resonance for him by the fact that the ashes of the writer Bruce Chatwin are scattered around the church there. More than ever, he sensed the sacred elements of nature. The magnificent result was a body of painting that shimmered with heat and light.

I went to see Jackson in his creative utopia in Cornwall, to ask him to take me on a journey into the heart of my picture. This became an excursion into pure sensation: the nowness of the act of painting in which 'all time is eternally present', in the words of T.S. Eliot. Wearing his big straw hat, Jackson walks into a day of punishing heat, of screaming cicadas, during which all five senses will be stretched to breaking point. The fig leaves are scented, but the fruit gives off a sweet, rotting smell as countless insects and birds feast on its decadent richness. The thickening air is infused with the subtle, dry aroma of olives and the pungent, herby fragrance of the undergrowth. Sweat stings and its odour rises because it is so hot.

Soon Jackson is driven mad by the cicadas, and scrawls as much on picture after picture ('*...the cicadas deafen you... Don't the cicadas ever want to be quiet?*'). When he becomes frustrated because the work is not going so well, he yells at them to '*Shut up!*' and his own voice bursts into what, on paper, looks like a quiet

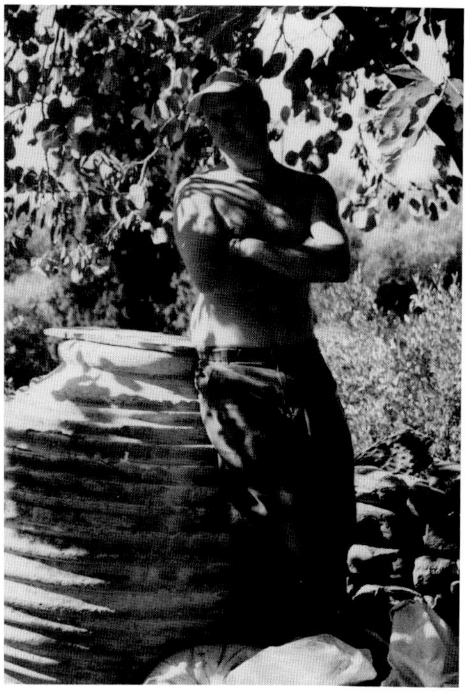

67
Kardamili, 2005

68
For Bruce Chatwin, August 2005
Mixed media and collage on hessian, 74 × 71 cm (29 × 28 in)

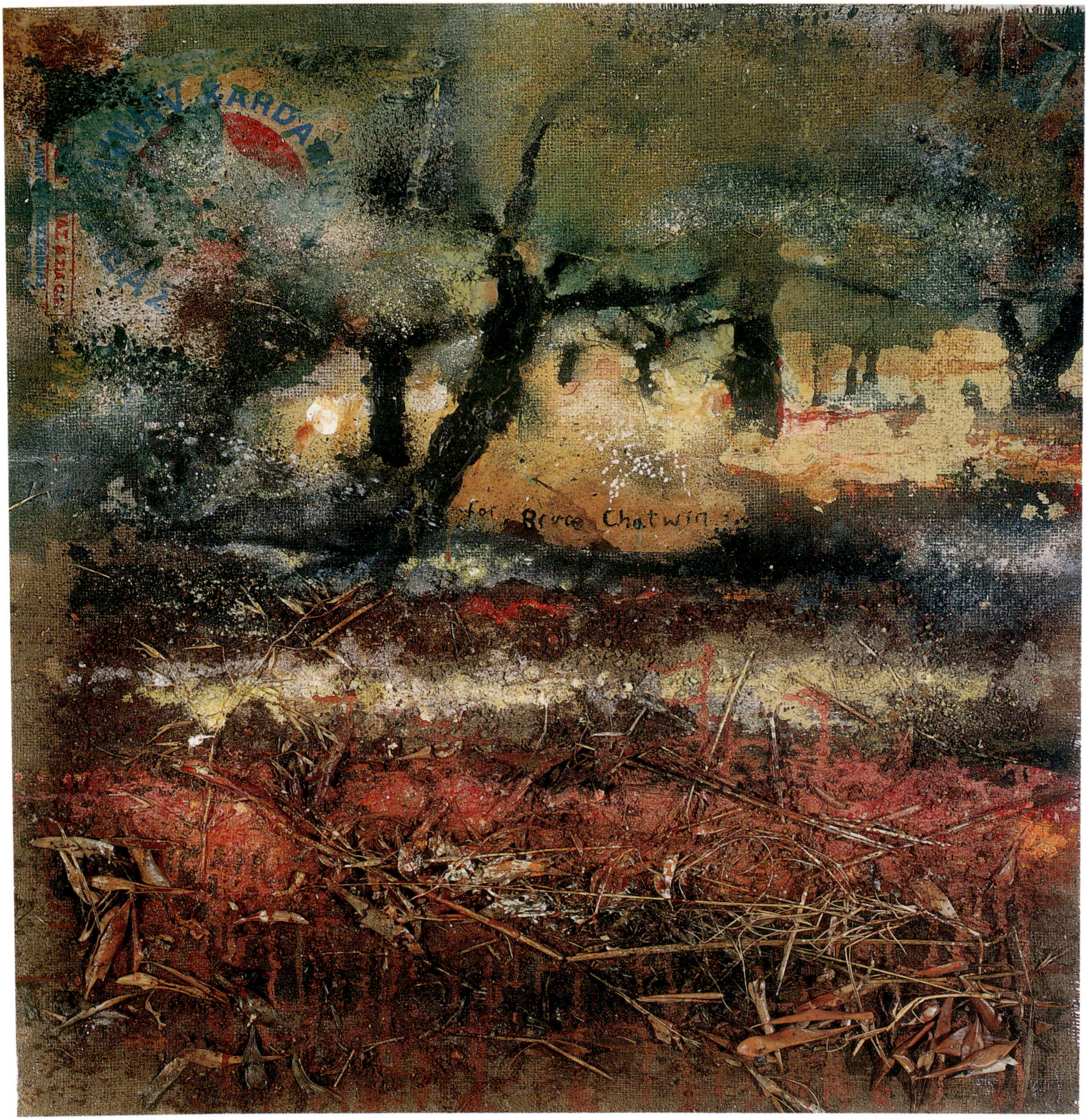
for Bruce Chatwin

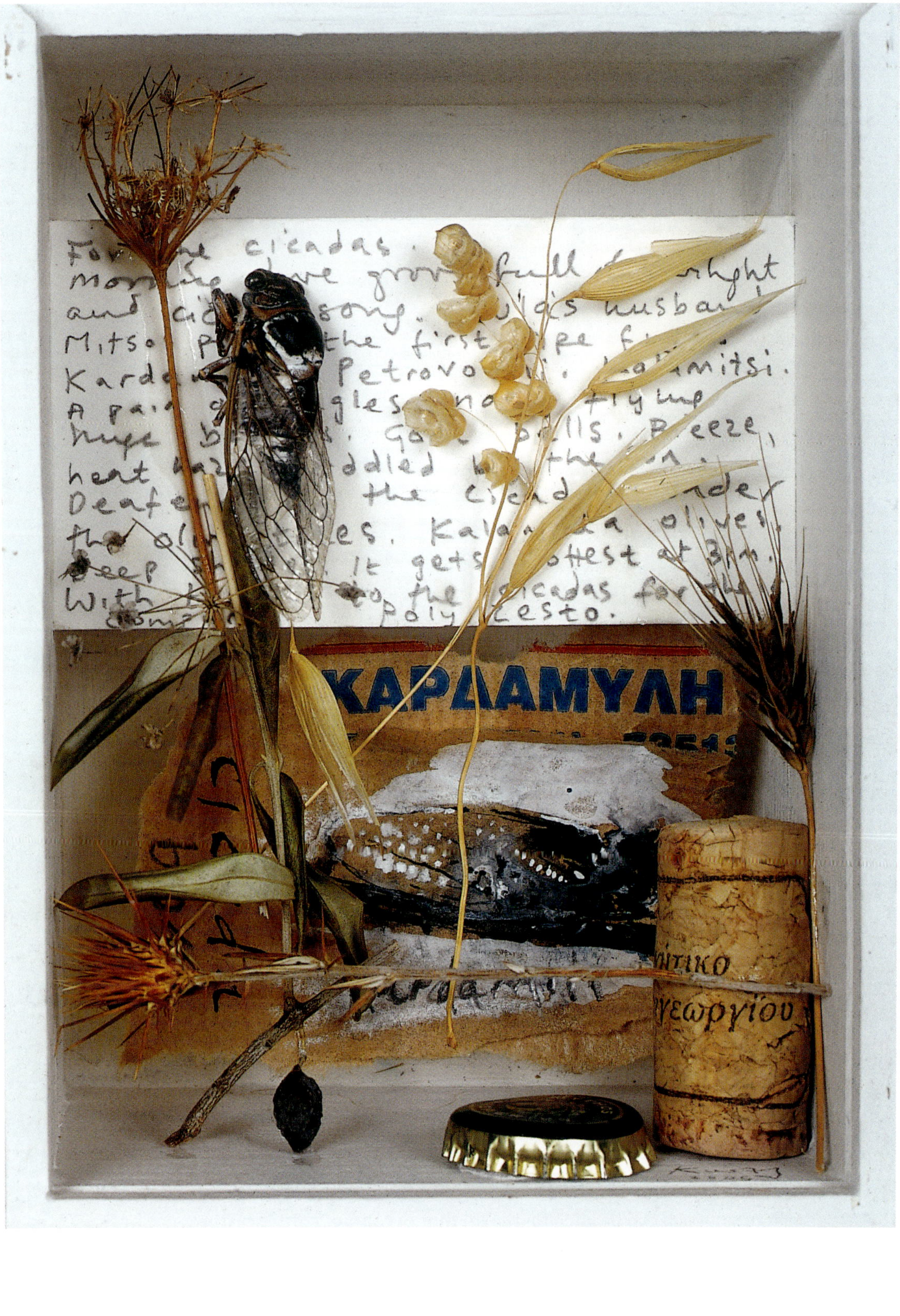

69
***Kardamili cicada box*, 2005**
Box construction, 16.5 × 11.5 × 9 cm (6.5 × 4.5 × 3.5 in)

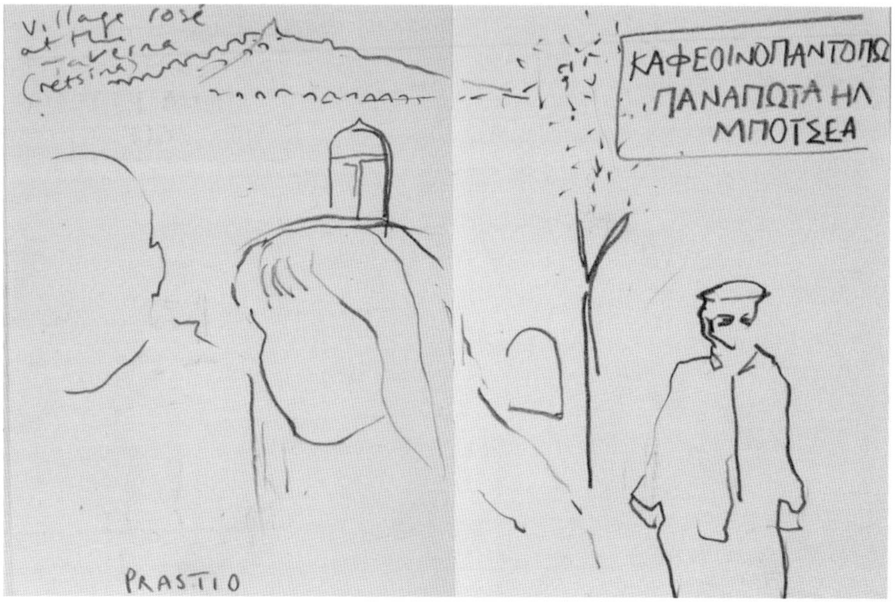

70
Village rosé at the taverna, Kardamili, 2005
Sketchbook and pencil, 15 × 21 cm (6 × 8 in)

idyll. But it is not what it appears. Jays scream in the treetops. Across the bay float excited voices from the Kalamitsi fiesta. Yet the precious time comes at the moment when he is painting my picture, just before dusk, when the cicadas stop. The quietening is odd, as if the olive grove is waiting for a sacred visitation as its ancient right. Then, as though a second choir has filed into shadowy aisles, the crickets begin their softer song, and he can finish and seek a cold beer.

Smells, sounds and, of course, sights form the overall aesthetic: Jackson scrutinises the architecture of two different trees, both of which are very productive. He observes the way the light falls off the leaves and filters through the distant trunks, the sun moving through the day and the shadows continually changing, darkness beneath the trees and a blaze of light on burning earth. Always the artist is looking, not just at the fingers of leaves or the topography of the whole place, but seeking what lies beyond it – what it actually *means*.

The landscape tastes of heat and dust, and maybe some sweat runs into his mouth, to be washed away by the bottles of refreshing water that he pours into him and over him to cool down. For in August this is the hottest place in Europe and that makes working very hard. The feeling of sweat running down his head, arms and back while he is trying not to let it drop on to the painting. Insects buzz all around, attracted by the paint; they sometimes make little tracks on a work, which can be good for the texture, or commit suicide on the painting. They plague

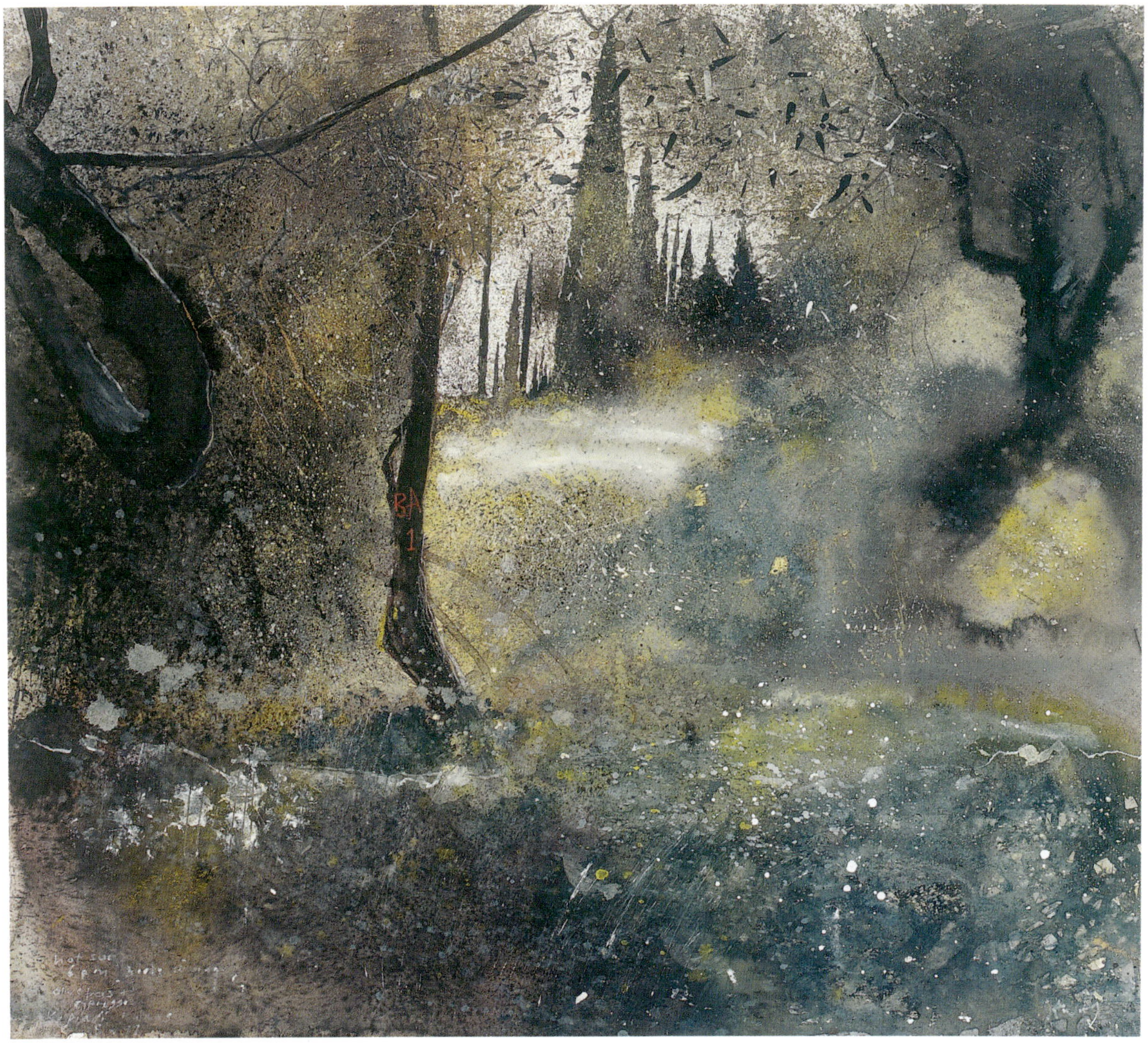

71
Hot sun, 6pm, olive and cypress trees, Kypiadi, Paxos, June 1999
Mixed media, 57 × 62 cm
(22.5 × 24.5 in)

him, stinging the back of his neck, until his whole body is itching and uncomfortable. The ground is hard. Columns of ants parade over his feet and he shifts, in case they change course for his shorts. He props the paper up on his lap, leaning against a rough tree trunk. His legs get cramped and his back aches – from all the jumping up and down to look, assess, pour paint, mix and scrape the work. The stickiness of paint builds up on his hands and clothes. More insects create a 'smack' and he swats his own neck again and again. This is not landscape painting as a dreamy exercise in skilful recording; this is being clutched at by the environment, punished, overwhelmed and, beyond the frustration, sometimes possessed by Dionysian ecstasy.

To what end? Jackson's work is infused by joy. He chooses to embrace every aspect of the places where he situates his work, whether in Cornwall, a Somerset woodland, Andalucia, the Dordogne or Mali. The artist's own physicality reaches out to meet the teeming, testing, tantalising aspects of life: air, leaf, grass, bark,

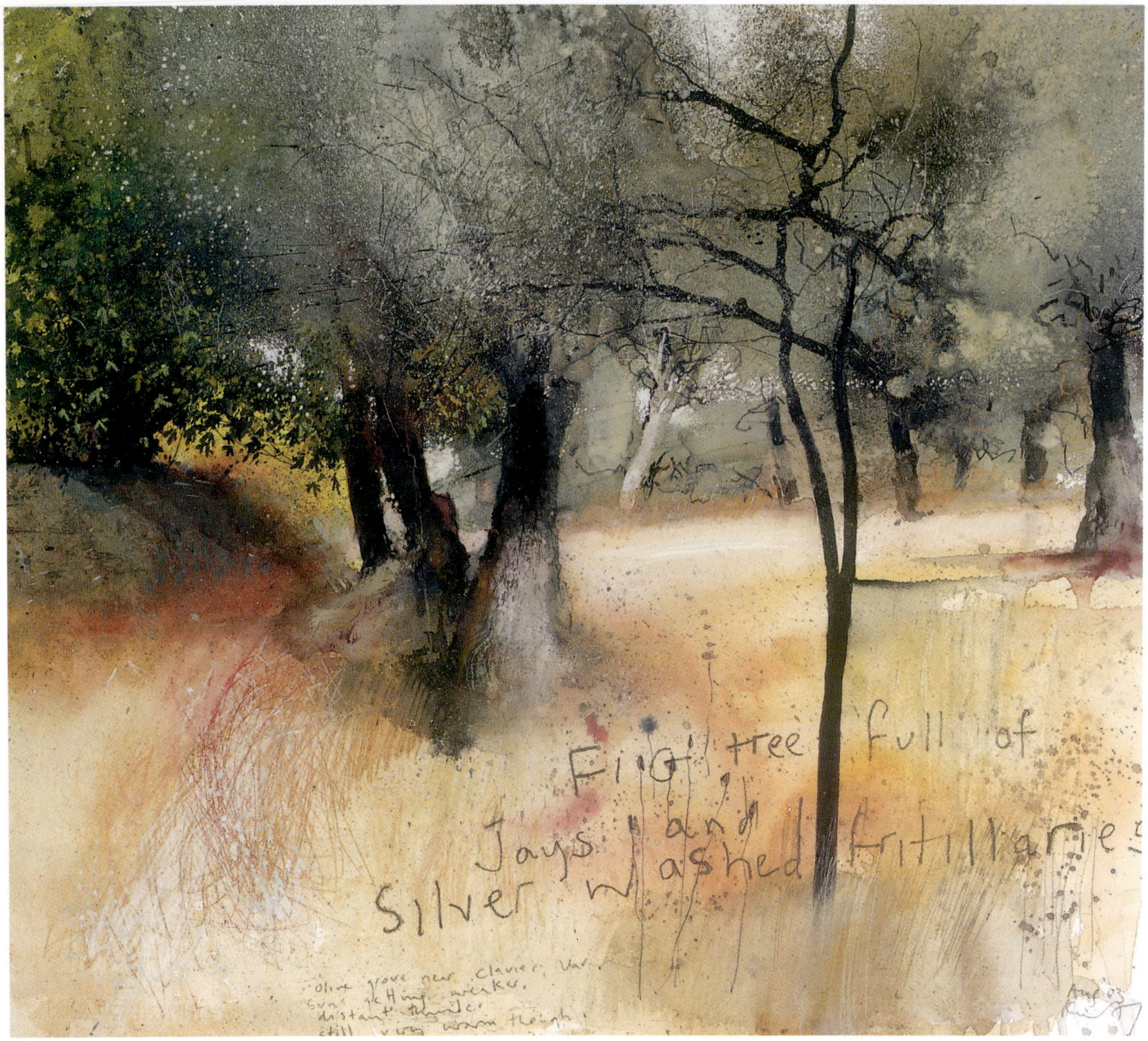

72
Fig tree full of jays and silver-washed fritillaries, 2003
Mixed media, 56.5 × 63 cm
(22 × 25 in)

flower, water and stone. Each painting transcends what is merely observed: it is a totality of experience, and even the smallest work on paper has as much *gravitas* as one of the huge canvases he will work on in his Cornish studio.

However, there are always deeper issues at stake as each painting is made. Past and present lead all of us inexorably towards a future we have to contemplate, even as the present minutes pass. With the wider dimension in mind, the olive tree in my own painting is transformed into a significant emblem. Jackson loves places that are passed on through generations, where people work the land as their forefathers did. That is how it would have been in England once: the sweetness of apple orchards nurtured organically, sustaining generations. But that is no longer the way of life, except in areas as remote as Jackson's adopted Cornish home. So the olive groves of Kardamili represent an ancient transaction between humans, culture and the land. There has been a settlement in this region since the ancient time of Homer, and the olive – symbol of peace, wisdom, plenty and a

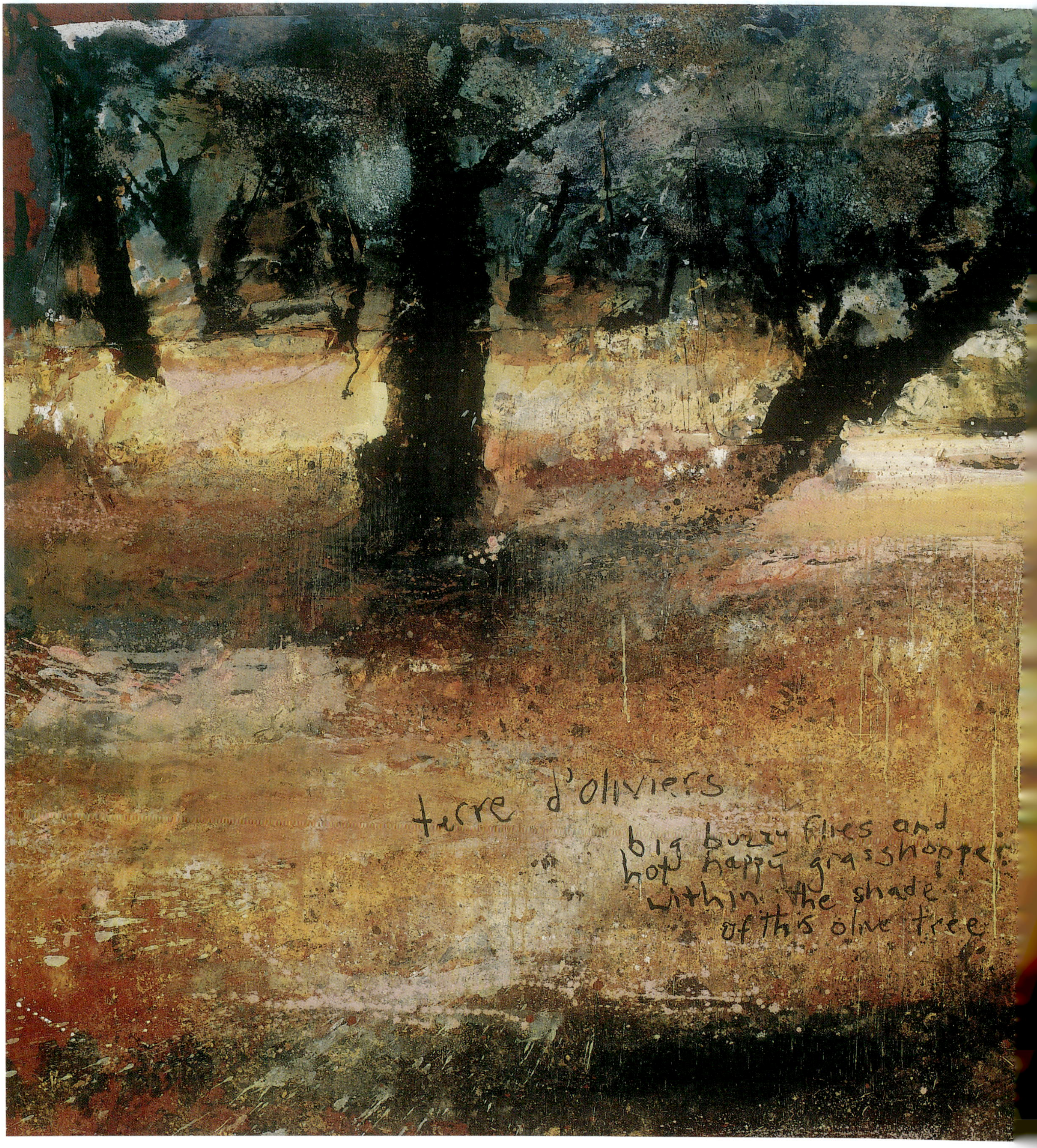

73
Terre d'Oliviers, big buzzy flies and hot happy grasshoppers within the shade of this olive tree, 2003
Mixed media on my duvet cover, 171 × 180 cm (67.5 × 71 in)

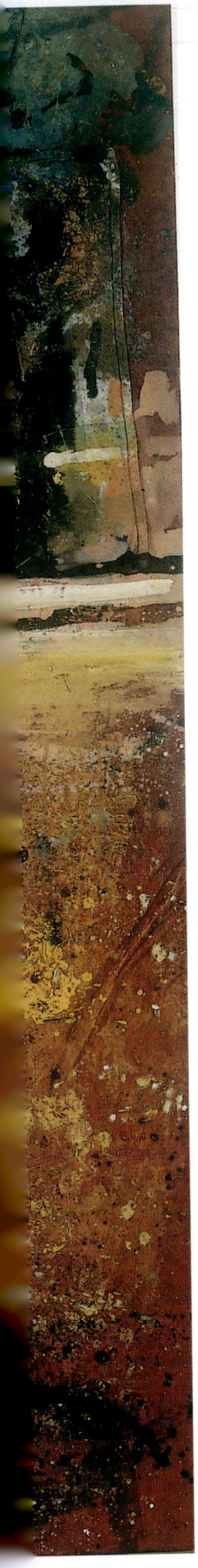

victor's crown – has supported people with wood, useful foliage and, of course, in Homer's phrase 'liquid gold' for food and light. Some olive trees are thought to be more than one thousand years old and fossilised leaves are about fifty thousand years old. For eons, *Olea europaea* has sustained the daily life and customs of peoples of the Mediterranean.

What's more, the olive tree is a basic element in maintaining the stability of a whole eco-system. Because it can take eight years before one produces its first crop, dependable cultivation needs an unchanging environment, which in turn requires political and economic security. This can be seen in the correspondence of the historical decline of the empires of Greece and Rome to the destruction of olive orchards. Since 2000, more than half a million olive trees have been destroyed by Israeli bulldozers – an act of destruction blasphemous to those who revere the ancient symbolism of the olive branch, as well as an ongoing annihilation of the Palestinians' essential livelihood, which depends on the olive tree for fruit, oil and wood. In Homer's time, courts sentenced people to death if they destroyed one olive tree. Those reduced to helpless despair and rage at the destruction of the rainforests and the corresponding oppression of indigenous tribes might think that an entirely appropriate retribution.

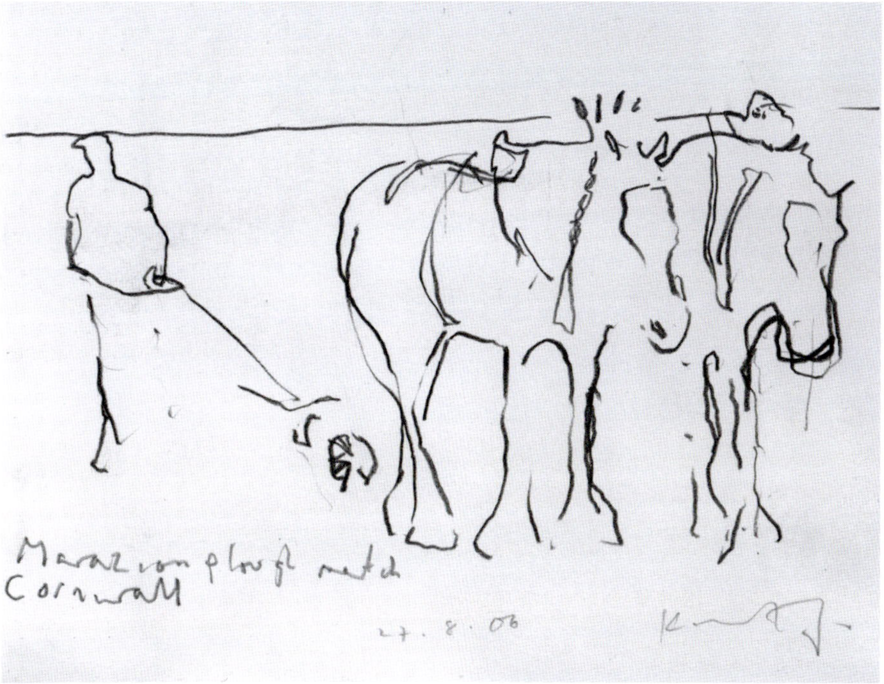

74
Marazion ploughing match, 27/8/06
Pencil, 25 × 25 cm (10 × 10 in)

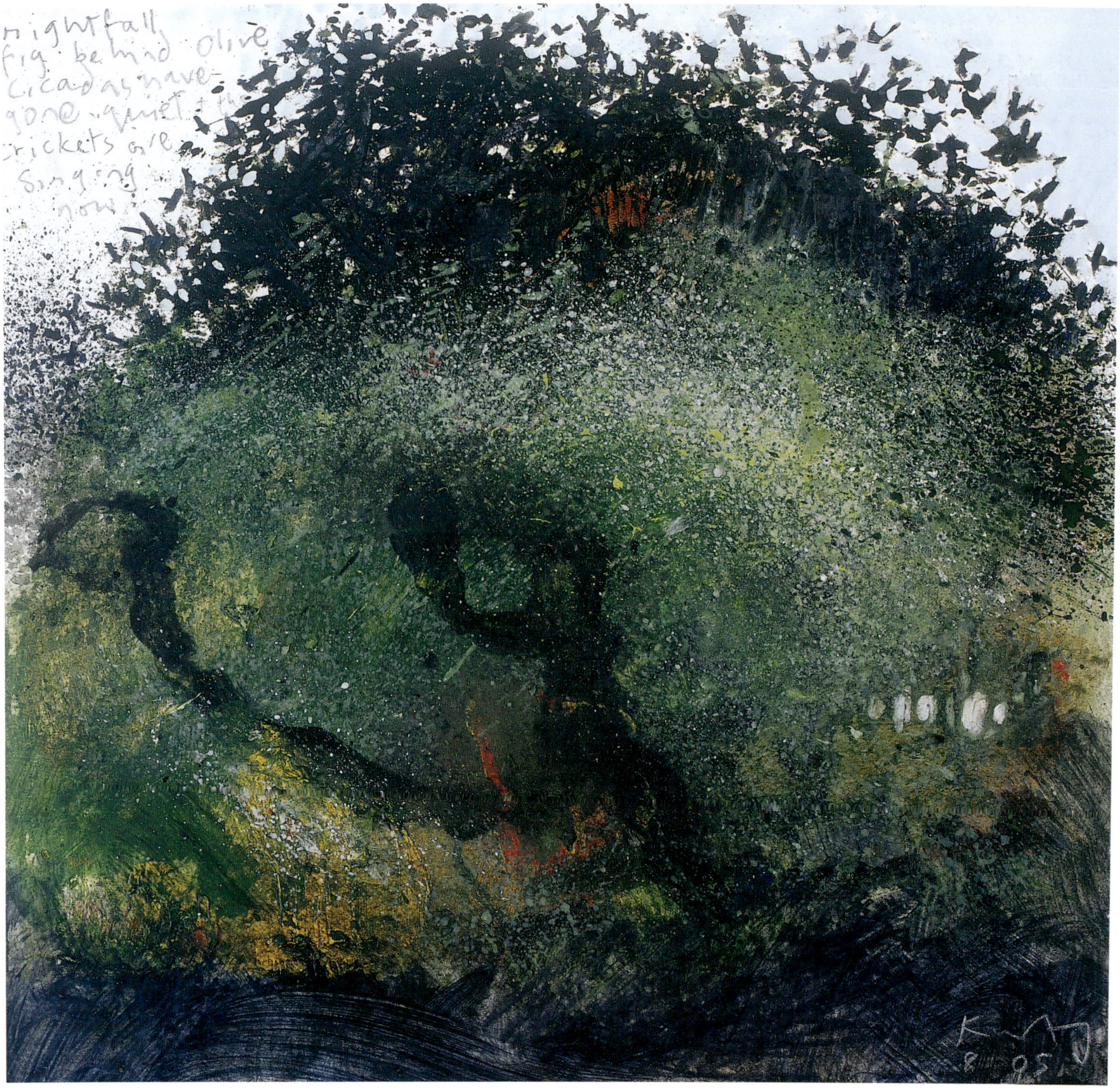

75
Nightfall, fig behind olive, August 2005
Acrylic, 21 × 21.5 cm (8 × 8.5 in)

If the olive tree is freighted with so much meaning, what of the majestic fig tree that waves its leaves behind, demanding the viewer's attention? The tree can be traced back at least two thousand years and its mythology links it to the race of giants (Titans), whose mother was, of course, *Ge* – the Earth. The first tree mentioned in the Bible, it is a holy tree to Hindu and Muslim faiths alike, and gave shelter to Buddha. A noble, productive tree, *Ficus carica* bears fruit in periods of drought because it retains humidity in its wood; it is no wonder that the fig is a symbol of abundance and the many seeds once signified the universality of true understanding.

Surely we need to meditate on the *generosity* of these grand, ancient trees, sustaining humankind in times of hardship and plenty. But are they still respected? There is no doubt that our future survival depends on a true understanding of the old Mediterranean proverb in which the olive tree promises its owner: 'Care for me and I will nourish you.' That covenant is sacred. Jackson knows it and this awareness permeates his work, wherever he is painting. I believe his greatness as an artist stems directly from his reverence for a natural world which, being constantly threatened by human folly and greed, is nevertheless restored to power and glory in his art. Two trees and five senses lead us into a pictured world where human beings, when they appear, are merely parts of a much greater whole, in which humility is essential.

Yes, these truths are whispered by the olive and fig trees from the old stone wall of my study, invoking (in Kurt Jackson's own words), 'the interface between us and the lives of other animals and plants, with peoples' traditions and cultures'. This can all be seen in the greens of one picture.

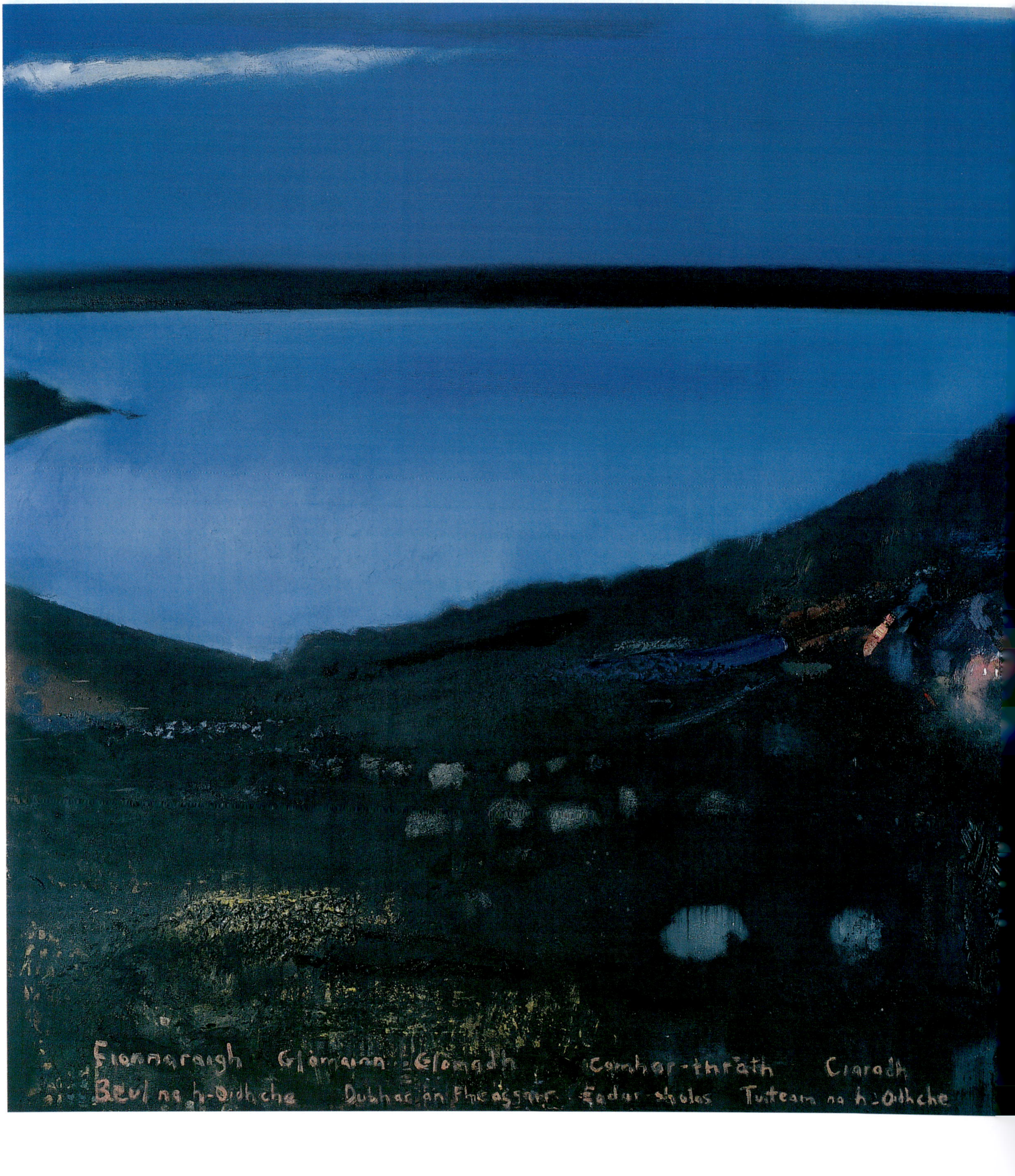
Fionnaraigh
Glómainn
Glomadh
Comhar-thráth
Ciaradh
Beul na h-Oidhche
Dubhar an Fheasgair
Eadar-sholas
Tuiteam na h-Oidhche

6 View from the South

Bill Hare

If you Scotch people don't know a bit of your own country when you see it, who is to help you to know it? – John Ruskin, 1858[1]

From this highly selected list of names, what have the following got in common: Paul Sandby, J.M.W. Turner, Sir Edwin Landseer, Queen Victoria, Sir John Everett Millais, John Ruskin, Joan Eardley, Richard Long and Kurt Jackson? Each of these English-born artists, with varying degrees of talent and genius, have at some time been drawn to the Scottish natural environment as a delight to their eye, as an inspiration for their art and a revelation to their soul. All of them, within the limits, or excesses of their artistic abilities, cultural circumstances and demands of their own historical periods, have turned their attention to creating an image of Scotland that is indelibly linked to the Scottish landscape and its evolving histories. It is therefore a salutary reminder to us Celts that Sassenachs have also played a considerable role in creating the concept of Scottishness, particularly with the visual representations of Northern Britain. This essay will place Kurt Jackson's Caledonian works in the context of this sustained and vital tradition of British landscape painting. It will delve into the rich and rewarding complexities of the artist's multi-layered practice and bring out the links and developments that it has with this particular tradition.

English taste set much of the agenda for the aesthetic opinions towards the landscapes of Scotland in the eighteenth century following the Act of Union of 1707 and the subsequent Jacobite uprisings. At that time Dr Johnson epitomised the critical approach with his infamous jibe that the only good view in Scotland was the road to England. He was not alone, of course, in taking such a hostile attitude. The English spy, and later author of *Robinson Crusoe*, Daniel Defoe also viewed the Scottish scene as 'wild and most hideous'[2] and, even as late as the final decade of the century, a visiting painter from the south, Joseph Farington, was bemoaning the fact that he could 'recollect in no part of the world such a length of country without objects to engage notice'.[3]

In fact it was not a conventional artist, but a military man, Paul Sandby (1731–1809), who was the first English observer to appreciate and record the rich and

76
The gloaming, 2006
Oil on canvas, 152.5 × 152.5 cm (60 × 60 in)

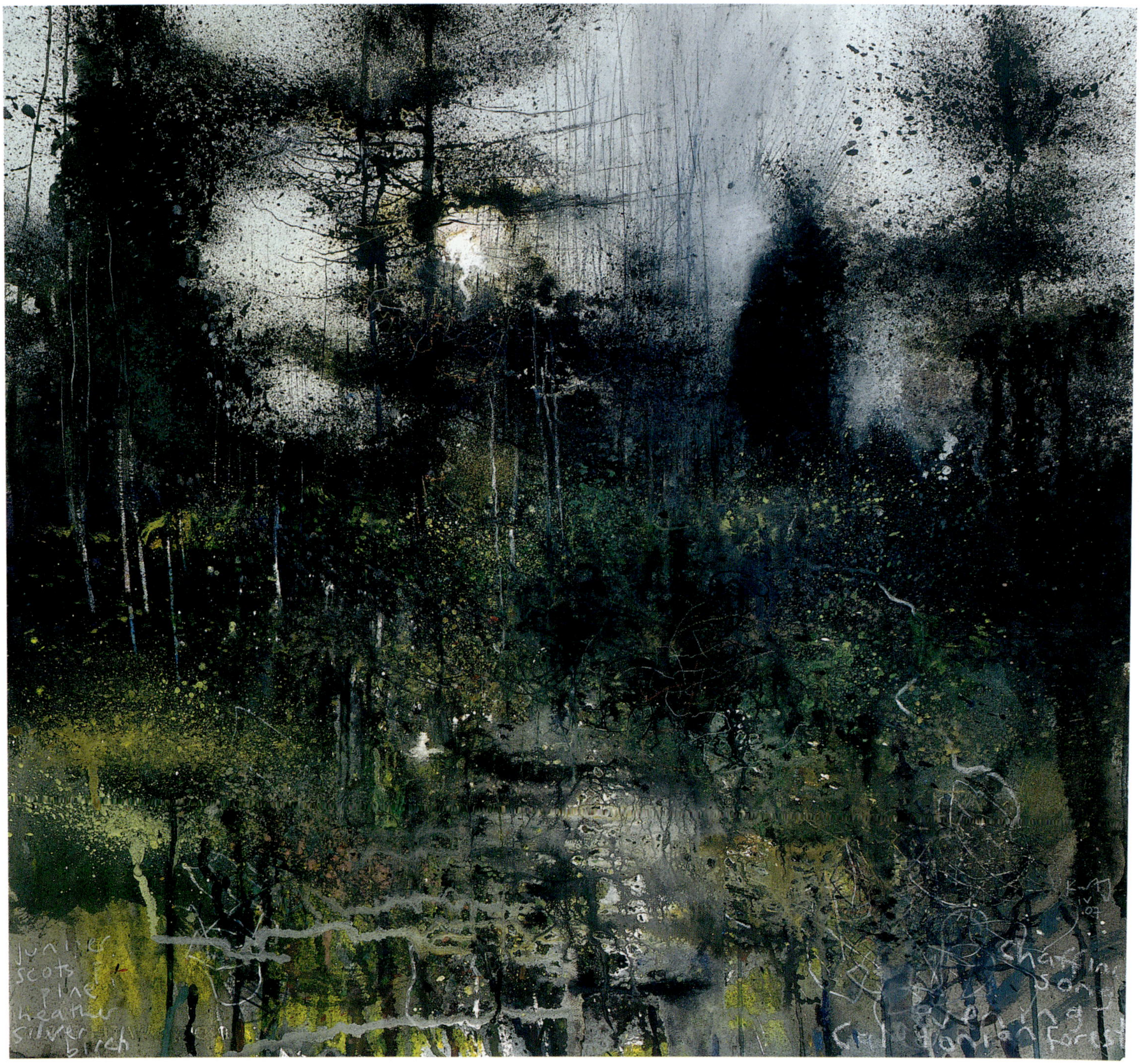

77
Juniper, Scots pine, heather, silver birch. Evening, Caledonian Forest, April 2007
Mixed media 57 × 60 cm (22.5 × 23.5)

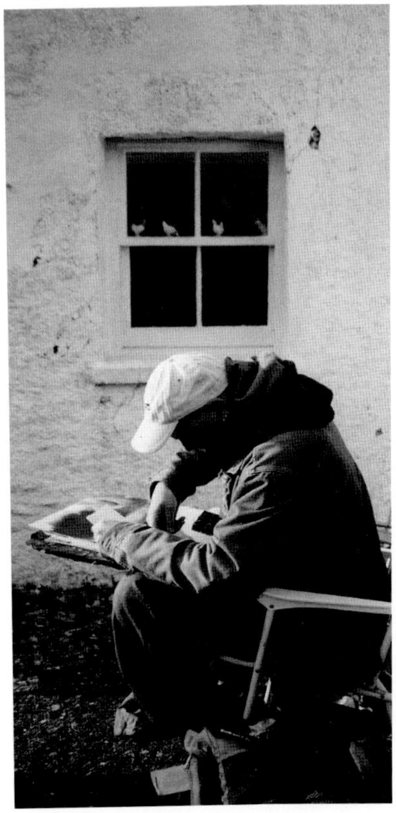

78
Diabaig, 2005

varied character of the Scottish landscape. Like Jackson, he did not have a formal academic education in the visual arts but came from a scientific background. In his case, he had worked as a topographical draughtsman for the Ordnance Survey of Scotland. He was given the task of mapping and consequently systematically controlling the truculent terrains of the Scottish Highlands after the last land battle on British soil at Culloden in 1746. Ironically it was out of this situation that British landscape painting in Scotland began.

As everyone who admires his work knows, Jackson paints in light of ecological concerns over the future of our planet today, but Sandby also faced a highly politicised environment in the middle of the eighteenth century. The art of both these landscapists, in different historical contexts, is a reminder that our natural world is not a fixed entity – a piece of scenic backdrop ever on call to please the eye and lift our flagging spirits when the need arises. On the contrary, over the centuries, our environment has been turned into a military and ecological battlefield in which man and nature are always threatening to deny each other the right to co-exist in what should be an enriching and harmonious relationship. As a military observer, Sandby witnessed the beginning of the mass depopulation process that would lead to the tragedy of the Highland Clearances. Not surprisingly then, it was the more congenial scenic attractions of lowland Scotland that mainly drew his artistic attention. As might be expected with his background in Ordnance Survey cartography, a dominant characteristic of Sandby's approach to landscape is its topographical accuracy. This particular approach also strikes a chord with Jackson, whose university training as a zoologist must have emphasised the vital role of empirical observation. Regardless of what physical and climatic conditions prevail, Jackson builds his art on the topographical foundation of immediate visual scrutiny and direct graphic response. This is borne out by his innumerable on-the-spot sketches and film recordings of titanic battles with the elements, which reach Turneresque dimensions in the artist's undaunted pursuit of nature's elusive and sublime effects.

As with most highly creative individuals, Jackson's artistic personality is driven by dynamic contradictions. Even though he initially trained in scientific methodology at Oxford, in many crucial ways his mode of working as a landscapist is markedly contrary to this empirical approach. Merely recording the appearances of his subjects in a detached objective manner would only hold limited appeal to such a passionate artist. Although he prefers to build up his engagement with the motif through the strategy of accumulating studies in the form of distinctive

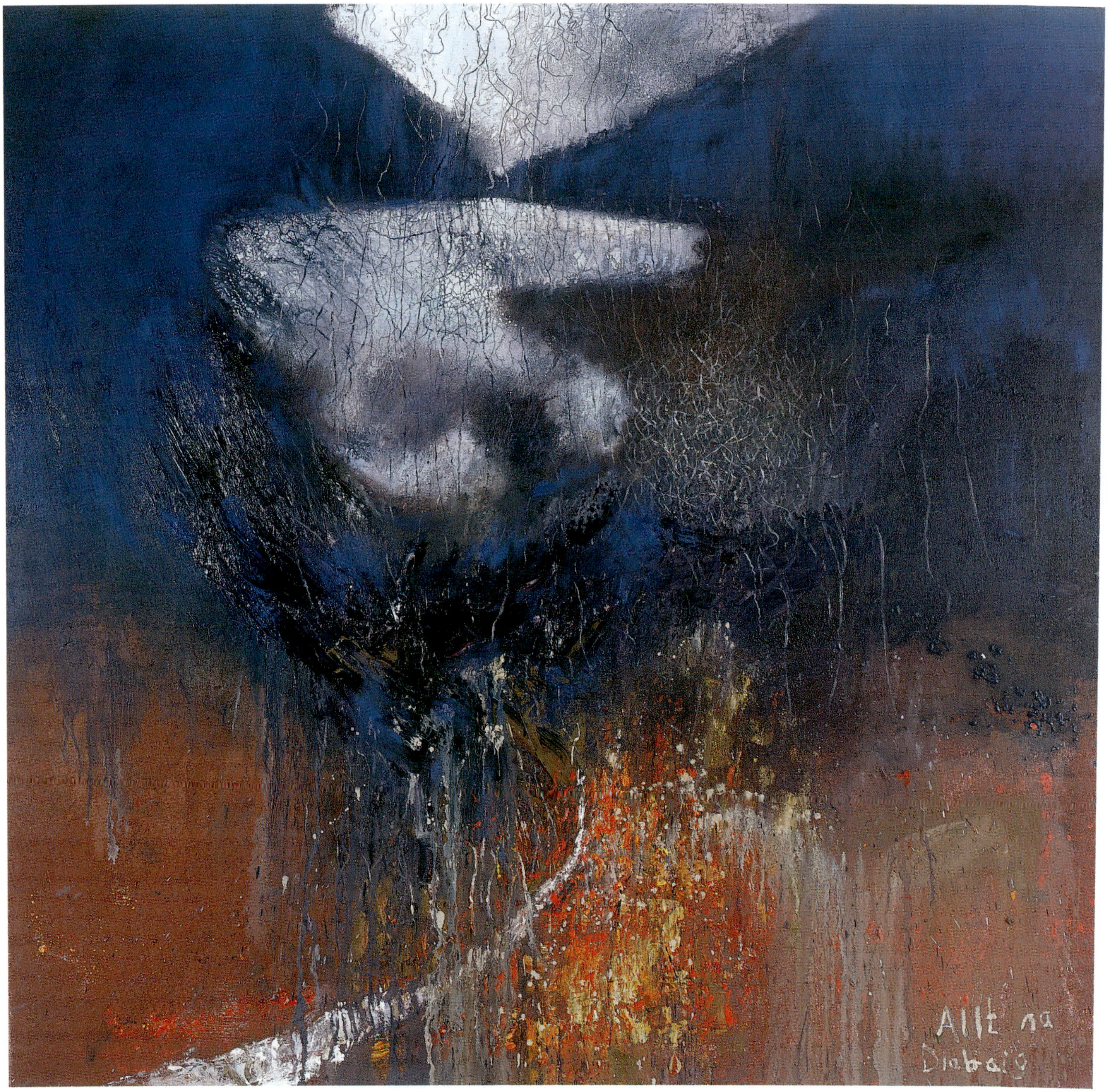

79
Allt na Diabaig, 2006
Oil on canvas, 122 × 122 cm (48 × 48 in)

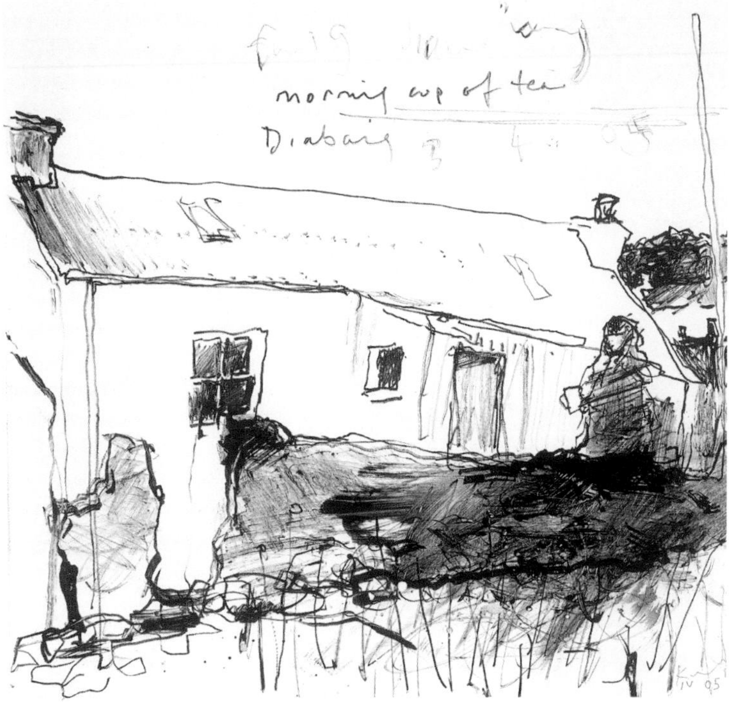

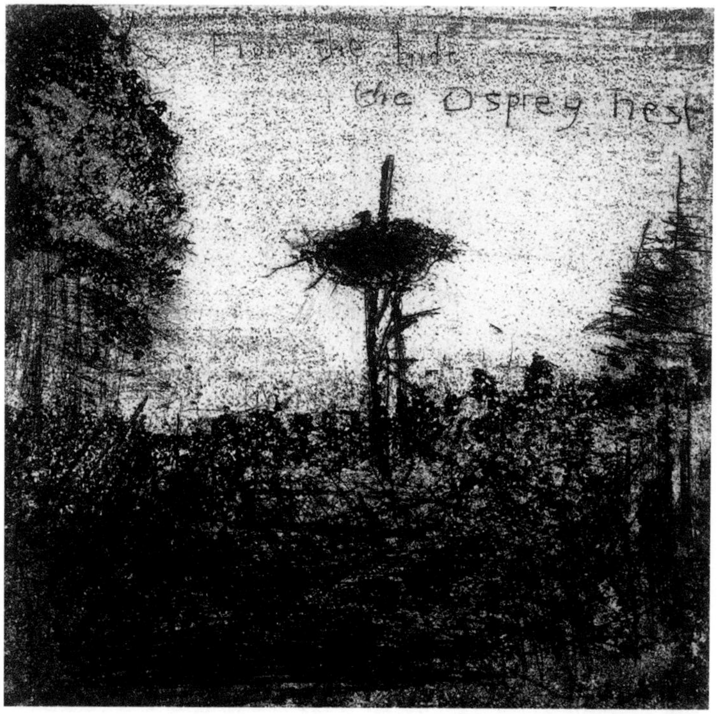

80 (this page, left)
Morning cup of tea, Diabaig, 3/4/05
Ink, 30.5 × 30 cm (12 × 12 in)

81
Osprey nest, 2008
Etching and drypoint, 10 × 10 cm (4 × 4 in).
Edition of 30

series, to follow rigidly a prescribed systematic approach to the art of landscape as seen in the eighteenth-century cult of the Picturesque would have a deadening effect on the vitality of Jackson's deeply empathic relationship with nature. This clearly suggests a strong Romantic dimension to Jackson's art. In fact, his particular relationship to the Scottish landscape has much in common with that of his illustrious English predecessor, J.M.W. Turner (1775–1851).

Throughout his long and peripatetic career, Turner developed a special bond with Scotland and came north for at least six working tours. On the later occasions, it was to meet and specifically work on illustrations for the 'Wizard of the North', Sir Walter Scott (1771–1832). These two renowned artistic and literary figures undoubtedly did more than anyone else to forge the Romantic image of Scotland in the public eye. Furthermore, it was those very things, for example the 'naked mountains'[4] which had been anathema to the Picturesque pilgrims (such as the English cleric William Gilpin), that were to provide vital inspiration for later artists and writers such as Turner and Scott. By the early nineteenth century, critical attitudes and tastes concerning the character of the Doric domain had radically changed. Thus Scott could dismiss earlier conventional attitudes to scenic beauty

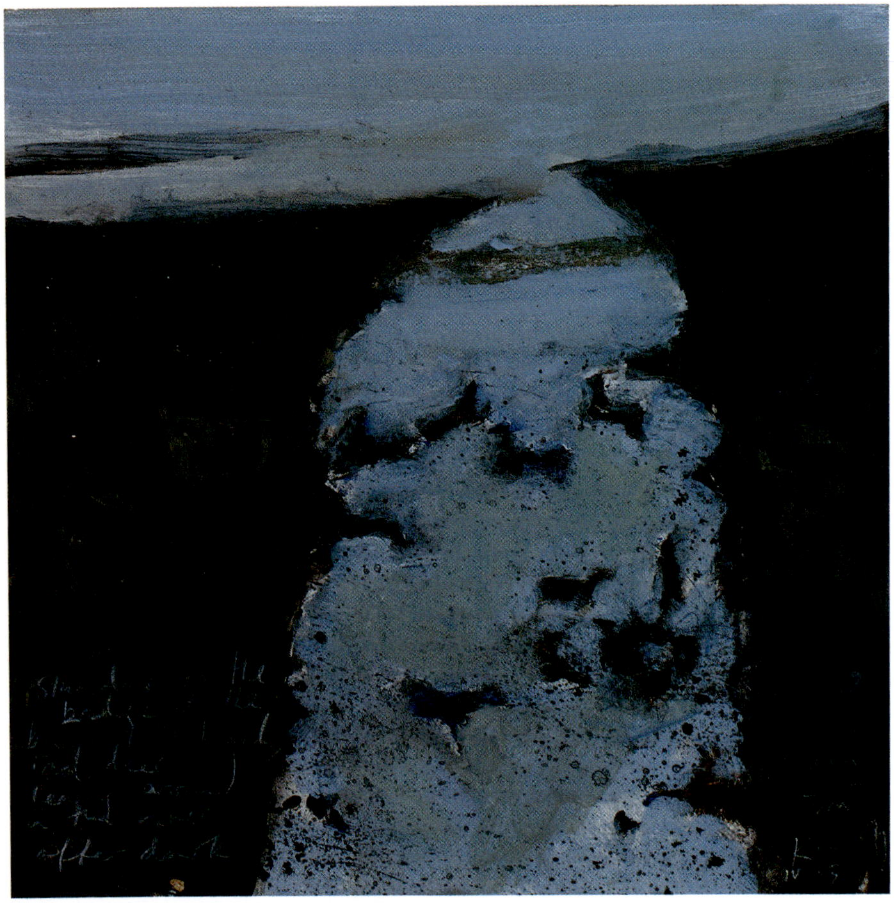

82
Jura. Standing on the bridge at the back of the beach, red deer leaping around in the river after dark, 2003
Acrylic and ink, 18.5 × 18.5 cm
(7.5 × 7.5 in)

by proclaiming, 'I like the very nakedness of the land; it has something, bold, and stern, and solitary about it.'[5]

In landscape painting Turner set an agenda that has had powerful reverberations down through Sir William McTaggart, Joan Eardley and on to Kurt Jackson himself. The prosaic approach of topographical recording and the gentilities of the Picturesque were swept aside by the highly subjective poetics of the Romantic Sublime. Now the worshippers of nature strove to capture the individual appearances of what they beheld – but more crucially, they also battled to express as directly as possible what they physically experienced and emotionally felt at the same time. Jackson's painting exemplifies this deep desire of the artist, not just to present an observed scene, but also to transmit, through the power of expressive mark-making and sonorous colour harmonies, a visionary event of profound significance. Furthermore, a vital part of that significance is due to the pervasive power of historical associations permeating the actual landscape. Such associations transcend time, so that when Sir Walter Scott wrote of the lyrical beauty of Scotland, it forever echoed its turbulent past: 'every stream sings a song and every field laments a battle'.[6] Jackson's landscapes are redolent with the echoes of past voices and traces of bygone human presences: the shifting

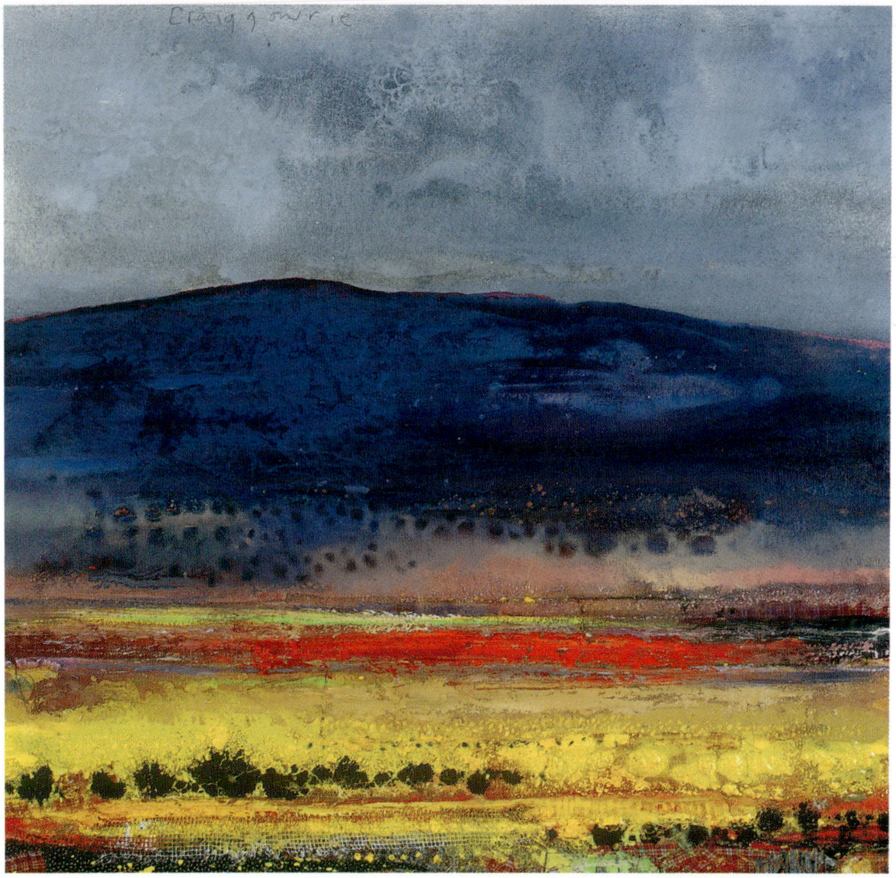

83
Craiggowrie, 2007
Oil and collage on canvas, 91.5 × 91.5 cm (36 × 36 in)

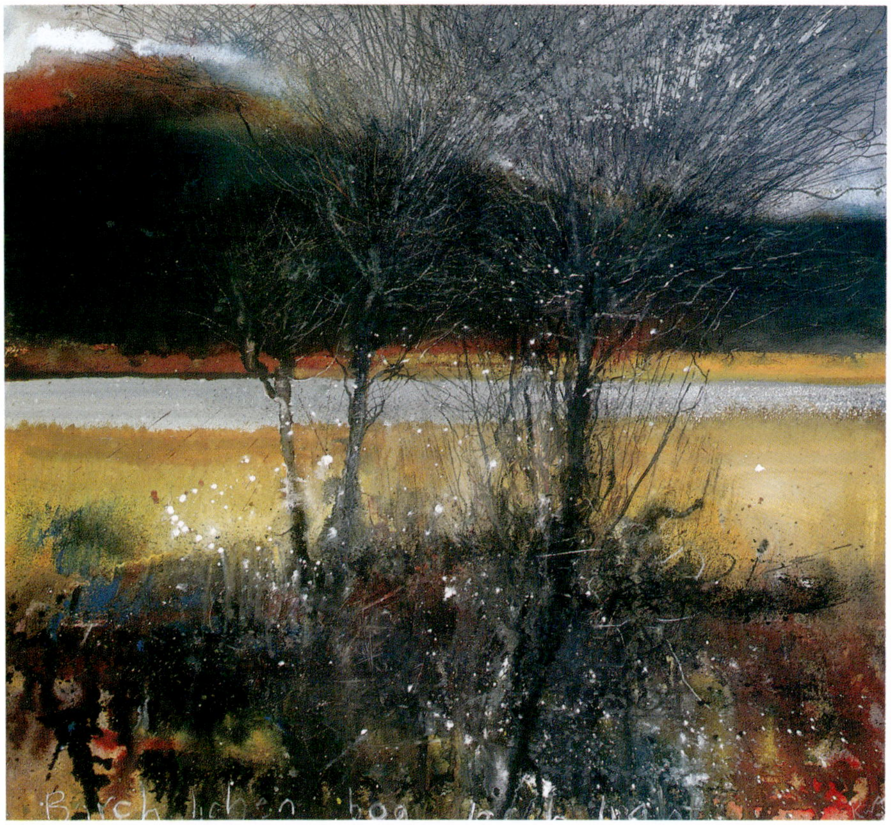

84
Birch, lichen, bog, loch, light, April 2007
Mixed media, 57 × 60 cm (22.5 × 23.5 in)

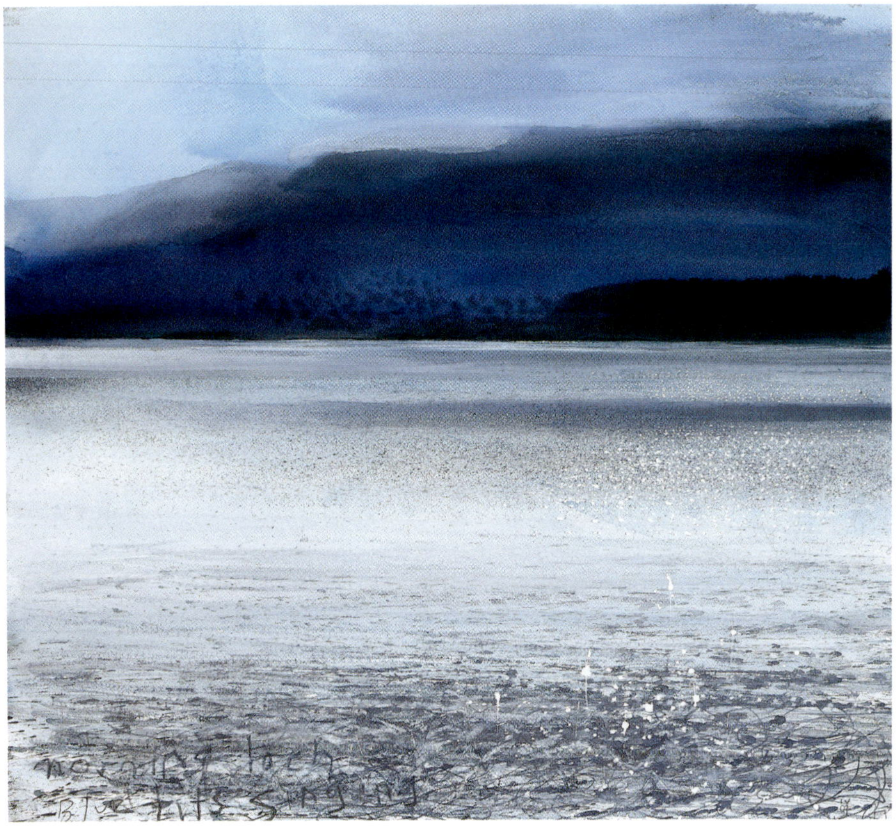

85
Morning loch, blue tits singing, Loch na Eilain, April 2007
Mixed media, 57 × 60 cm
(22.5 × 23.5 in)

historical relationship between mankind and nature provides a central theme that runs throughout his work. Undoubtedly, Jackson can readily identify with the great Sir William McTaggart (1835–1910), who declared that 'it is not grand scenery that makes a fine landscape. You can understand the older Scottish landscape painters going to the Highlands in the footsteps of Sir Walter Scott, but humanity is the thing'.[7] Unfortunately, with the opening up of previously intractable areas of the northern Highlands by modern railway, too many of the 'older' landscape painters were inclined to portray their Scottish subjects with the Victorian bathos of postcard-style tourist imagery, as exemplified by the sentimental paintings of Balmoral Castle by Sir Edwin Landseer (1802–73). Fortunately out of this wilderness of tasteless tartanry came the powerful and arresting voice of the latter-day aesthetic prophet John Ruskin (1819–1900). He passionately urged his Pre-Raphaelite followers to go directly to nature and pay scrupulous attention to every detail that confronted them. Such a concern for the particularities of each aspect of the natural world has not been lost on such a dedicated ecological landscapist as Jackson. He too shares the fundamental respect for the material integrity and moral sanctity of our inherited environment held by his Victorian predecessor. It should, however, be pointed out that such a multifarious artist as Jackson would never get so bogged down in the minutiae of pictorial description as seen, for instance, in the image of Ruskin standing by the Falls of Glenfinlas by Sir John

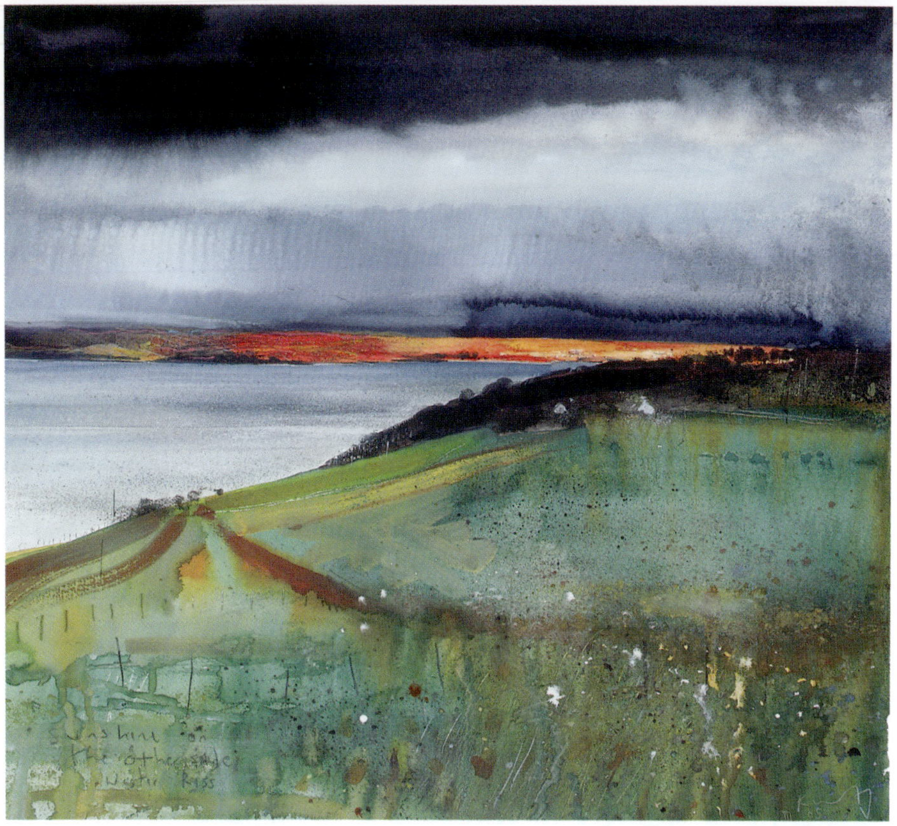

86
Sunshine on the other side, Wester Ross, March 2005
Mixed media, 56 × 60.5 cm (22 × 24 in)

Everett Millais (1829–96). Yet the Pre-Raphaelite concern with the distinct physical structure and material character of the natural world in all its different manifestations is very much in tune with Jackson's own direct mode of observation and hands-on approach to art.

That increasing emphasis on the physical and tactile nature of making art is a marked feature of modern landscape painting. In Scotland, this modernist concern with the medium and its expressive potential reached its triumph in the art of Joan Eardley (1921–63), especially in her celebrated late seascapes of Catterline. Jackson has spoken of his admiration for Scotland's great English-born modern landscapist. Both exhibit a receptive approach to the nature and role of their art, as expressed by Eardley in her need 'to leave one's mind completely open to all things political and social as well as plastic and visual'.[8] The art of these painters is an outcome of a creative visual dialogue and material exchange between the artist and their inspiring subject. Neither of them are 'Impressionists', merely concerned with superficial appearances. On the contrary, their paintings 'must be more than only visual reactions to things', as Eardley said.[9] Thus each artist seeks to capture transient optical realities and turn their observations into something tangible and enduring. This can involve not only the thickly layered application of paint in a very visceral fashion, but also the search for and attachment of physical materials to the picture surface. This process can reach such levels in some of

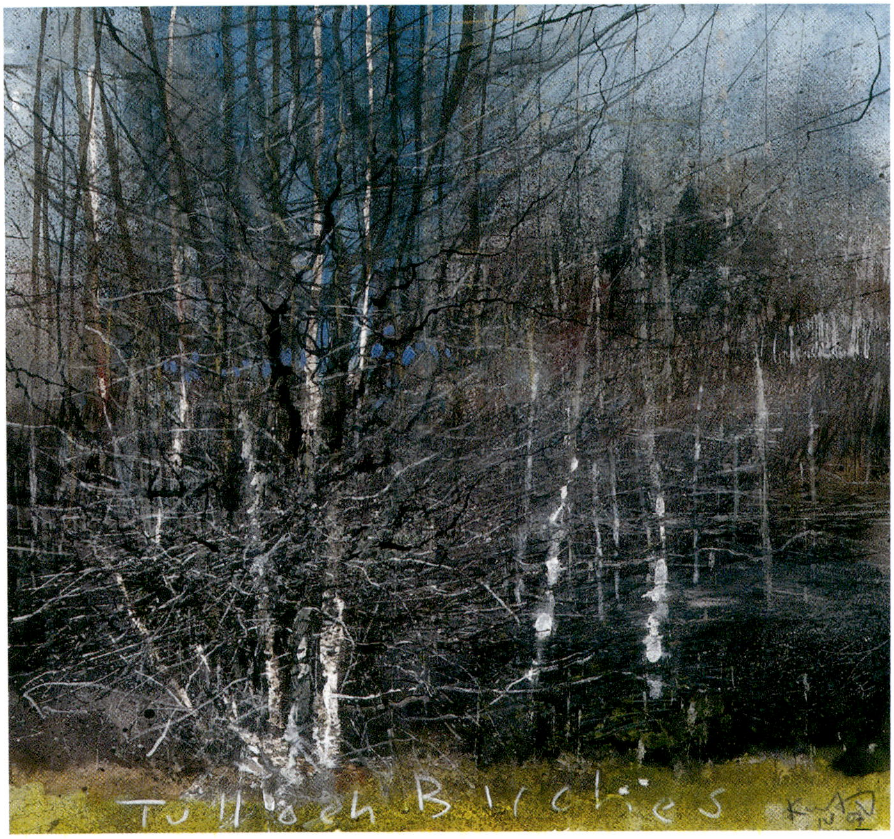

87
Tulloch birches, April 2007
Mixed media, 28 × 30 cm (11 × 12 in)

Jackson's more challenging pieces that the distinction between picture and earthwork, painting and performance becomes blurred.

It is understandable that in our postmodern era there have been critical attempts to link this archaeological aspect of Jackson's work with the practices of Land artists such as Richard Long (*b.*1945). What Jackson has managed to achieve through such experimental engagements with the landscape is to expand the range of possibilities of his art and the alternative ways in which it can be experienced and enjoyed. Through the complex approach that Jackson has developed to the art of landscape, the viewer is not merely presented with a scene they can admire, but is invited to witness and become absorbed in a multi-dimensional event in space and time.

It is hoped that this essay has shown that over the last three centuries Scotland has been fortunate in attracting a series of distinguished English artists to contribute their own visual interpretations of the distinctive qualities of the Scottish landscape. Jackson is not only one of the more recent contributors to

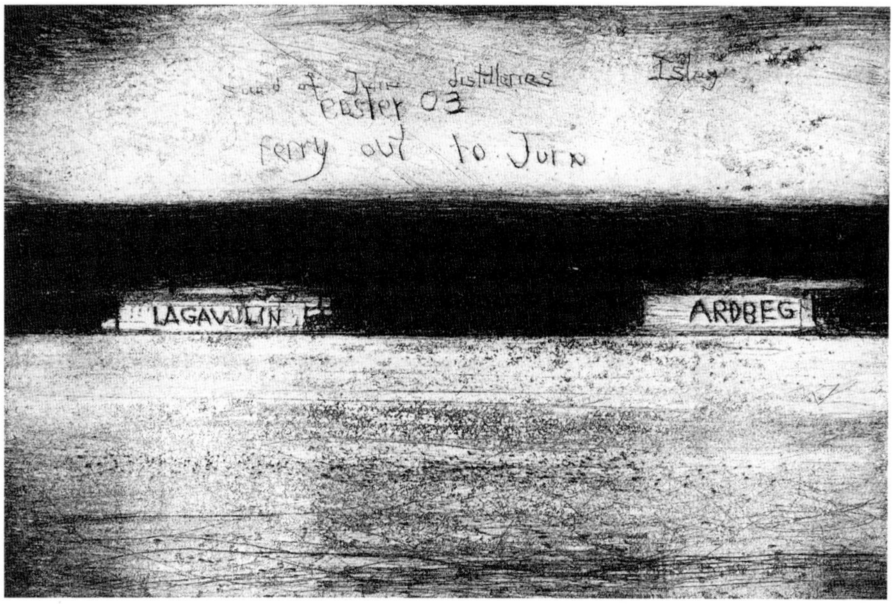

88
Sound of Jura, distilleries, 2003
Etching and dry point, 10 × 15 cm (4 × 6 in). Edition of 5

this continuing tradition, but his richly layered work builds on many of the important achievements of the past. Coming from the other edge of the British Isles, Kurt Jackson gives a geographical link to this Anglo-Scottish artistic alliance. Unlike Dr Johnson, he is always welcome north of the border.

Notes

1. John Ruskin, in a letter to *Witness*, Edinburgh, 27 March 1859, in James Holloway and Lindsay Errington, *The Appreciation of Scottish Scenery through Two Centuries of Painting*, National Galleries of Scotland, Edinburgh, 1978, p.129.
2. Daniel Defoe, *A tour thro' the whole island of Great Britain*, 1724–26, ibid, p.3.
3. Joseph Farington, *Journals of Farington's Scottish Tours*, 1792, ibid, p.87.
4. William Gilpin, *Observations on the Highlands of Scotland,* 1789, ibid, p.87.
5. J.G. Lockhart, *The Life of Sir Walter Scott,* 1893, ibid, p.93.
6. ibid, p.93.
7. Sir William McTaggart, *Black and White*, 1905, quoted in an unpublished lecture *William McTaggart, W. D. McKay and the Glasgow Boys – A Continuing Tradition,* M.A. Forrest, Royal Scottish Academy, 1989.
8. Joan Eardley, *Italian Notebooks*, 1948–49, in Fiona Pearson, *Joan Eardley*, National Galleries of Scotland, Edinburgh, 2007, p.24.
9. ibid, in Cordelia Oliver, *Joan Eardley RSA*, Edinburgh, 1988, p.32.

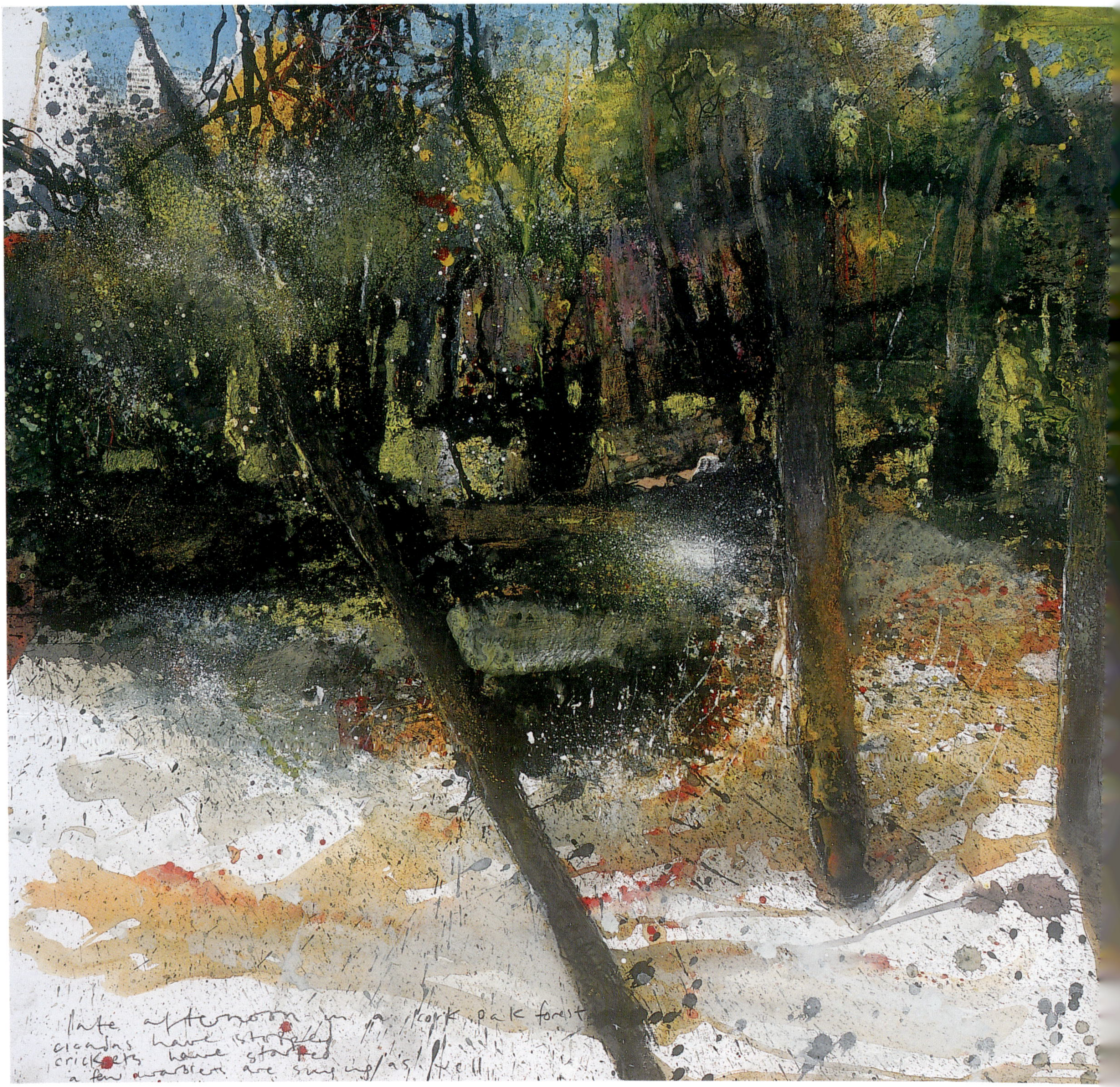
late afternoon in a cork oak forest
cicadas have started
crickets have started
a few warblers are singing as well

7 Green Chaos: Painting the Forest

Richard Mabey

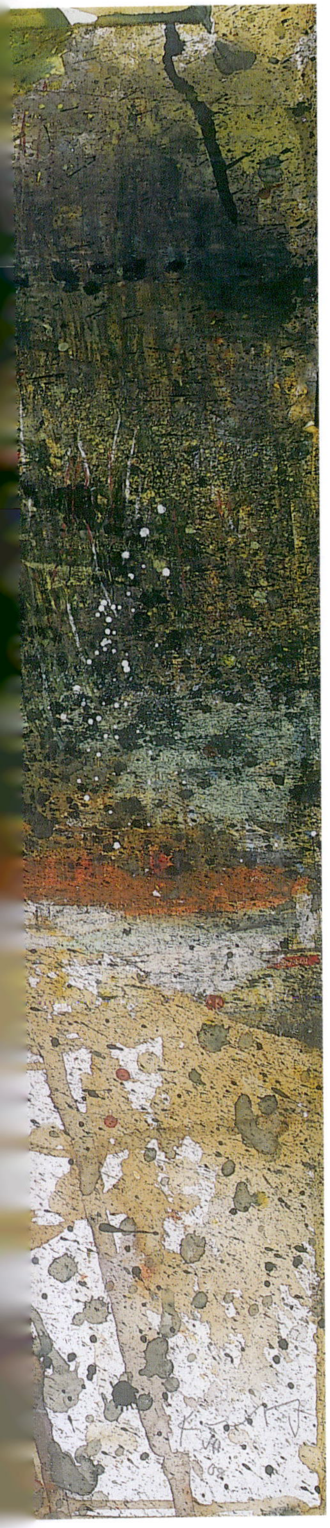

89
Late afternoon in a cork oak forest, cicadas have stopped, crickets have started, July 2008
Mixed media, 60 × 73 cm (23.5 × 28.5 in)

'You are God', challenges Annie Dillard in her roller-coaster exploration of nature's luxuriance, *Pilgrim at Tinker Creek*, 'You want to make a forest, something to hold up the soil, lock up solar energy, and give off oxygen. Wouldn't it be simpler just to rough in a slab of chemicals, a green acre of goo?'[1] Landscape painters, faced with the comparable challenge of expressing the most intricate environments on Earth, have for the most part taken that simpler option, and settled for the slab of undifferentiated green, viewed from a safe distance. But I suspect that is not because this is an easier route, but rather that the energy and complexity of the real forest challenges our fundamental notions about the superiority of civilisation.

For a tradition that has glorified individual trees in every detail from bark fissure to bursting bud, the way woods are generalised in English landscape painting is striking. Trees have been marginalised, domesticated and simplified. They sit as amorphous lumps on hilltops, or nestle in deep valleys like comfortable green hearthrugs; they ornament formal views and are reduced to political symbols of status and wealth. If trees are brought into the foreground, or into closer focus, it is to frame other, more significant business. In surveying three centuries of the English landscape tradition, it is hard to think of paintings that revel in the florid internal energy of the forest. Thomas Gainsborough's *Cornard Wood* (*c.*1748) is a pleasant, naturalistic scatter of young trees, busy with men turning them into firewood. The few Pre-Raphaelite woodland interiors are still lifes, frozen in time for all their radiant detail. Paul Nash's obsessive *Wittenham Clumps* (1912–44) is a distant symbol of mortality, rather than a thriving beech plantation.

Even the best-loved painting of our master landscapist does not avoid side-stepping the forest. The soothing pastoral image in Constable's 1826 painting, *The*

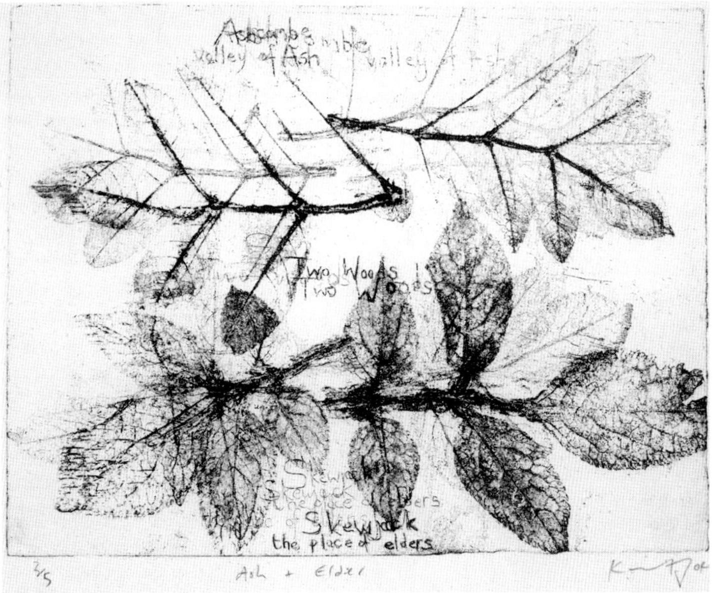

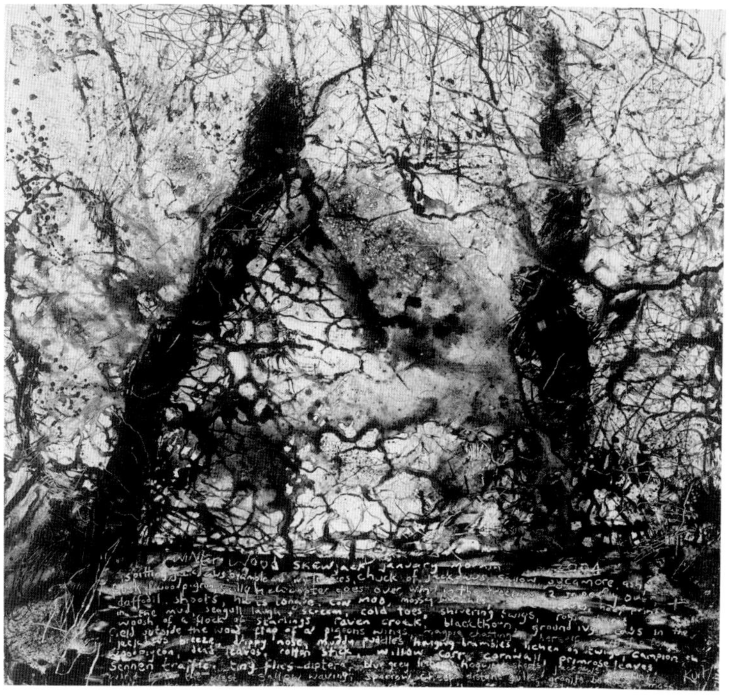

Cornfield – the boy drinking in the stream, the trees framing the ripe corn and the working labourers, the church in the distance – is a parable of England as we believe it once was, of a harmonious dwelling with nature. However, it is also an evocation of a woodland refuge, a spy-hole among trees. The eye of the viewer is drawn through the arch between the dappled ashes and oaks, out into the sunlit and orderly world of farm and village beyond. This is the archetypal view of the forest in English landscape painting. It is a place to look out from or back at, but never *into*.

This artistic diffidence towards the forest parallels our social and cultural retreat. The wildwood of the hunter-gatherers morphed into the managed woodlots of farming communities, then into the timber factories of the commercial forester. What had once been seen as the dwelling place of benign spirits became the imagined haunt of outlaws and barbarians. By the eighteenth century, the forest was understood to be the contrary to civilisation. 'In a country full of civilised inhabitants', wrote John Morton in 1712, the forest could not be 'suffered to grow. It must give way to fields and pastures, which are of more immediate use and concern to life'.[2] We now know better, of course, and have a greater scientific understanding of the importance of this natural vegetation.

90 (left)
Ash and elder, 2004
Soft-ground etching, 24 × 29 cm (9.5 × 11.5 in).
Edition of 30

91
Skewjack winter morning, 2005
Photogravure and etching, 51 × 52 cm (20 × 20.5 in).
Edition of 30

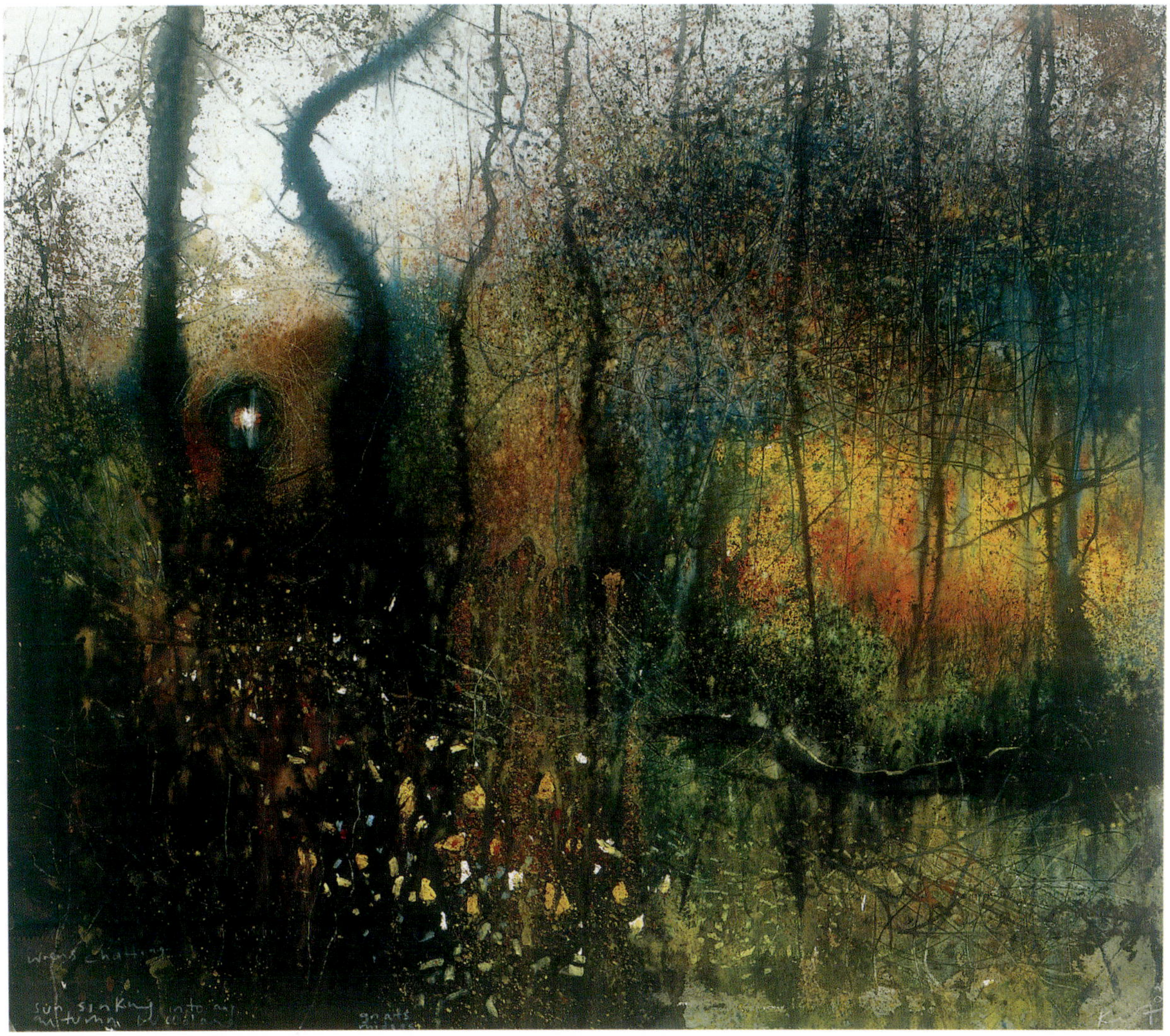

92
Wrens chatting, sun sinking into an Autumn woodland; gnats and midges, October 2003
Mixed media, 57 × 63 cm (22.5 × 25 in)

The forest is the great reservoir of life's diversity, the touchstone by which we can understand our own origins, the generator of oxygen and regulator of climate. But in our psyches, as in painting, it is still an alien and mysterious presence. The forest has become our backdrop.

Early on, Kurt Jackson questioned this short-sighted, conventional perspective and sought to explore nature in more depth. He remembers that 'the enjoyment I experienced as a child was in knowing what was happening in the bottom of that hedgerow, or what was migrating overhead at certain times of the year'.[3] He went on to study Zoology at Oxford, but found the scientific perspective too

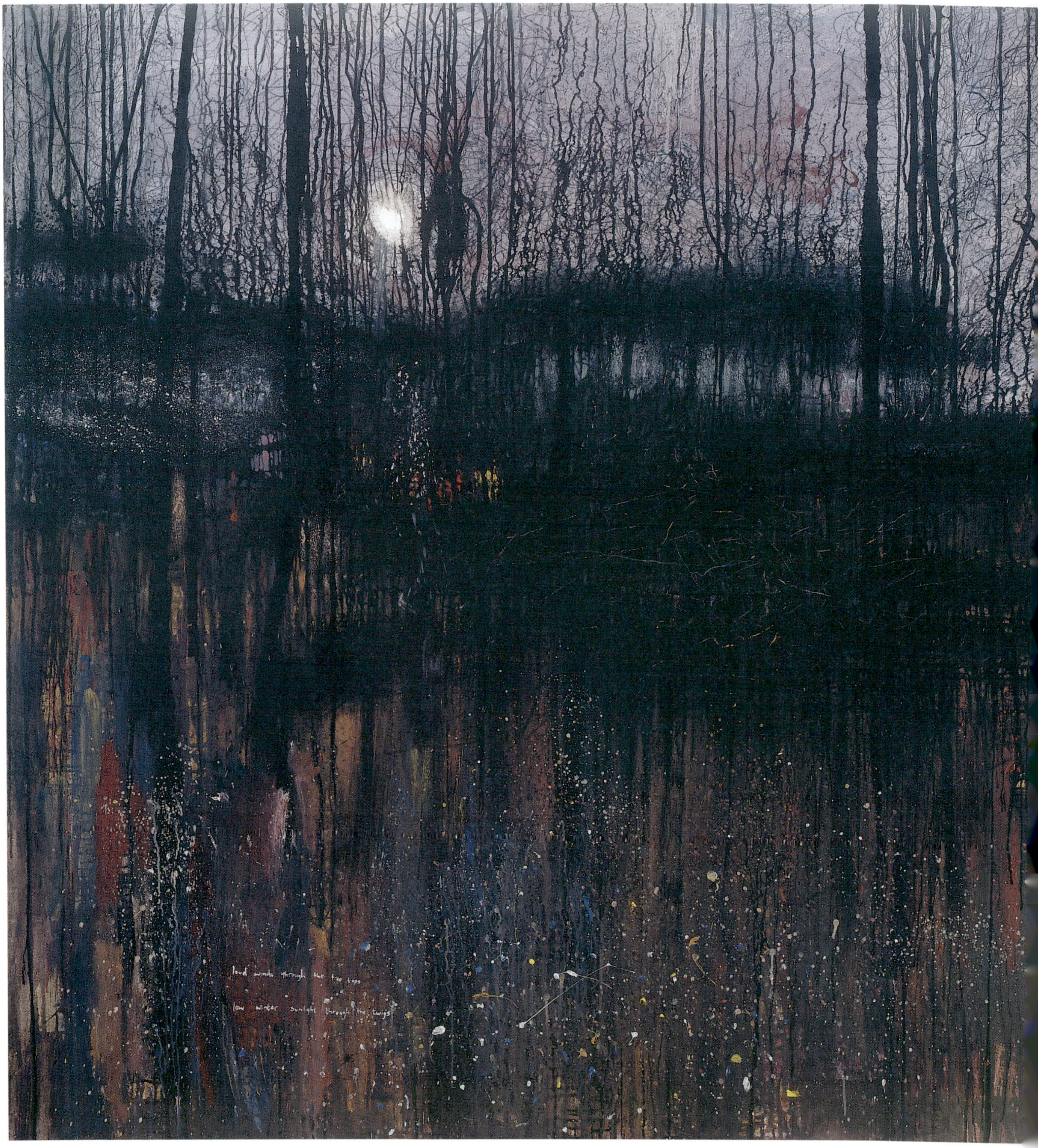
loud winds through the tree tops
low winter sunlight through the twigs

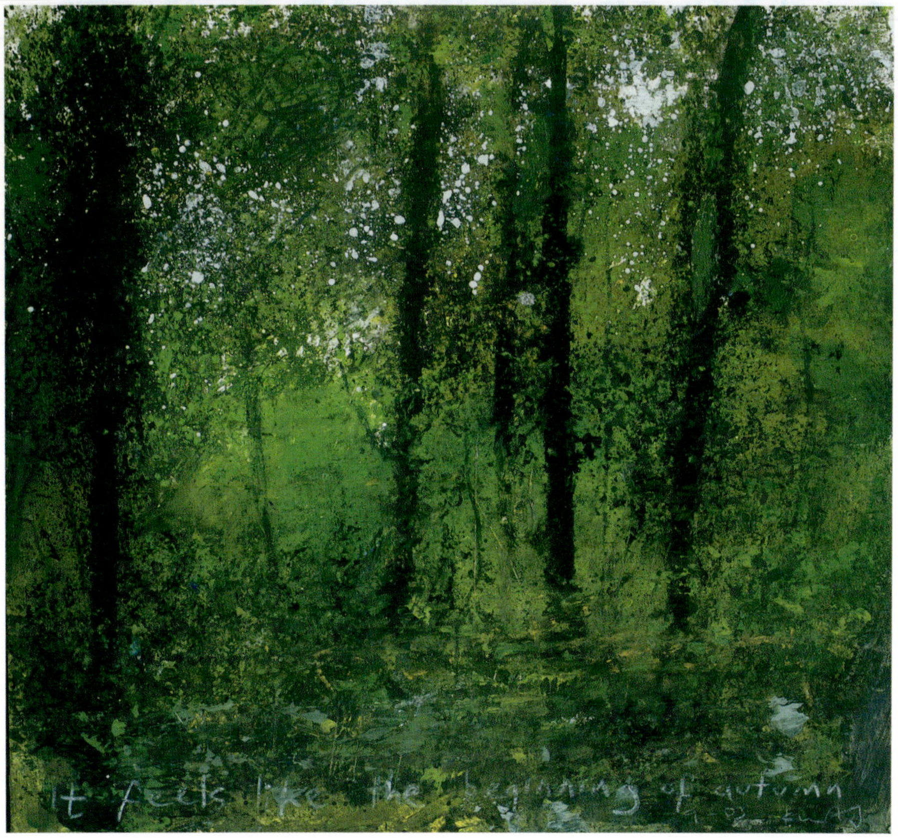

94
It feels like the beginning of Autumn, 2003
Acrylic, 19 × 20 cm (7.5 × 8 in)

disciplined and instead spent his time painting in the water-meadows of the River Thames. Wood and water have been two key themes in his work, and are often painted in contrast. In a series on ponds, 'Ponds, Pools and Puddles' (2006), he writes of these small bodies of water as if they were holes in the earth, 'entrances into the unknown', and makes it clear that his job as a painter is to dive in, not to play the detached and superior observer. *Pond in a woodland of sallow and ivy, January 2006* shows just such a place, a dark and occult surface, the colour of pewter and latticed over with branches – and the reflections of branches.

Even through their modest elevation, Jackson's woodland pictures challenge the grand, colonial tradition of prospect painting. These are landscapes seen literally from the grass roots. You are in a thicket, enmeshed with greenery. In his many pictures of Cornish lanes and streams the track invariably leads into the wood, not away from it, and you are reminded not so much of any other painter but of the Romantic poet John Clare. The start of his poem 'The Nightingale's Nest' captures the sense of wonder that draws the viewer into one of Jackson's wooded landscapes: 'Up this green woodland-ride let's softly rove | And list the nightingale – she dwells just here | ... Creeping on hands and knees through matted thorn | To find her nest and see her feed her young'.[4] He respects too the individuality of specific moments in the life-cycle of the forest, as seen in his studies of a hawthorn tree at Morvah

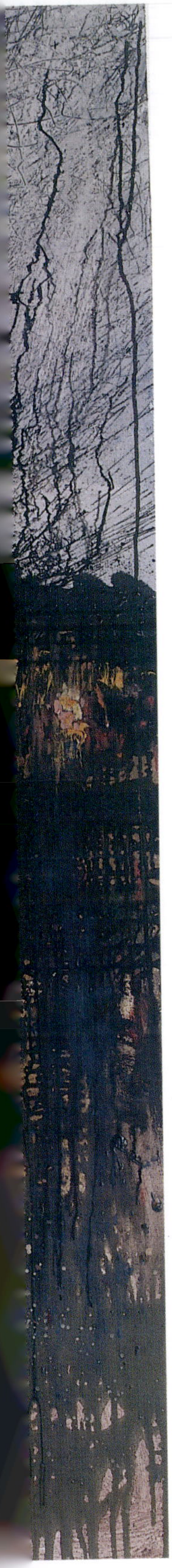

93
Loud wind through the tree tops, low winter sunlight through the twigs, 2003
Mixed media on canvas, 183 × 183 cm (72 × 72 in)

(1992–93), a small farming community on the north coast of Cornwall, which captures every declension of the tree from winter torpor to blowsy blossom.

What is impressive is his painterly translation of the ecology of wild places. The patterns of light and shade, the thick impression of the paint, the sudden detonations of colour and embryonic forms, echo the vitality and inventiveness of the natural processes they signify. Jackson's series 'Two Woods' (2004) explores the interior life of two contrasting habitats: Ashcombe Wood near Bath and Skewjack Wood in Cornwall. The first, Ashcombe, is believed to be a wood with origins dating back to the end of the last Ice Age. It is a place of airy trees – ash, maple, hazel – and the long continuity of forest cover means that it has its share of the scarce and fastidious wild lilies that haunt the Wessex limestone. *Green light, Ashcombe* and *Ashcombe, sun sinking, sycamore, hazel, oak, September 2003* (plate 95) are both studies of the depths of the wood, and in their dappled latticework suggest the intricate transactions between light, time and living tissue that create the fabric of these ancient places. *It feels like the beginning of Autumn* (plate 94) is a more spacious painting. Light filters in through the treetops. The tree trunks are straighter, more gracious. The text hints at uncertainty, at a palpable mystery in the surfaces of the wood. It might, in fact, be the beginning of spring. Woods lock their history inside them, but they reveal cyclical traces, and the spring bud is already formed at the moment of the leaf's fall.

The second subject of the 'Two Woods', Skewjack in Cornwall, is almost certainly a younger, and possibly even a planted, woodland that demonstrates the refusal of natural growth to stay inside the fence defined by the tidy categories of scientists and aesthetes. The farmer who owns Skewjack insists that it is not a 'wood' at all, but an overgrown orchard, as if it were impossible for the one to turn into the other, and upset the sacrosanct lines between nature and culture. Kurt chose Skewjack because it is the most southwesterly patch of wild woodland in Cornwall, and thus in Britain. It is a small copse surrounded by Cornish hedgebanks and full of burgeoning willow carr, dead elms throwing out suckers, scrub, bogs and badgers, and what Jackson simply refers to as 'woodlife'.

'Woodlife' is what his pictures capture in their depictions of animals in the landscape. *Skewjack afternoon, sunshine with jackdaws* is a portrait of a June wood erupting like a supernova. The sky is just visible in the background and defines the woodland's fragmentary existence. But in the centre of the painting a huge fountain of woody spray, of dense, ambitious clusters of twigs, of gold light scattering on leaves, gushes up from the earth. It signifies the future growth that

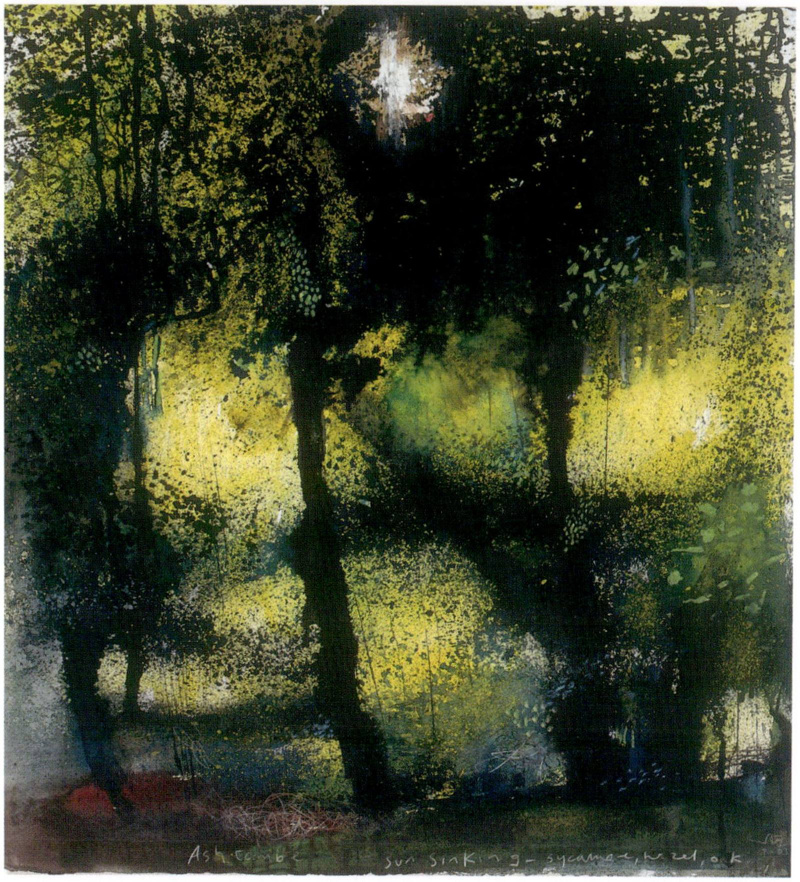

95
Ashcombe, sun sinking, sycamore, hazel, oak, September 2003
Mixed media on paper,
63 × 57 cm (25 × 22.5 in)

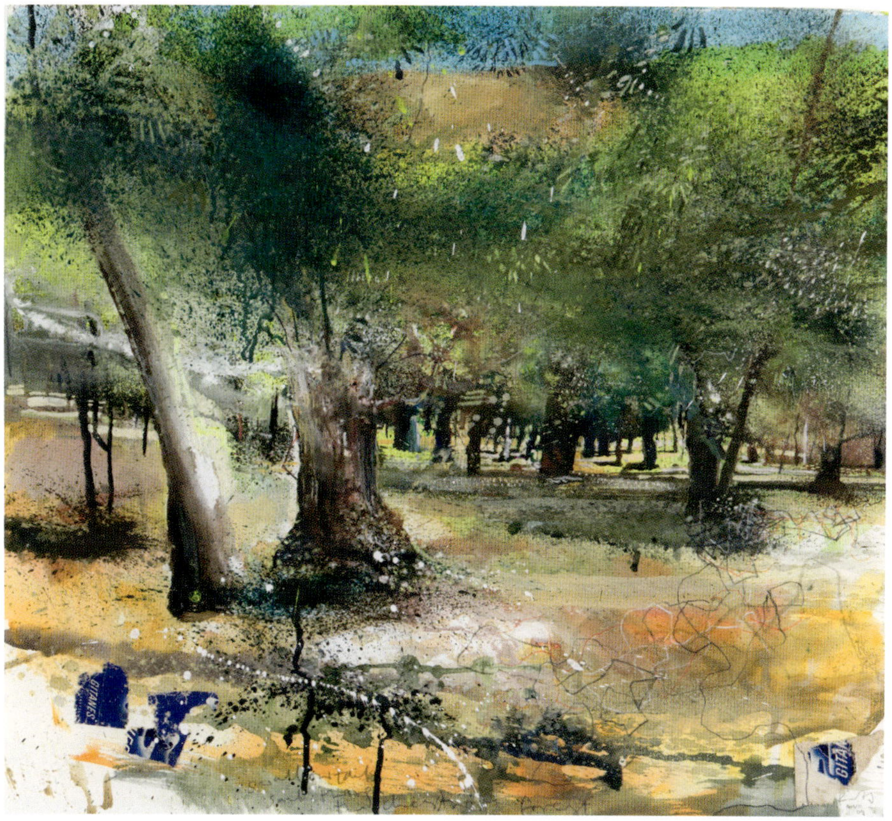

96
Swallowtails sail through the chestnut forest, July 2008
Mixed media, 57 × 62 cm
(22.5 × 24.5 in)

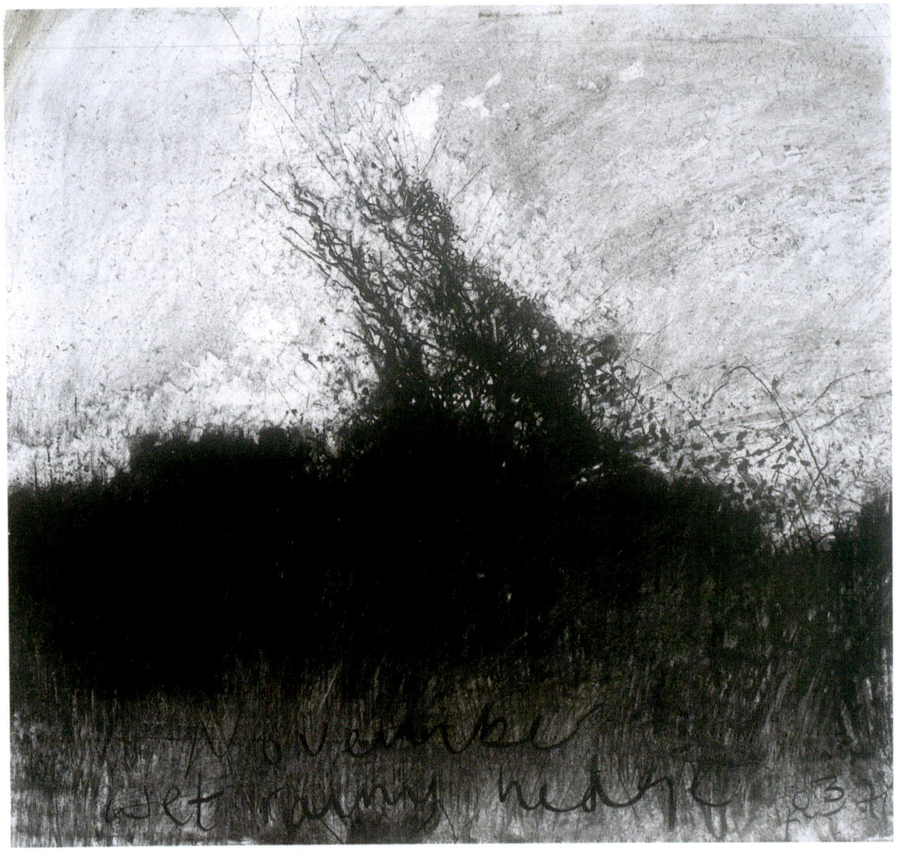

97
November, wet rainy hedge, 2003
Charcoal, 50.5 × 54 cm
(20 × 21 in)

will spring up. Skewjack might not be an ancient wood, but it is undeniably in the act of *becoming*. As the poet and ecological philosopher Gary Snyder writes: 'This present moment | That lives on, | To become | Long ago.'[5]

The contrasts and similarities between Ashcombe and Skewjack raise the question of human intervention in the forest. Kurt explores this shifting territory more explicitly in the series 'Forest Gardens' (2009). At first glance the title sounds like a contradiction. The wilderness and the cultivated plot appear to be archetypal opposites, symbols of a stand-off between nature and culture that goes back ten thousand years. But we are trapped by our own narrow concepts here; if we look back into history, we realise that harvested forests existed long before the invention of agriculture. The chestnut grove and the apple orchard represent ancient compromises between the worlds of the hunter-gatherer and the farmer, places where humans could provide for themselves without obliterating whole eco-systems.

These forests are a natural subject for Jackson; he has championed the idea that humans can be participants in natural eco-systems, not just external manipulators. He is an artisan painter, having worked in these fruitful treelots, tracking down rare apples in his own West Country redoubts, helping with the almond harvest in the valleys of the Alpujarra in Southern Spain. It appears odd, then, that you rarely encounter other people in his paintings of these places. However, that is the

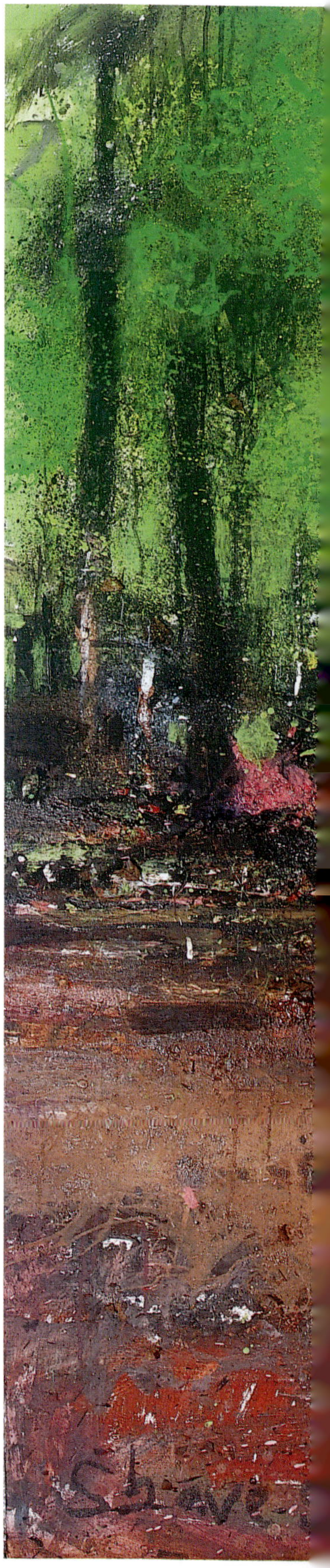

98
Shave Green greens, 2005
Mixed media on canvas,
153 × 169.5 cm
(60 × 66.5 in)

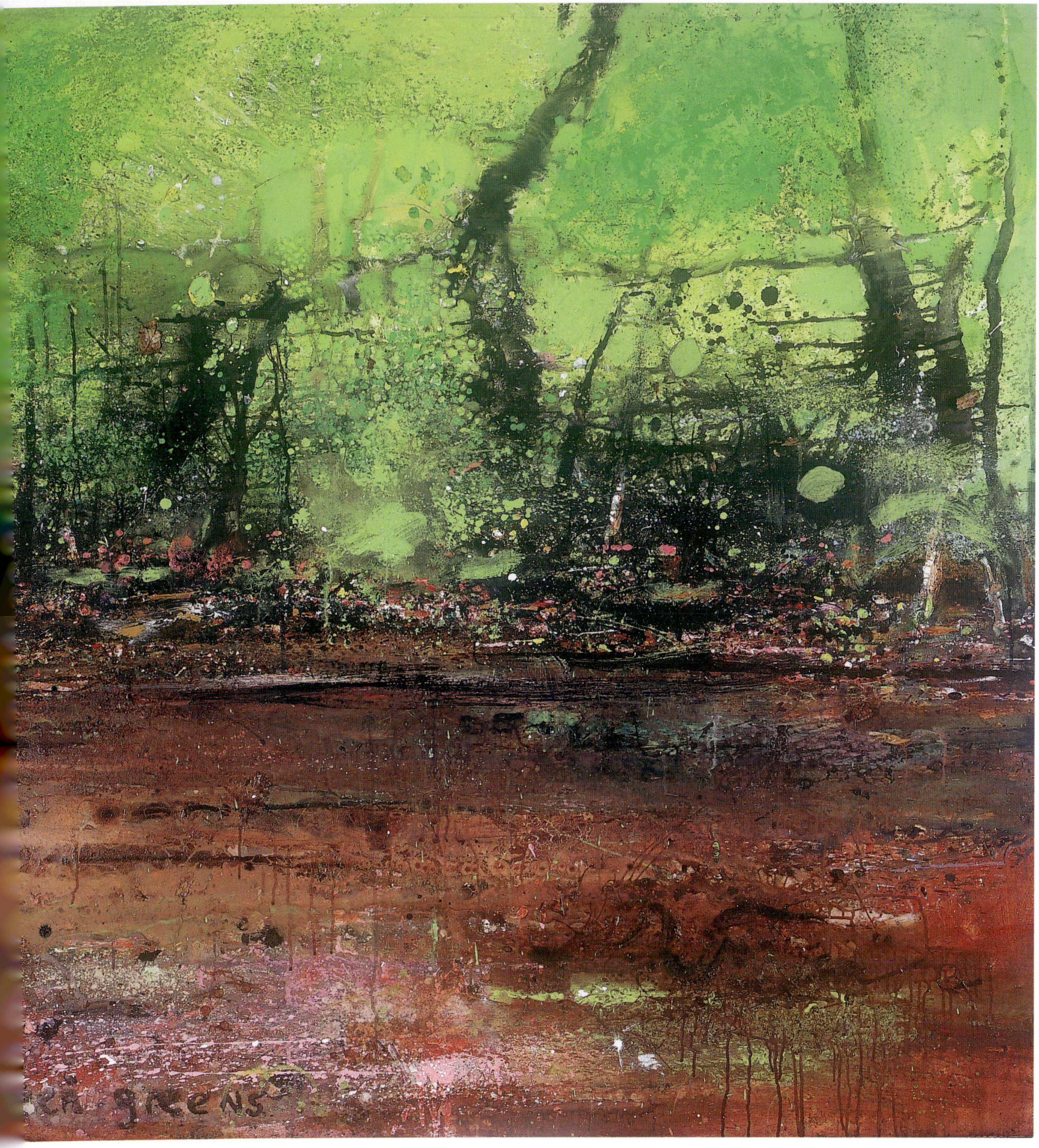
greens

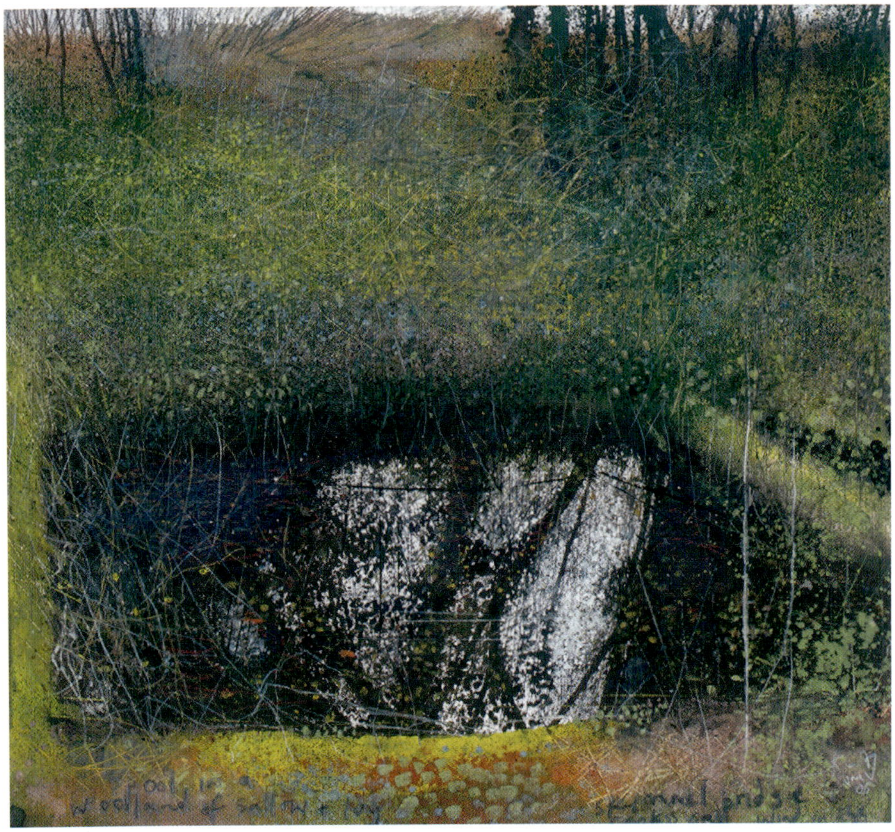

99
Pool in a woodland of sallow and ivy, Skimmel Bridge, January 2006
Mixed media, 29.5 × 30.5 cm (11.5 × 12 in)

special quality of forest gardens: they are not under *occupation*, as are so many conventional agricultural landscapes. Their human tenants enter to prune and harvest, but for the rest of the year leave the places to their other inhabitants. Jackson is also aware of the difficulties associated with inserting human figures into natural scenes. The history of landscape painting is strewn with failed attempts to colour in the relationships between the two. Humans as picturesque ornaments, as beasts of burden, as gods and idealised heroes: clichés swarm around the ambivalent power relationship that exists between the figures and their setting. Jackson prefers to suggest a human presence implicitly by registering the solid fact of a worked landscape's endurance.

However, the continuity of nature itself permeates 'Forest Gardens'. What is exceptional about these works is that few of them are *composed* in a conventional sense. There are no obvious foregrounds, no distant prospects artfully framed by trees. At times, they almost have a two-dimensional feel, as if, in the moment of painting, nothing else exists except this plane of living tissue. Jackson has turned

100
Tree of 431 fruit, 2008
Bronze and granite, 147 × 75 × 75 cm (58 × 29.5 × 29.5 in)

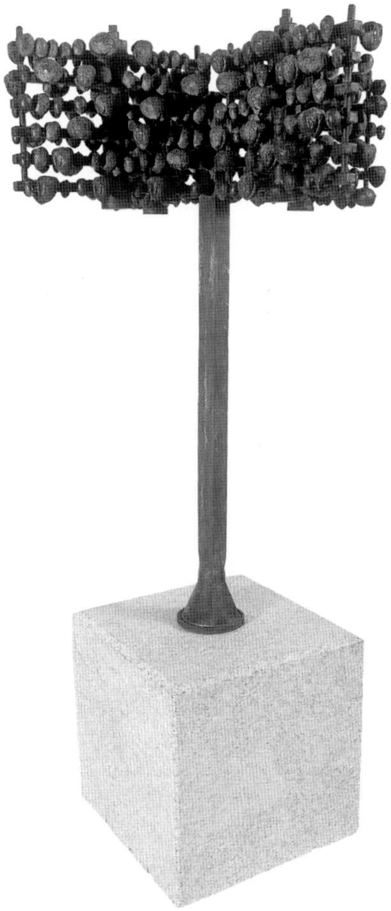

the conventions of landscape painting back to front. Since Claude Lorrain (1604–82) set out his idealised prospects of the Italian *campagna*, painters have typically portrayed a scene that seems to flow out from them, that is composed as if they were at its focal point. They *command* the scene. In this sense, traditional landscape painting faithfully reflected, and helped to consolidate, the conventions of land ownership and management. Property and fertility lay in the soil, and the business of farming was to organise and cultivate this, to break it into submission.

In Jackson's forest garden paintings, there is no sense in which the 'view' has been composed or possessed either by the painter or forest-farmer. The prospect hangs nebulously in the middle distance, a shape-shifting cloud of living matter, a green gauze across the walnut trees, a pink froth of blossom over the almonds. It seems not to be unrolling from your feet, like a tidy surveyor's plan, but to expand *towards* you, and up to the sky. The artist's pictures are, in the precise sense of the word, atmospheric: they celebrate the biological fact that the true life of forests hangs in the air, where the alchemy of photosynthesis creates green tissue from light and carbon dioxide, and where the sun's rays open the flowers and ripen the fruit.

In his significant book *Forests: The Shadow of Civilizatio,*[6] Robert Pogue Harrison argues that contact with the energy of the wild wood is crucial to us as a species, in reminding us that we have both 'left' the forest yet still have inextricable links with its creativity and life-support systems. Kurt Jackson, painting from deep inside the 'green chaos', brings us close to that energy, both in the intimacy and attention of his studies, and in the sheer vitality of his paintwork.

Notes

1. Annie Dillard, *Pilgrim at Tinker Creek*, Jonathan Cape, London, 1974, p.129.
2. John Morton, eighteenth-century naturalist and topographical writer. *The Natural History of Northamptonshire*, R. Knaplock and R. Wilkin, London, 1712, pp.12–13.
3. Interview with the artist in catalogue of *Paintings of Cornwall and the Scillies*, White Lane Press, Plymouth, 1999, p.10.
4. John Clare, 'The Nightingale's Nest', *c.*1832, in *The Midsummer Cushion*, ed. Anne Tibble, MidNAG, in association with Carcanet Press, Manchester, 1978, p.201.
5. 'This present moment', from *The Gary Snyder Reader*, Counterpoint, Washington, 1999, p.608.
6. Robert Pogue Harrison, *Forests: The Shadow of Civilization*, University of Chicago Press, Chicago, 1992.

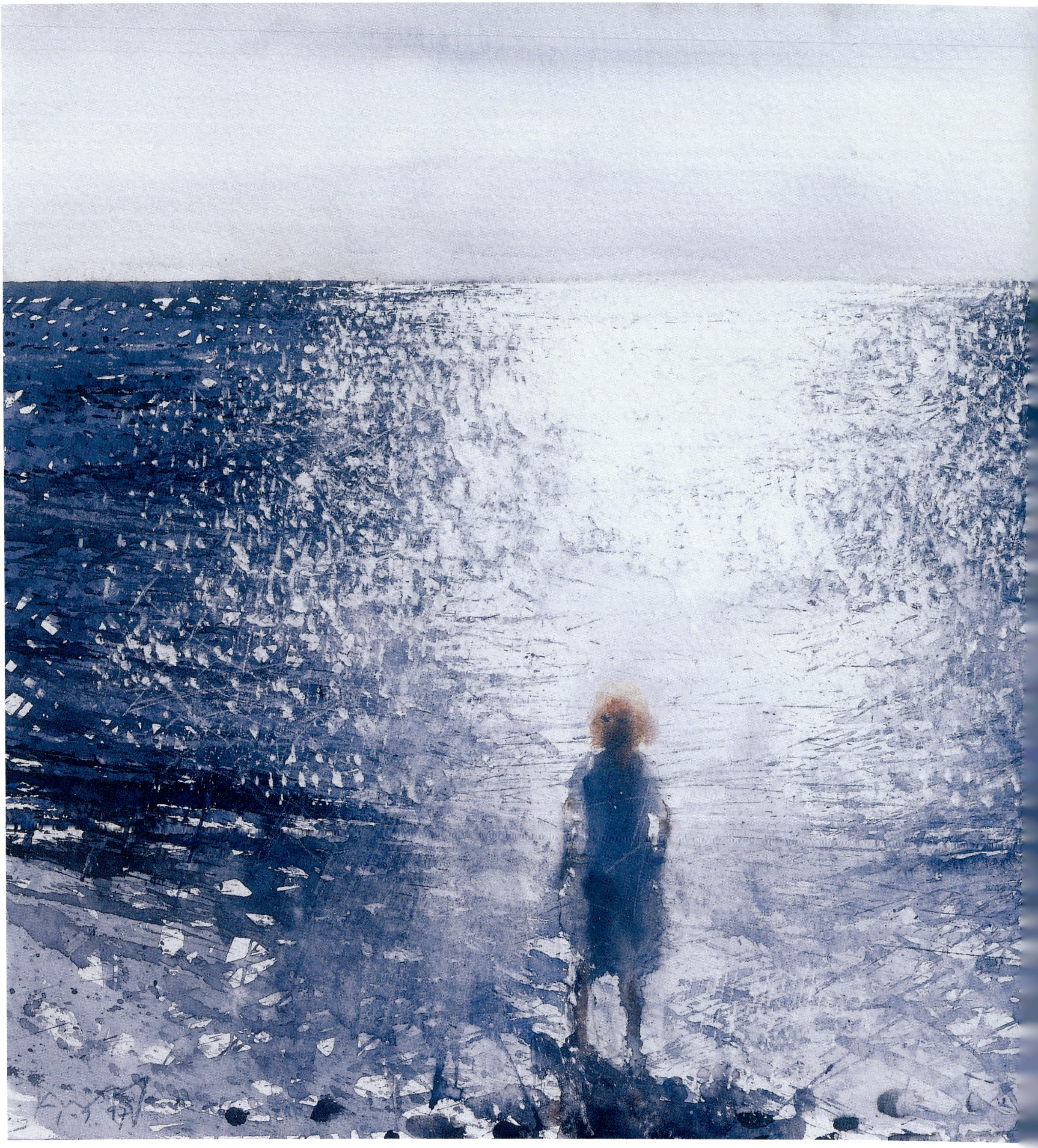

8 Mordros: A Portrait of Kurt Jackson

Mark Cocker

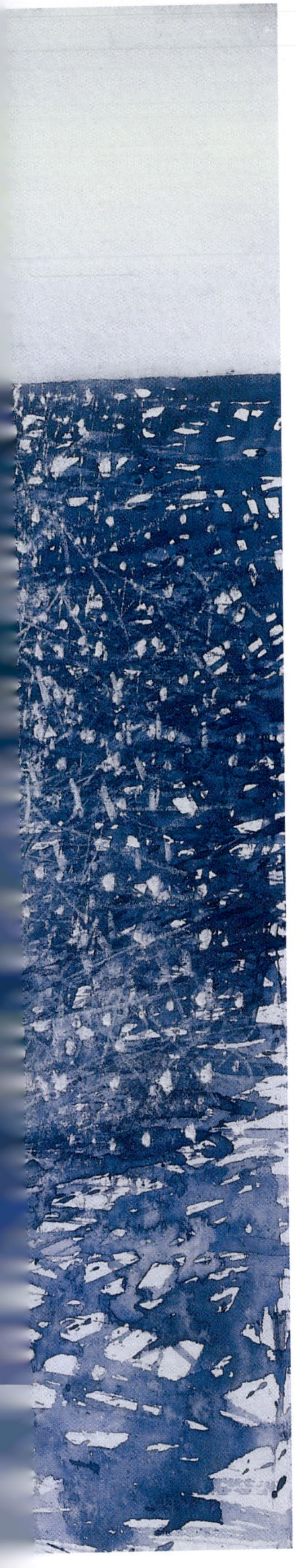

101
Sealight, Chloe, 1/9/97
Watercolour, 28 × 30.5 cm
(11 × 12 in)

We face southwest towards the Isles of Scilly. To our left is a coastal hill, Carn Gloose. On our right lies Cape Cornwall and beyond, exactly a mile offshore, is a group of rocky outcrops known as the Brisons. In Priest Cove, we hop from boulder to boulder in the direction of a series of larger weed-mottled granite monoliths. They stand closer to the edge of the sea and offer us a perfect vantage point on the incoming tide. 'Hear that?' he asks me as we search for a seat among the rocks. 'In the Cornish language, that is called *Mordros*. It's the only language, along with Greek and Polynesian, I think, that has a word for the sound of the sea.'

Almost without pause, he continues: 'If you look at that line in the beach, you can see the exact place where the basaltic mudstones meet the granite.' Just these few fine details, such as his translation of the Cornish place-name (*Carn* as rocky hillock and *gloose* as grey/green), and his awareness of the precise distance that the Brisons lie offshore, tell me that this is a man deeply embedded in his landscape. In fact, part of the scene before us is visible from his kitchen window.

I'm with the artist, Kurt Jackson, who, after growing up in Hertfordshire, moved to Cornwall with his family in the early 1980s. Jackson has lived here ever since, first in Boscastle on the north coast, and now in sight of the spot where we are sitting. His passion for the peninsula's landscapes and its Atlantic-pounded coast has resulted in tens of thousands of mixed-media paintings, sketches, etchings, prints and sculptures. In return, Cornwall has come to embrace its most prolific interpreter as one of its own. Nine immense reproductions of his work greeted me on the day that I arrived, along the south wall of Penzance railway station. Jackson is now regarded as one of the most important landscape artists in Britain and his annual exhibitions at the Lemon Street Gallery in Truro now sell out even before they have opened.

The spot where we have chosen to sit is sheltered from the wind and close to the edge, but in the summer Jackson has to take special account of his visibility to passing tourists. People now seek out these customary painting localities. The success of Jackson's works has made their creator himself a celebrity, a living embodiment of the artistic tradition long associated with this part of Cornwall.

My guess is, however, that should anyone find the place, they might easily overlook him. I quickly realise that Kurt Jackson is a plain-dressing sort of man. There is little that immediately conjures the *artist*, and much that seems distinctly workman-like, even urban, in his physical appearance. The completely shaven head, the nose ring and three ear-rings rising up his left lobe, the DM boots, the jeans and the *keffiyeh* scarf are all resonant of life in the inner city. The only giveaway about his trade is the liberal splattering of paint over almost everything he wears. In a sense, the edgy modernity to Jackson's dress seems to offer a clue as to why he has had such a startling impact in the very traditional field of landscape painting for which he is famed.

Before I even begin to reflect on why this should be and how Jackson has refreshed this established genre, we should note that the description of 'landscape artist' does not really encompass his true scope. Some of his most glorious and ambitious paintings depict inner London, as far from the natural world as it is possible to be. Then there is the series of images narrating the lives of Cornish charcoal-makers, or workers in the local slate quarry at Delabole. There was also his exhibition of works, completed deep inside the Earth, on Cornwall's last working tin mines, and a parallel project in Iberia documenting Spanish and migrant Cornish miners. Furthermore, he makes annual visits to cover the stage performances at the Glastonbury Festival and has recently exhibited paintings of a surgeon friend working at Treliske Hospital in Truro. There was no fresh air except for the antiseptic interior of an operating theatre, no landscape but the unfamiliar terrain of human bodies under anaesthesia.

It would perhaps be more accurate to say that his real concerns are landscape *and* the multitudinous ways in which humans have impacted upon or have, in turn, been shaped by their environment. It is this two-way relationship between people and place, essentially a form of human ecology, which starts to unearth what is original and different about Jackson's approach to landscape art. He is a lifelong naturalist and displays a deep knowledge not merely of how the various parts of an environment are constructed, including the shapes of leaves, trees, rocks, birds and flowers, but also an understanding of the processes of interaction that occur in all natural environments.

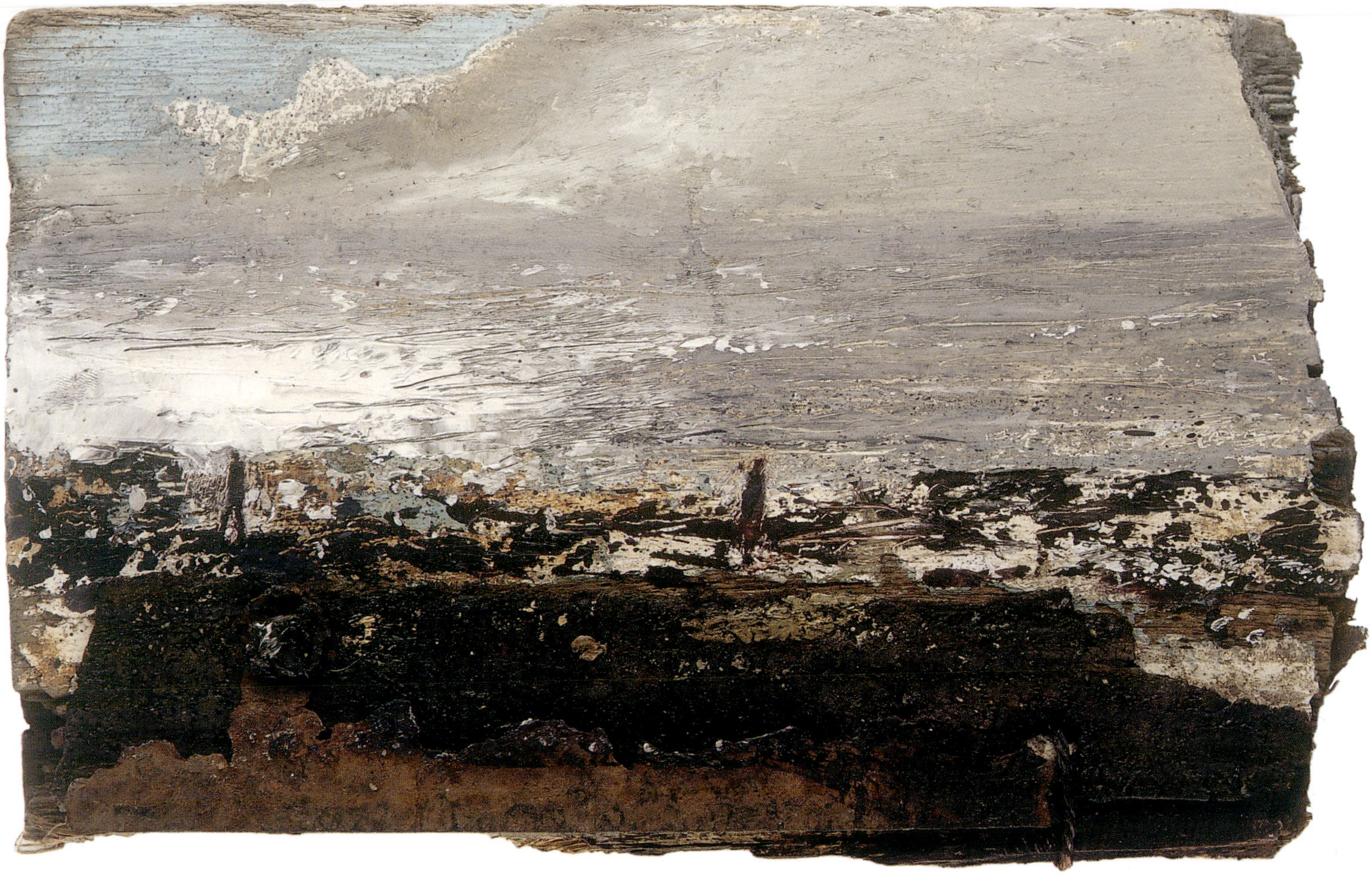

102
Priest Cove, figures, Winter 1994
Oil and collage on driftwood, 15 × 23 cm (6 × 9 in)

The author and naturalist, Richard Mabey, has talked about the state of '*becoming*', which is evident in the places that Jackson re-creates. This ecological approach explains why the same, habitual few places continue to exercise fascination for him. Where we are sitting in Priest Cove is a scene to which he has returned countless times, resulting in hundreds of images. The places are the same and yet endlessly different.

More than this, however, the artist understands that he too is party to a larger web of connections. There is an ecological relationship between Jackson and his paintings, which holds a fascination not merely for art lovers, but also naturalists. In this second role, as a watcher of nature myself, I have come to sit with Jackson over the next couple of days. I sense that one can only understand these deeper interconnections between art and place, not simply from looking at the finished works, but by seeing how they are created. For the next two days I want to watch him as I might study a species of bird, such as a rook or a jackdaw. The ecology of Kurt Jackson is my theme.

The trip starts to unfold almost as we begin to settle into our pitch, opening the boxes of paints and crayons, and adjusting our seats to observe our respective

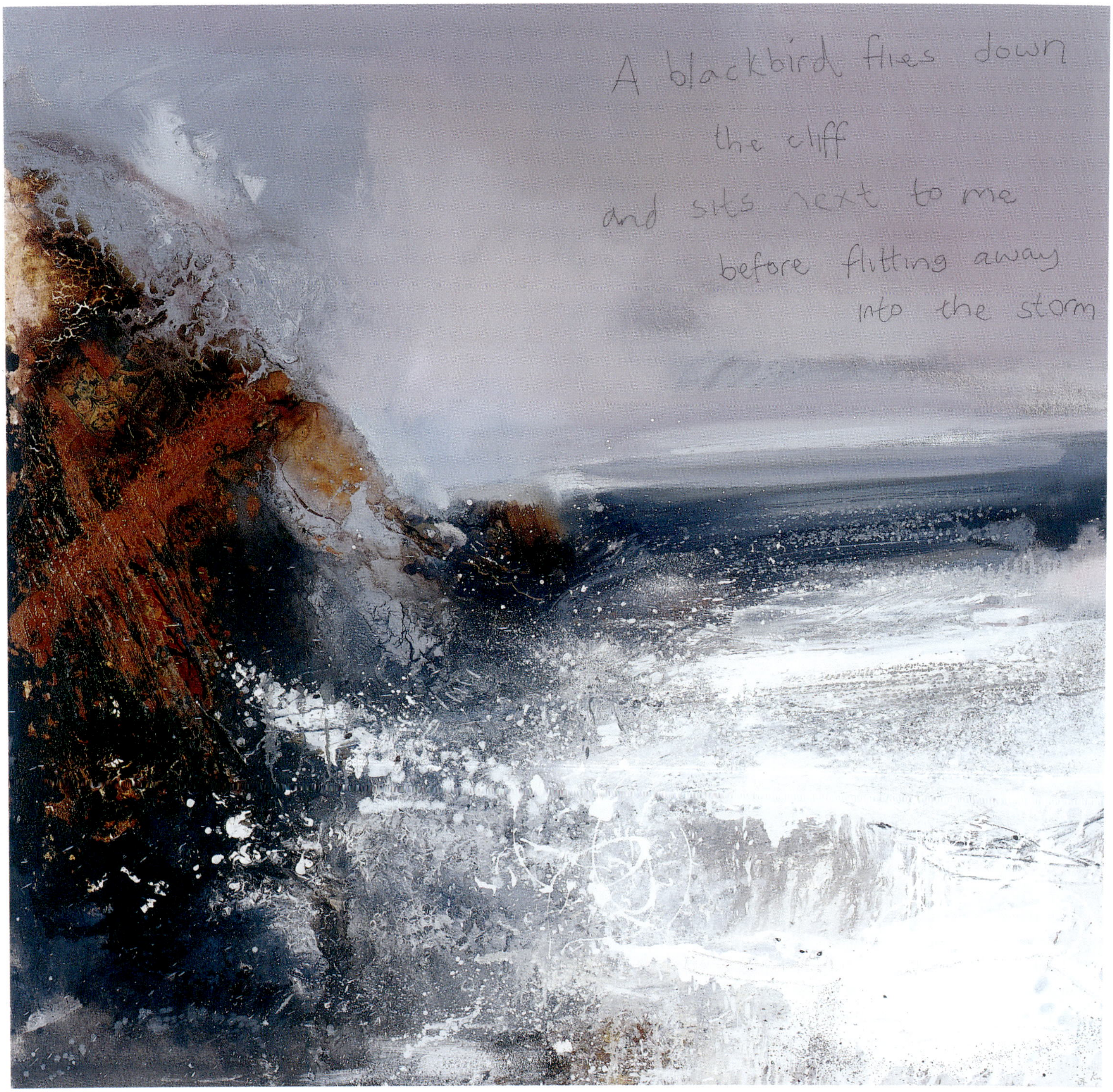

103
A blackbird flies down the cliff and sits next to me before flitting away into the storm.
2004. Mixed media on canvas, 122 × 122 cm (48 × 48 in)

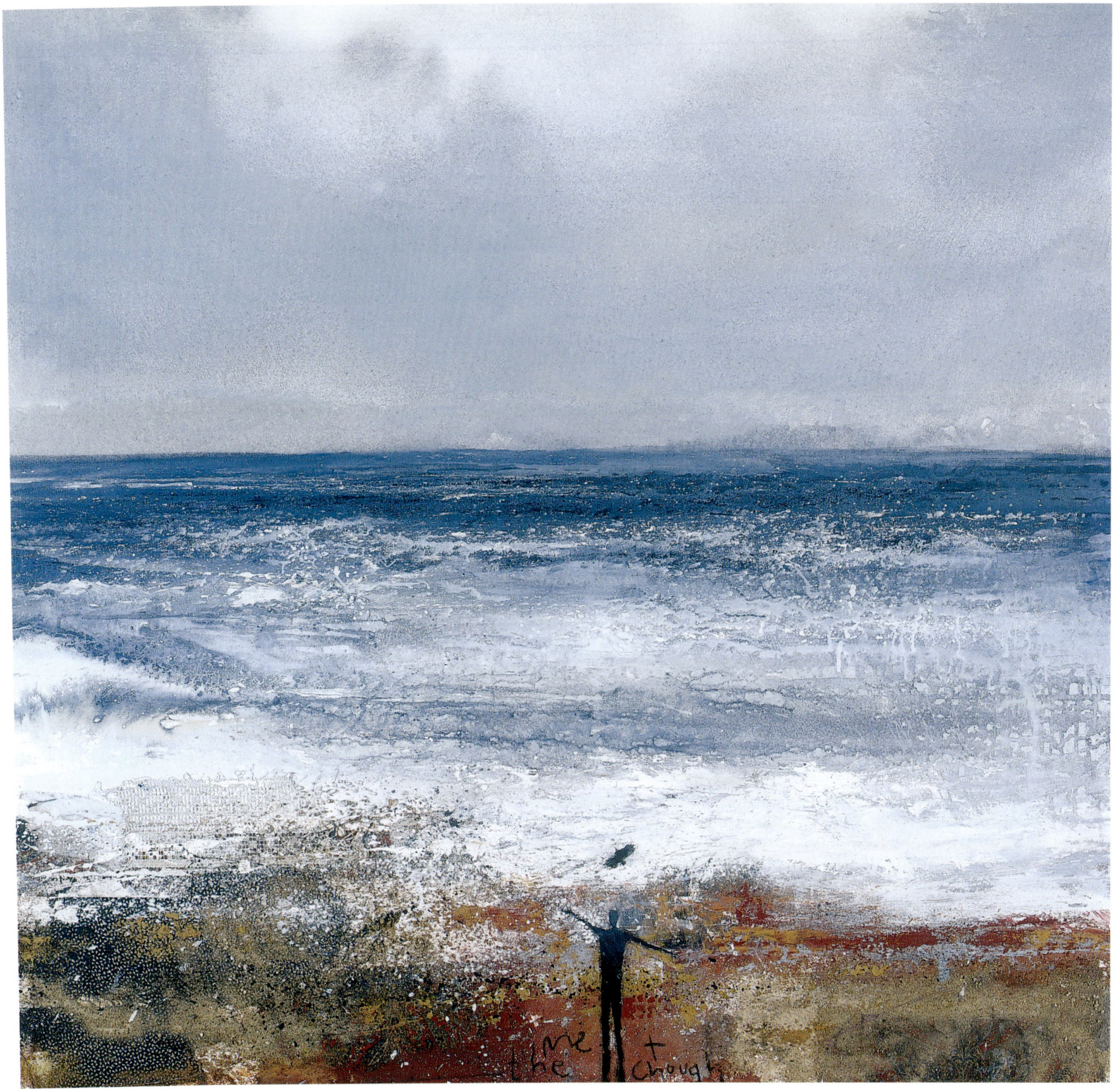

104

Me and the chough, 2007

Mixed media on canvas, 122 × 122 cm (48 × 48 in)

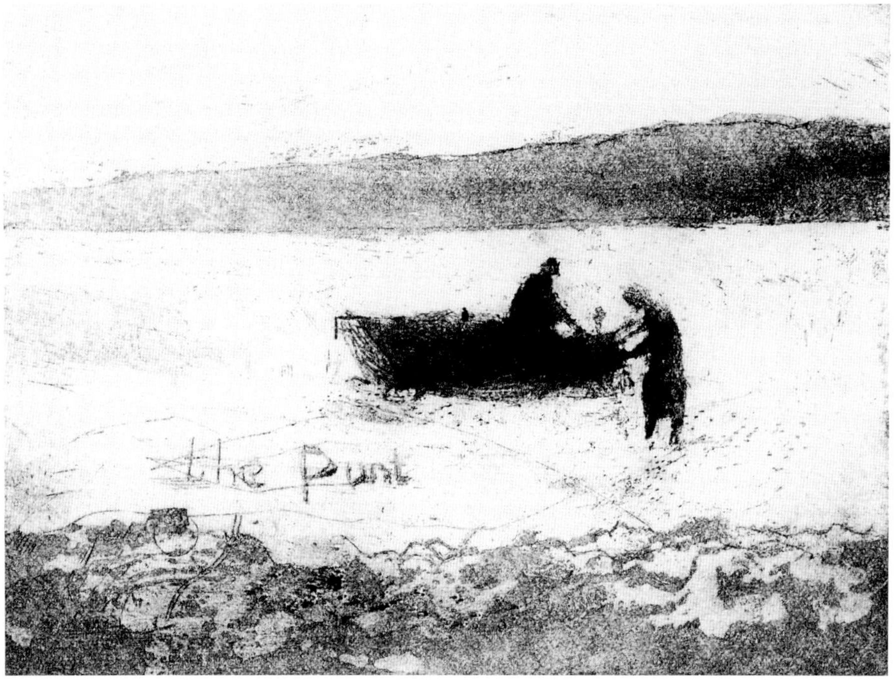

105
The Punt, 2005
Etching and drypoint, plate size 10 × 13 cm (4 × 5 in). Edition of 30

subjects. Suddenly, a small brown flake chips off the rocks ahead and acquires the powers of flight. It performs a circuit around our heads and returns to its perch. A high, clear insistent alarm call, a sound that punctures the *Mordros*, tells us that this inhabitant of the inter-tidal zone is alert to our arrival. It is a type of small grey-brown bird called a rock pipit.

Jackson notes the presence of the pipit and explains how, sitting in the same spot for hours, such creatures often begin to accept him as a congenial part of the landscape. Birds and other animals such as shrews, stoats and weasels, will come right up to him. But he gives the rock pipits special commendation: 'They are my friends. They are often the only companions I have all day. They will brush right past my face and even walk over my feet.'

In exchange for this act of faith, Jackson might make a note of the rock pipit on his painting. Incidental details – minutely observed parts of the scene, such as the weather or the sounds that he can hear, and often the other species which share the habitat as he paints – will be recorded in a little scribbled message on the canvas edge, and sometimes right across the top through the sky. These marginal inscriptions often become the titles of his paintings and are almost a signature for his art.

Occasionally these signs are even more intimate. In some of the largest canvases, Jackson works barefoot, moving around them and even directly across them to apply the paint – on one massive piece, I noticed a size-ten blue footprint. Like his scribbled marginalia about rock pipits, these marks are central to the message. Even in the quietude and detachment of a gallery space, they convey the living context for his artifice, the pressing contingency of the places that inspire it, the unseen inhabitants to whom the landscape truly belongs and the unseen artist who shares this moment. In short, they remind us of a complex of inter-relationships that inform our acts of creativity. It might be the artist's name on the canvas, but Jackson's marginal notes recall how paintings are democratic transactions set in real life. (Later that morning at Priest Cove I am astonished to see how he welcomes a bit of smudging as he slides the newly wet painting into its plastic sleeve.)

Another key motif stressing the deepest connection between place and art is Jackson's use of found materials. In fact, if the incidental marks that he makes himself are a personal signature, then his adventitious borrowings from a place seem like the landscape's own interventions in the painting. I love these material incorporations. Wool is a favourite, but you will also find feathers and seaweed, leaves and twigs, even bits of sand and gravel out of a streambed. A memorable recent work documenting the River Avon is notable for the plastic bottles and other indestructible flotsam, which have been engineered into the scene. However, one of the most moving examples of found materials is Jackson's usage of the mud, which he picked up off the shaft floor while working underground in a tin mine. It is exactly the same dust that once stained the faces and blighted the lungs of miners here in Cornwall and elsewhere. Dirt converted into art.

A piece that I was keen to see was completed on the stretch of coast where we are now sitting. This huge canvas of Priest Cove is smothered in the sand taken off that beach as an oblique commentary on the location. Jackson explains how most of the sand in the bay was dug up and removed long ago for its tin content, so although we see the place as an elemental, untouched scene of bare rock and salt water, it is actually a human artefact – just like the painting itself. Reflect briefly on the elegant symmetry in that conceit: a painting made from sand that depicts a place that looks real, but is actually man-made. It makes you wonder, what is a landscape and what is a landscape painting. In this extraordinary work, the two entities are fused or, to use the word that is almost a leitmotif for Jackson's oeuvre, one has *become* the other.

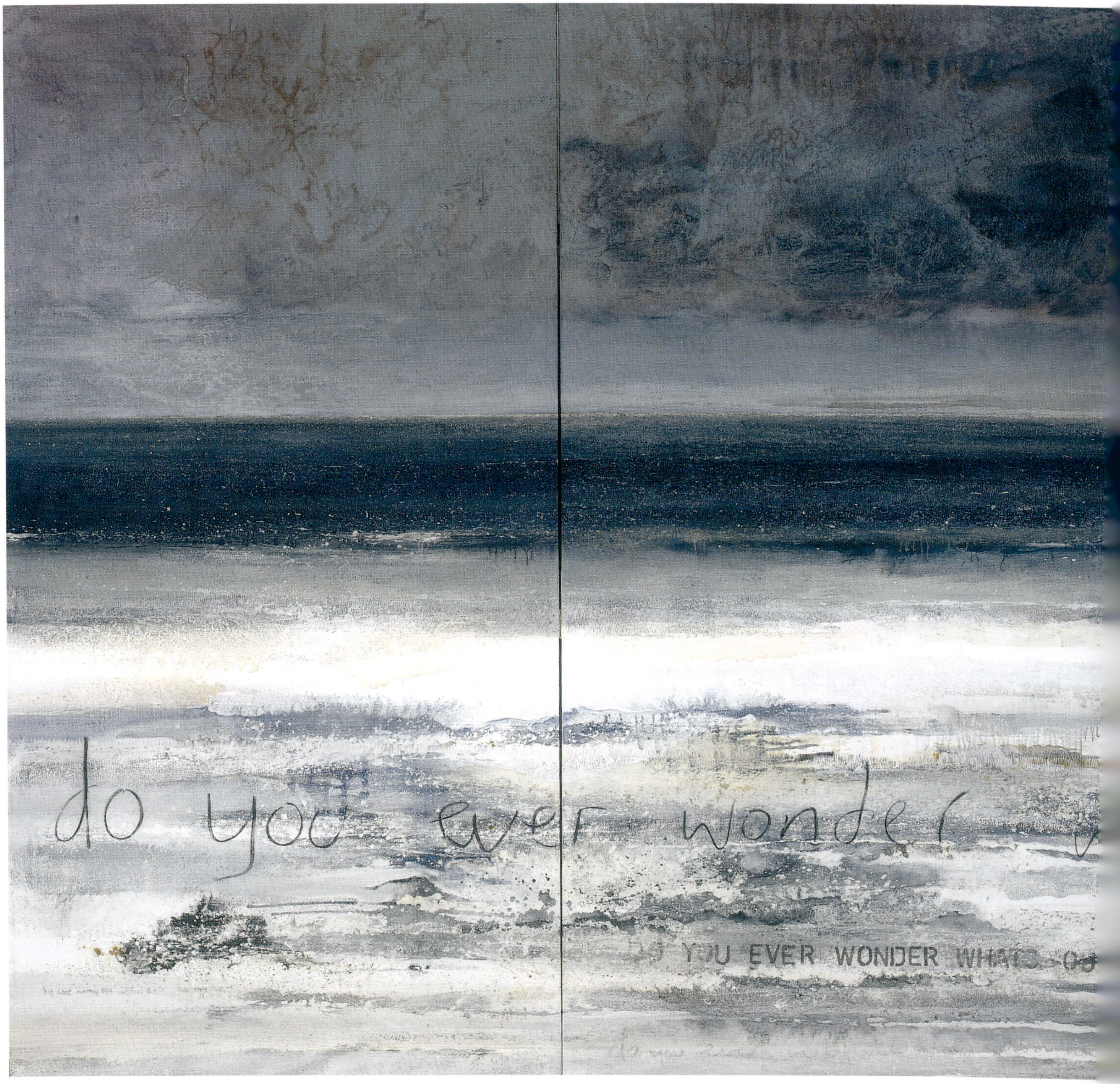

106
Do you ever wonder what's out there? 2002–03
Mixed media on canvas, 305 × 610 cm (120 × 240 in)

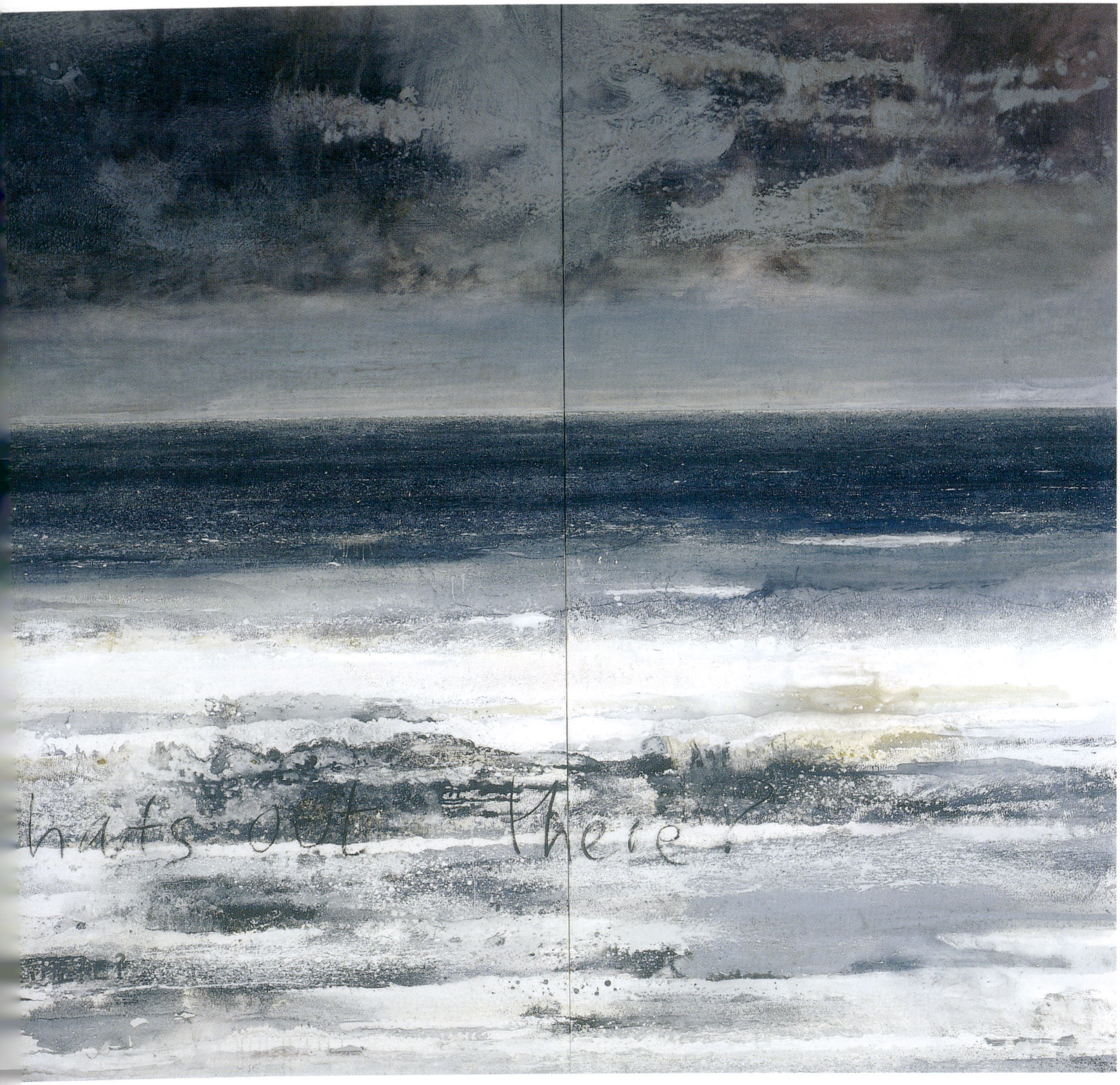
hats out there?

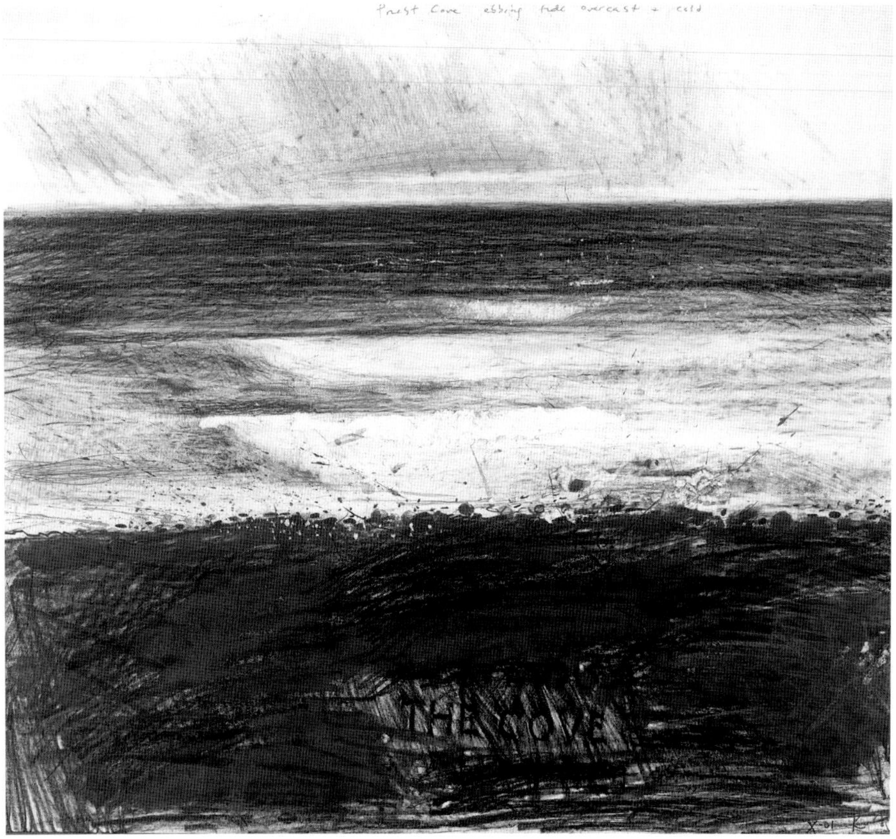

107
Priest Cove, ebbing tide, overcast and cold, October 2001
Pencil, 51 × 55 cm (20 × 21.5 in)

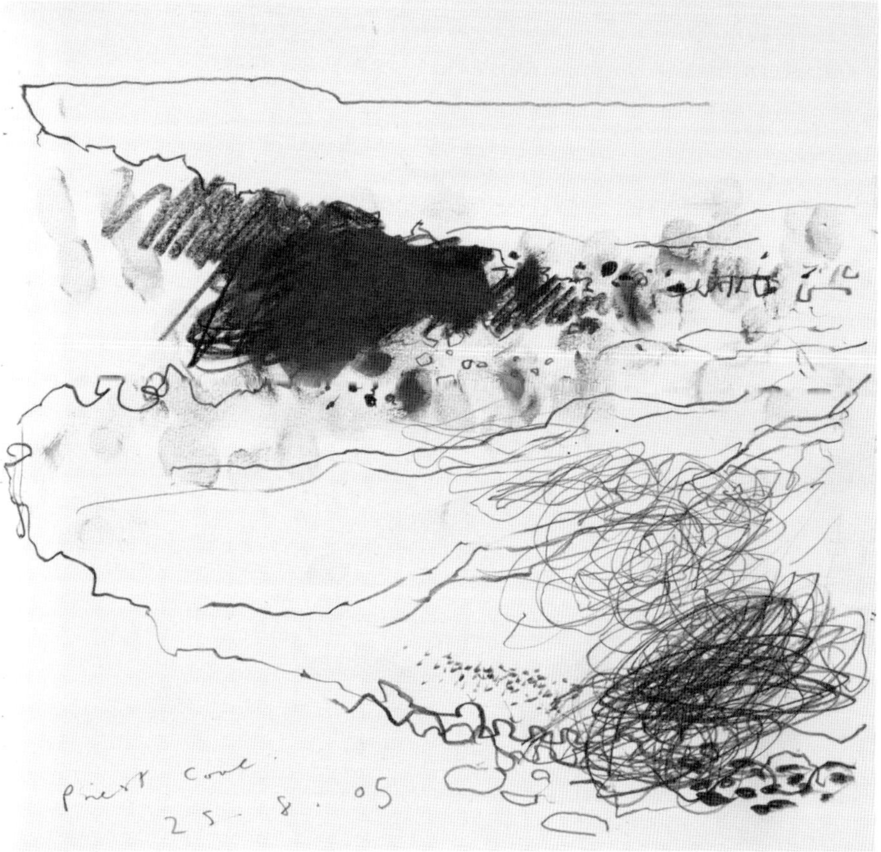

108
Priest Cove, 25/8/05
Pencil, 25 × 25 cm (10 × 10 in)

As we watch the Atlantic pounding the bay, and the *Mordros* slowly triumphs over our senses, I am lured away from my chosen subject of study by another rare bird. While Jackson sketches out a preliminary scene, I spot a peregrine falcon, probably a male, as it cruises over the sea. A slate-grey bullet, it steers south and west, but is blown gradually inland towards us. It rises over Carn Gloose and loiters, the air rinsing its wings, the bird wind-held. Jackson sees it with the naked eye as soon as it slips free of the Brisons and then turns back to his work, as he starts to push a fistful of brushes across the leaden sky from which the bird has just flown. 'Grey is such a beautiful colour', he reflects.

That *fistful* of brushes brings me back to my primary task. There is a final dimension present in Jackson's paintings that makes me feel it is necessary to sit with him and observe the creative process. A regular reference made in the context of his art is to the Abstract Expressionist Jackson Pollock (1912–56). The living Cornish Jackson is a great admirer of his dead American namesake. In both of their works, final layers of paint look to have been applied in big, rough, hectic splashes and dribbles. They suggest the volatile, performance-like nature of the painting process.

Jackson's art is also compared to the landscapes of J.M.W. Turner (1775–1851). In fact, having just seen *Rain, Steam and Speed* (1844) in London's National Gallery, I find the artist is now uppermost in my mind as I sit with Jackson. In Turner's great work one is never quite sure whether the Victorian age, with all its bright shiny trains and ambition-spanning bridges, is taking shape out of miasmic chaos. Or is Turner warning us how that same material world, whose permanence and order we take for granted, is only a mist veil away from the great elemental forces which could render it all back down into the Earth?

In Jackson's paintings, there is also a sense of the earthquake-like energies that initiated the proto-landscape from which the present scene evolved. When we see his works of Priest Cove, for instance, we have not only the finished granite boulders, but we feel the molten magma that gave birth to them, awkwardly and violently, eons ago. Immense elemental forces often lie just below the outer surface of a Kurt Jackson painting. One wonders if that appearance of great energy is borne itself of the same stuff.

As soon as I see that clubbed fist of brushes scouring back and forth across the paper, I sense the answer is at hand. There is a frenetic pace to the way in which Jackson works. A relentless, organic multi-tasking, hands roving for pencils and bottles, inks and crayons. This operates in a chaotic synchrony with the looking. In the initial phase the artist's head moves up and down from scene to canvas every few seconds. One can almost feel how the landscape is entering the optic nerves and is being pulsed through the synapses and ganglia of the central nervous system, then out once more via muscle reflexes in hands and arms, on to the paper.

Jackson then breaks off briefly to incise with a razor blade a bruised grey sky he has just laid on the paper. The act of slashing vigorously at his own canvas – and sometimes he tells me he goes clean through the sheet – makes me realise that the volcanic energies conveyed in the paintings are achieved by a gradual slackening of control over the forces that create them. The artist's release of himself into the process reaches its climax about half an hour later, as the roar of the sea imposes its ineluctable rhythm on us both.

I am struck most by two aspects of this creativity. The first is the sheer range of materials and techniques. I am not only referring to the spectrum of ink bottles, crayons, pastels and pencils – the material stuff he uses – but the odd things, such as the moment when he grabs the actual palette and drags it repeatedly over the layers of colour. Another moment, he empties the muddy water wholesale out of the palette, which he has used earlier to mix his pigments, on to the painting and starts working with that. The razor blade is deployed repeatedly, and if that does not create the desired effect, Jackson uses his nails and tells me that he cannot bite them precisely because of their instrumental value to him. At one point, in fact, he uses all ten digits from both hands and it looks as if he is playing the piano in his own wet paint.

The second aspect to this few minutes of picture-making is its sheer physicality. On one occasion, I can count the number of brushes in his hand. He has all 12 and wields them like weapons against his image. Then brushes might be held, not by their handle, pencil-wise, but laid flat in the palm of his hand, with the bristles flicked almost individually so that tiny specks of paint are sprayed on to the paper.

The subtlety of this last technique contrasts with another method, whereby he swipes the brush hard at the paper like a swordsman testing a blade, lacing the canvas with great raindrops of paint. Jackson has been filmed regularly for television, and he explains how he is a 'cameraman's nightmare', particularly for his impact on those big silvery plastic discs they use to reflect light on their subject. 'They collect paint splashes like they collect light', he remarks, 'I have ruined a good number of them in my time.' My coat too, I notice, now has the tell-tale signs of a day in the field with Jackson.

At last he blows hard at the paper and stands back. Jackson is hugely self-critical. Pieces are put away on completion and left for several weeks, untouched

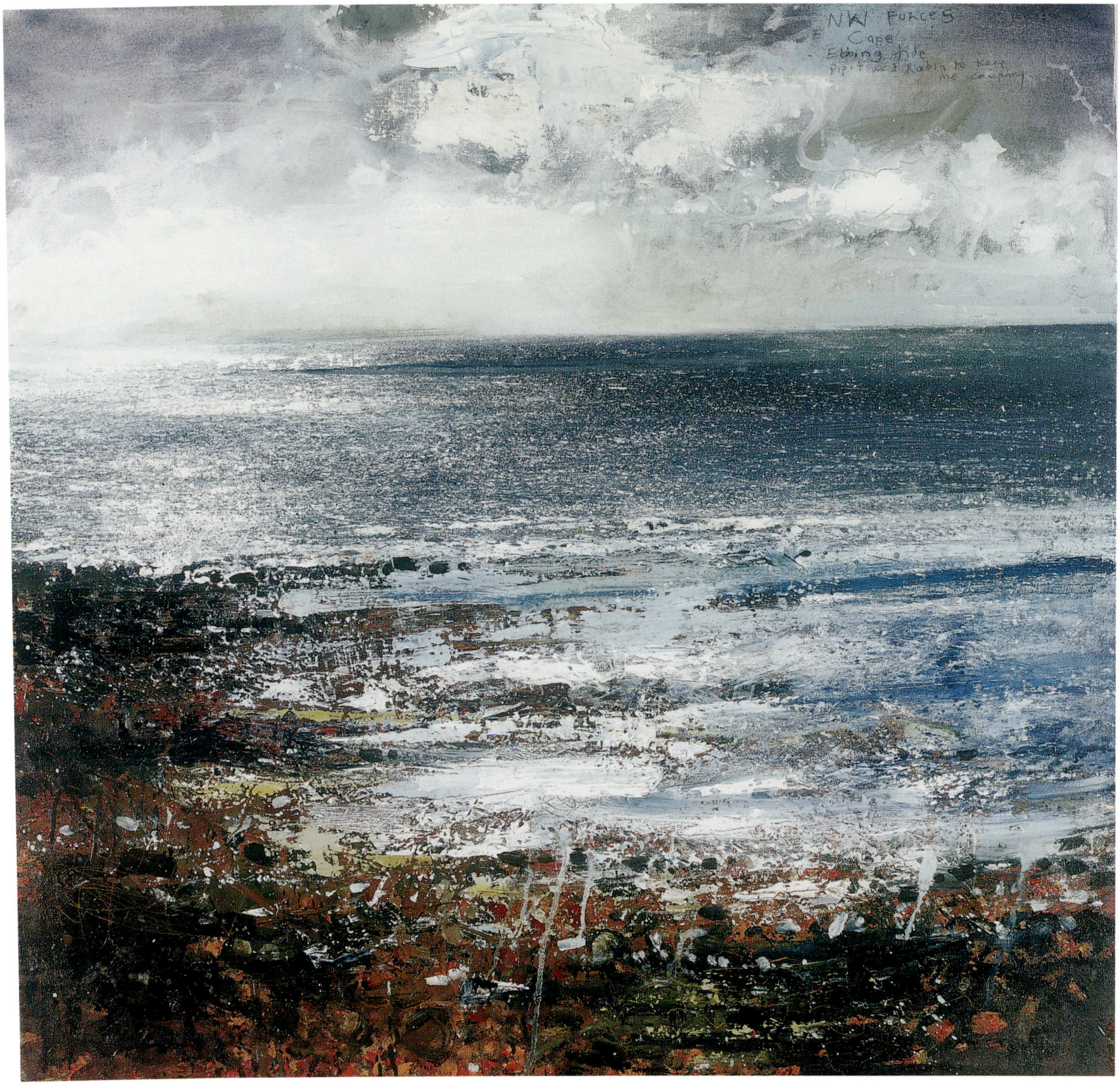

109
NW Force 5, Cape, November 2000
Oil on canvas, 91.5 × 91.5 cm (36 × 36 in)

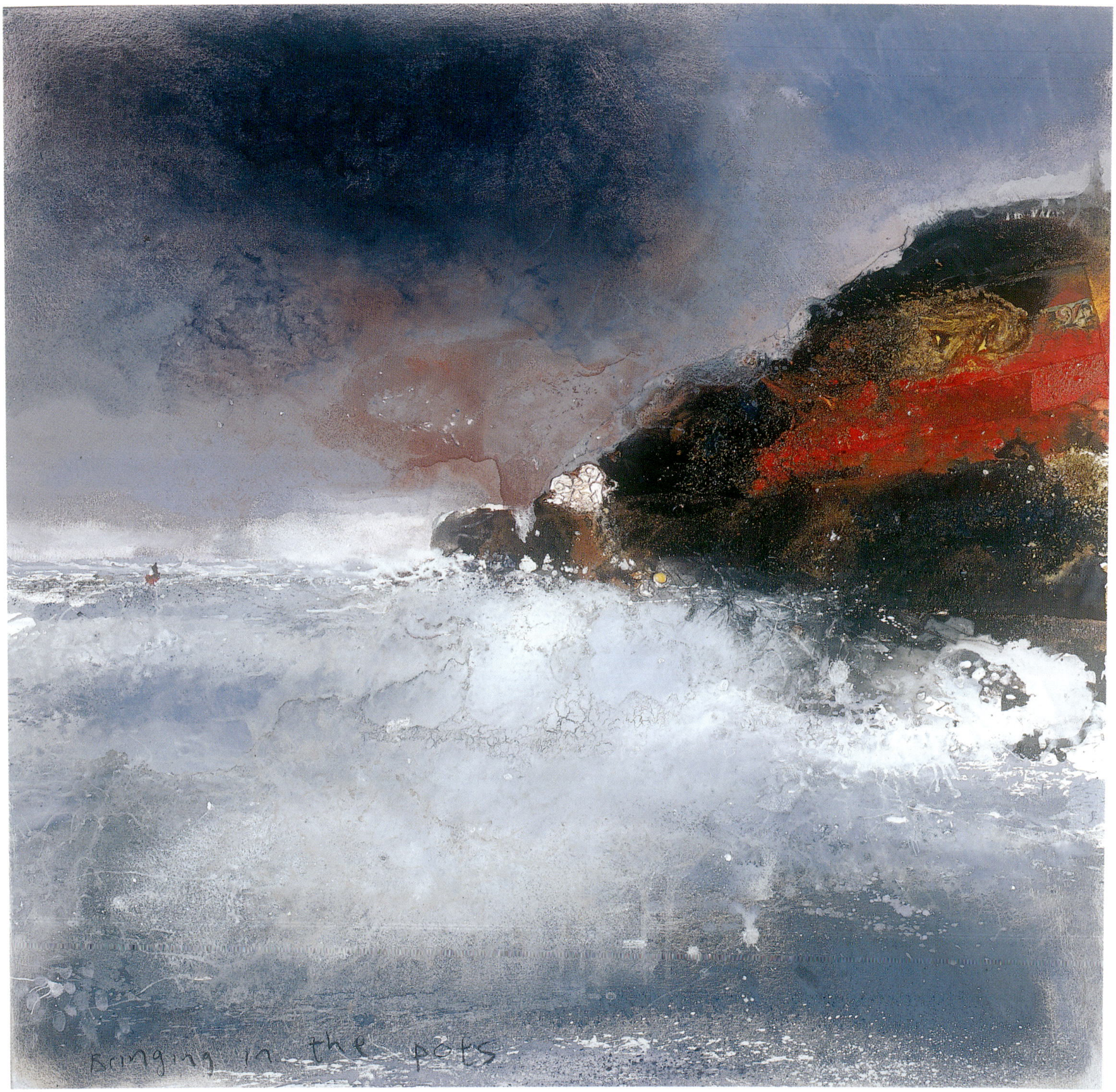

110
Bringing in the pots, 2005
Mixed media and collage on canvas, 122 × 122 cm (48 × 48 in)

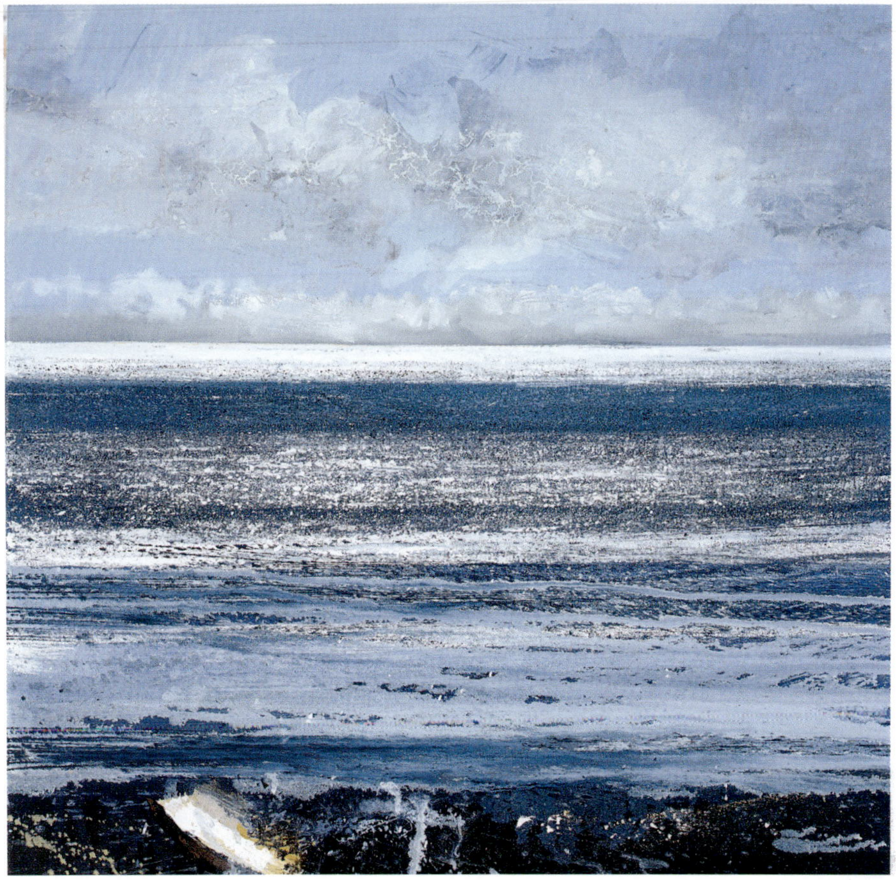

111
***Sun, sea, showers*, 2002**
Oil on canvas, 61 × 61 cm (24 × 24 in)

and unseen, before he takes them out again to see if they have succeeded. A significant percentage of them are destroyed immediately. The earlier crescendo of artistic methodology has taken five minutes, but it feels like the summation of 25 years of apprenticeship, a word that he cherishes. I calculate afterwards that the artist has used a different approach or technique every 13 seconds, and at times I have found it nearly impossible to observe him and write up the processes as they happened.

Improbably, given the intensity of his application to the changing landscape and to the even faster-moving portrait of it, Jackson talks to me all the time he is painting. Or rather, I should say, he is talking to himself. But I do manage to capture the last word: 'Mental!' He almost shouts it out, in his wonderfully flat, Southern-English street tone. It is odd, given the ecstatic tumult of the preceding minutes, that it is not a reference to himself, nor a comment on how I might be feeling. Kurt Jackson nods to the sea, 'Looks as if they are about to overwhelm you ... The Waves.'

There are two mental scenes before me. There is the Atlantic and the rock. Over his shoulder, I glimpse its twin: the grey-turquoise sea slump, calm and expansive, just behind an oncoming frenzy of white spume careening into the black basalt. This is the *Mordros* made visible – a thing of colour and elemental contest, and a scene of immense beauty.

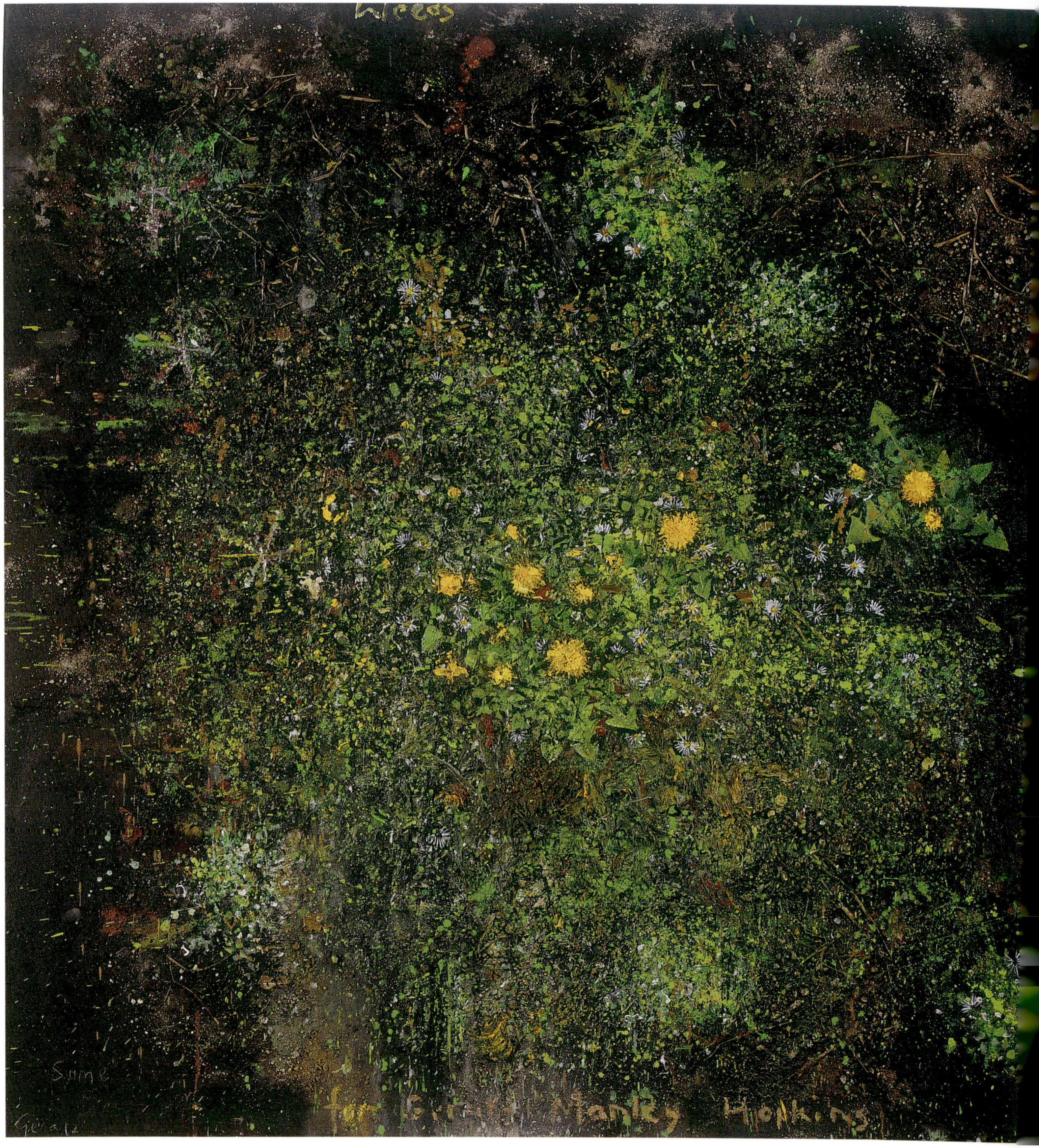
Weeds
Some
Manley Hopkins

112
Weeds – for Gerard Manley Hopkins. Early Spring, 2006
Oil and collage on canvas,
122 × 122 cm (48 × 48 in)

9 That's The Way To Do It

William Packer

Properly considered, a rule is a guide only, never a master. In the making of Art there are few enough rules. The only absolute law is for the artist to be true to himself, and to the needs of the work as they declare themselves, as the work grows, changes and develops in the course of its making. Brush, chisel, printing press, pencil: they are only tools, and paint, canvas, steel and wood are simply stuff. There is no hierarchy of material or scale. Big is not necessarily better, and small may be truly monumental. A watercolour on a scrap of paper may be a masterpiece, and a ten-foot oil painting a disaster. It is for the artist to make the best use of what is appropriate to the work in hand.

That is not to say the artist must reinvent the wheel every time the brush is picked up. There is technique in everything, the wise and useful accretion of generations of experience, and technique may be learnt. Do it in this way and you will miss the trap: that way is quicker, yet never be afraid to take your time. But no advice should hold you prisoner, and there is room for intuition and happy chance. Each start is a fresh start, and all true work is new. All Art is modern in its time. Originality is innate, and the last thing that should bother any artist – it is simply the surprise and bonus when the work is done.

In all these respects, Kurt Jackson is entirely an artist of his time, one as modern, radical and independent in spirit as he is in practice. The paradox is that while in so many respects he ticks all the right boxes of the right-on contemporary Conceptualist agenda – he is thematic, in tune with the natural world, socially responsible and engaged, and as green as the old man of the hills, with his windmill, solar panels and vegetable patch – he remains by his independence an artist apart. For there are also boxes on that Conceptualist agenda that he resolutely does not tick.

His carbon footprint may be small, but his boots are large and robust enough to take him as far into the wild as Richard Long, for example, whose diaries of the moment, the lists and texts incorporated into the very fabric of the work, are

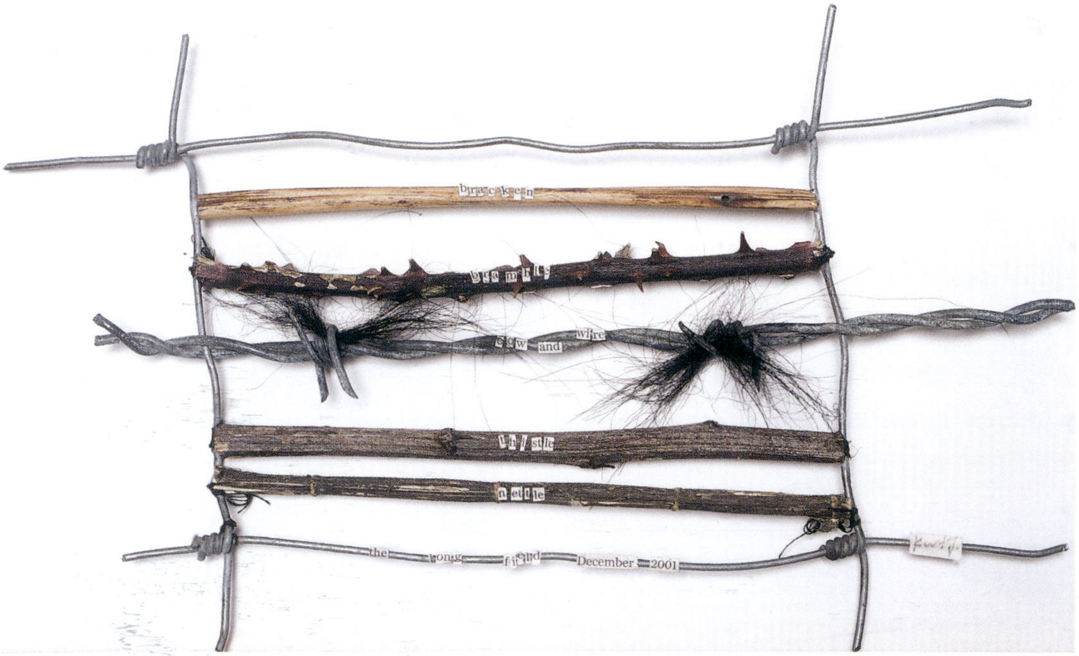

113

The Long Field, December 2001

Mixed media, 16 × 25.5 cm (6.5 × 10 in)

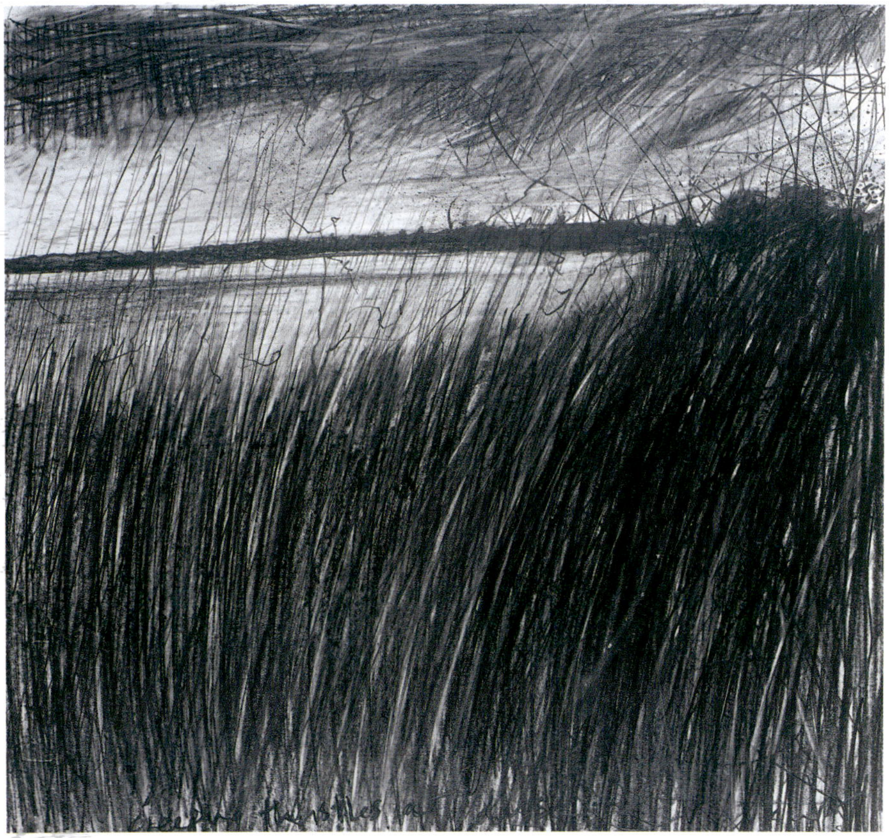

114

Creeping thistles at dusk, 2001

Pencil on paper, 39 × 39 cm (15.5 × 15.5 in)

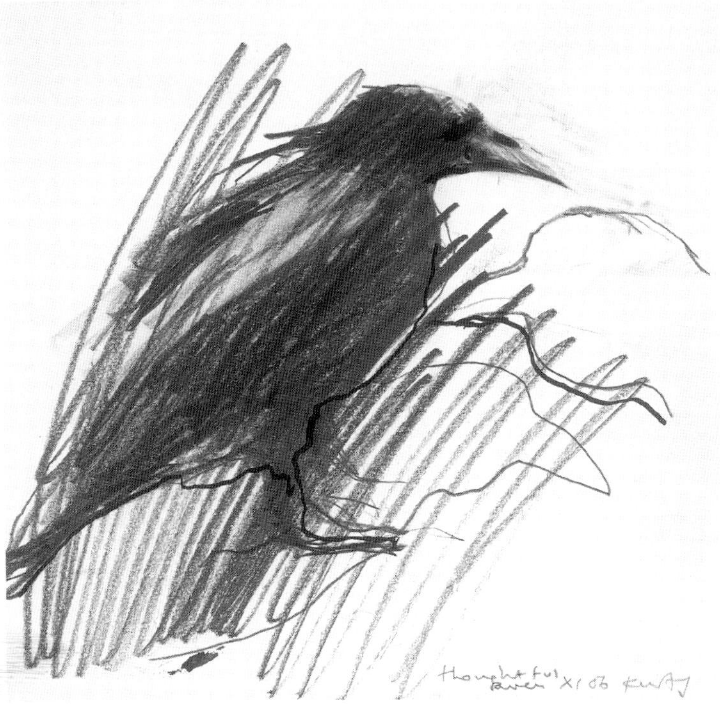

115
Thoughtful raven, November 2006
Pencil and ink, 25 × 24 cm (10 × 9.5 in)

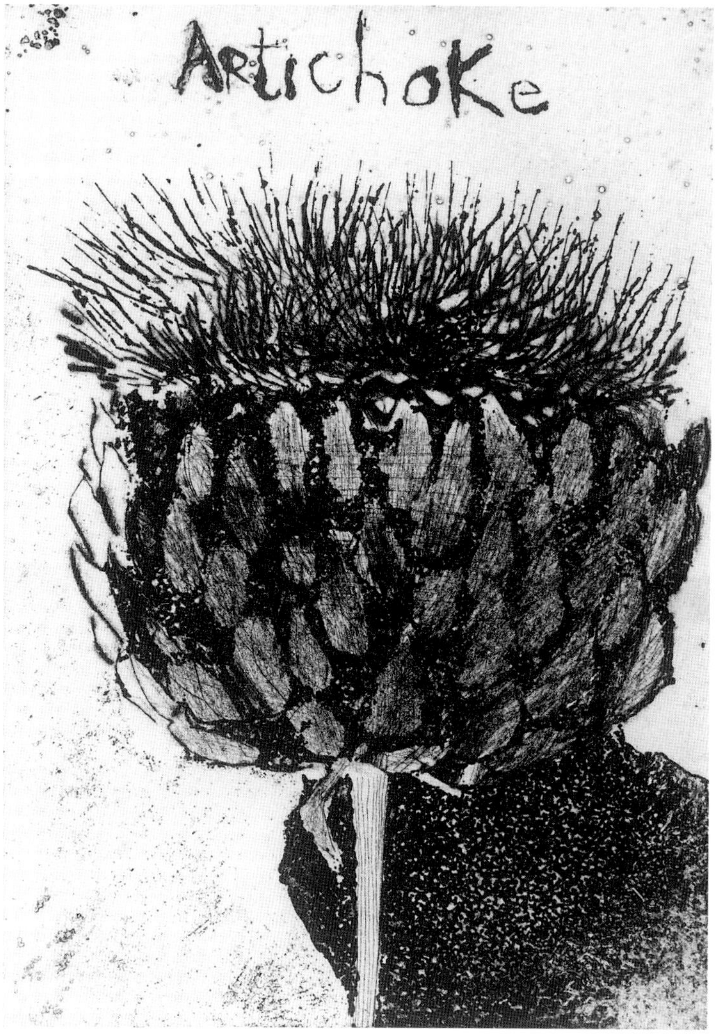

116
Artichoke, 2006
Etching and drypoint, plate size 14.5 × 9.5 cm (5.5 × 3.5 in).
Edition of 30

closely sympathetic to his own. The scope and physicality of so many of his paintings, with their mud and sand and branches worked into the surface, bring to mind the work of Anselm Kiefer, as well as Long. Jackson takes casts of natural forms, which he works into his assemblage sculptures, part modelled form, part found object. How close he is in spirit to Arte Povera, and indeed to artists of his own generation who work closely with landscape and nature, such as Andy Goldsworthy or David Nash.

Yet for all his environmental probity, his schemes and projects, his expeditions and journeys, his lists and investigations, and for all his spectacular material success, the public arbiters of the Modernist orthodoxy – that committee world of major museum curators, right-on critics and fellow travellers – seem scarcely to have noticed him. It must be said he has often shown in galleries where those arbiters never seem to tread. Is that the trouble? More to the point, he paints directly from and in the landscape and the natural world. Photographs would be easier, and certainly more fashionable. That perhaps is the heart of the matter. He does not make statements, or videos, or gestures. He paints, in mucky, awkward paint, on board or canvas, card or paper, and he makes paintings. He draws too, from nature, beautifully.

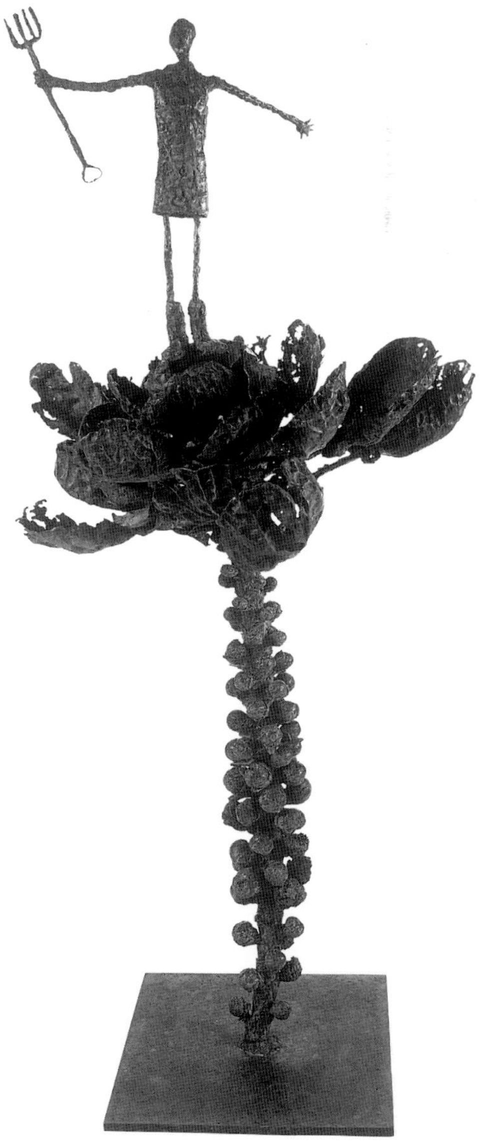

In all of this, to have had parents who were artists and teachers of art certainly did him no harm, but less in terms of any particular advantage, than in the sense of art being an unexceptional, but serious engagement, and a natural part of ordinary life. For his own early interest, amounting to an obsession, was with natural history, and in particular with the plants and creatures that he observed so closely and drew as a matter of simple study and record. It was just that personal commitment that led him to Oxford to read for a degree in Zoology, which he took in the normal way. Even so, he continued to draw and paint as a matter of course, and it was at Oxford that the twin forces of Art and Nature, which have driven his life ever since, were finally joined. His, therefore, has always been a position of fundamental independence, unbeholden alike to the imperatives of academe or art school, but free to take what he chose from either.

Jackson is, in short, a most paradoxical and contrary figure, an artist who is at once radical and traditional in his imaginative approach and practice, ever unorthodox in his orthodoxy, and at his most surprising and radical when he is at his most straightforward and direct. So it is back to that first principle: that the artist does what he must, by whatever means are appropriate to the work in hand. Its gift and blessing is an absolute and wonderful freedom, and one which, given

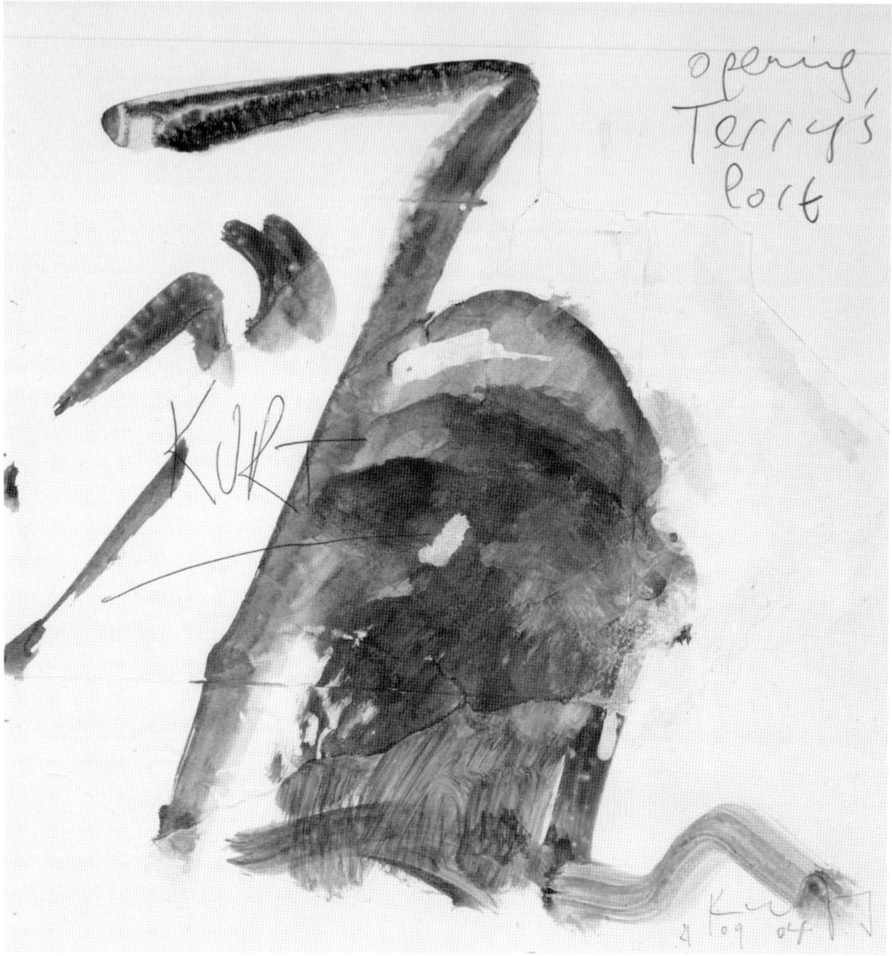

118
Opening Terry's port, Self-portrait, 21/9/04
Ink and collage, 26 × 24 cm (10 × 9.5 in)

so artistic an upbringing, interests and education, Jackson of all people was likely to exploit to the full.

So it is that as an artist he counts himself free to work in whichever medium he chooses, indifferent to any supposed hierarchical distinction between them. He will use oil, acrylic, ink, watercolour, gouache, oil crayon, pastel, charcoal and pencil, as needs be, on wood, metal, board, or paper. He makes etchings, relief prints, collages and sculptures. His one constant concern is never to allow himself to slip into a habit of work, and so he is for ever varying the medium and scale of his paintings, always mixing things up and experimenting with different approaches and combinations of medium, re-working prints, or even photographs or sheets of newsprint in ink or pastel. So too he is always changing his subjects and looking on to the next great project – the entire course of the Thames, Crows, all the islands off Cornwall's coast.

In every case, his eternal stimulus lies in the natural world – rivers, islands, fruit and veg, trees and flowers, the ancient Cornish fieldscape, its lanes and 'hedges', which is to say the field walls and banks that have stood there since time out of

117
Sexy sprouts, 2006
Bronze [unique], 117 × 50 × 50 cm
(46 × 19.5 × 19.5 in)

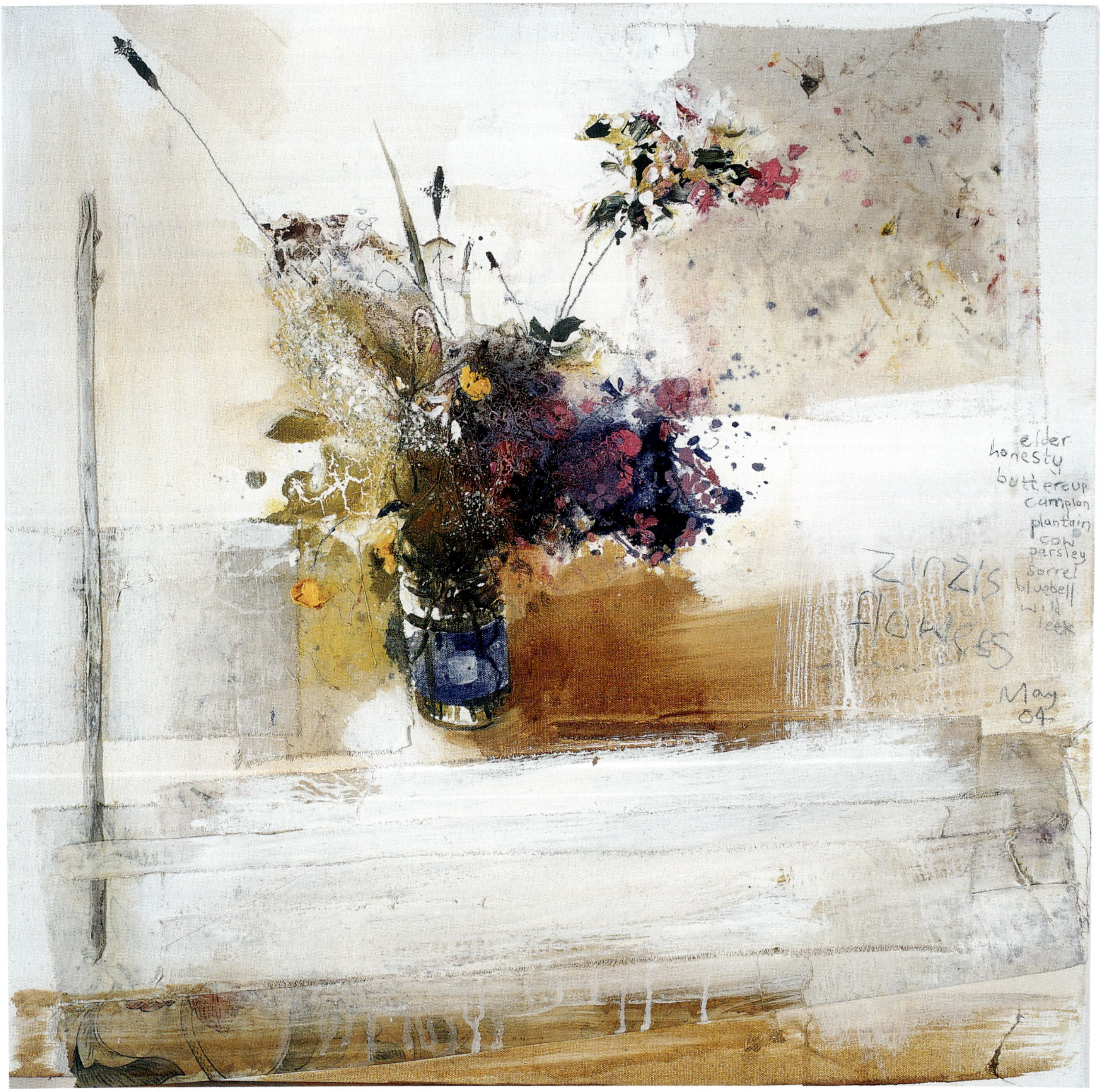

119
Zinzi's flowers, 2004
Mixed media and collage on canvas, 61 × 61 cm (24 × 24 in)

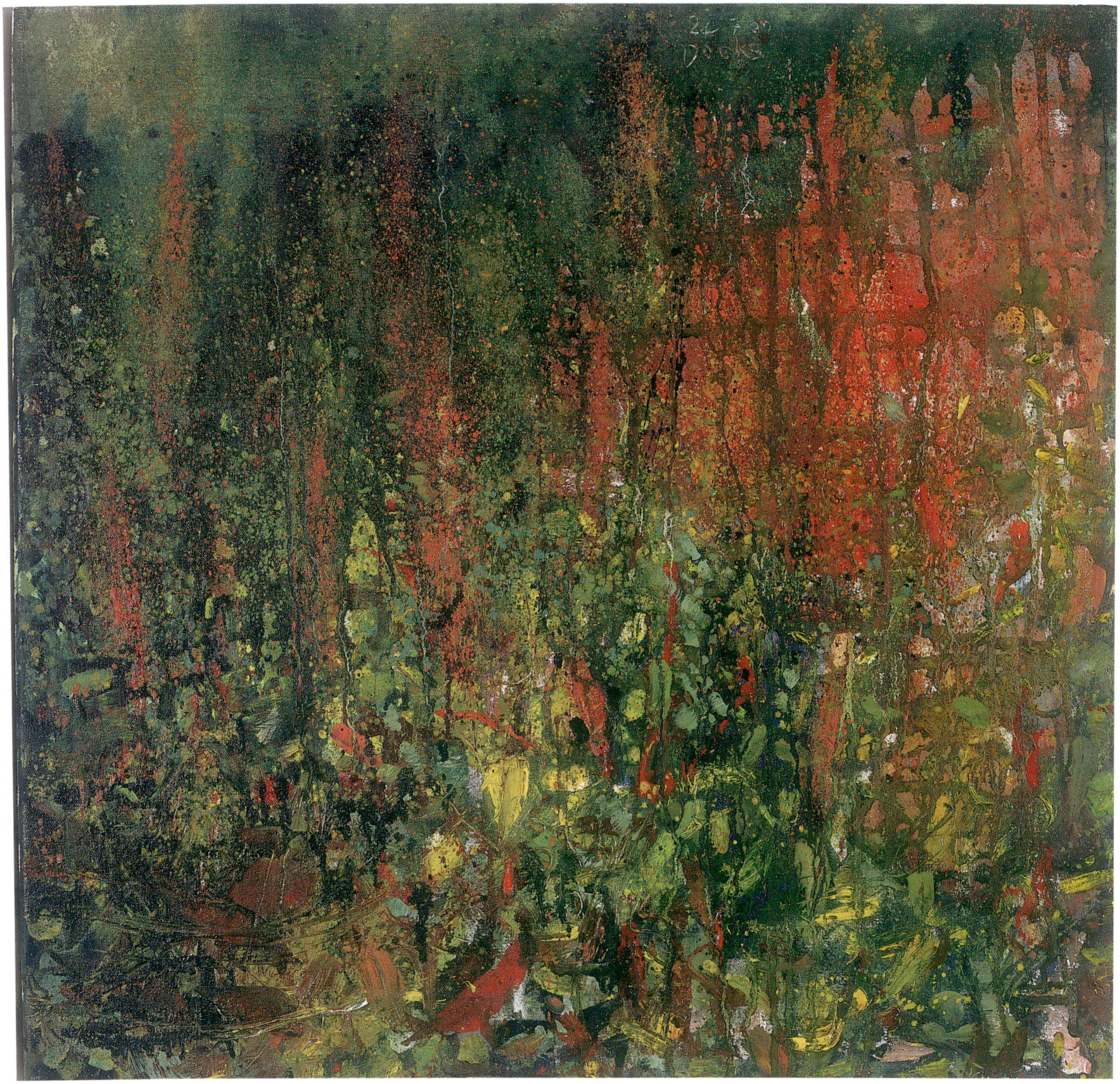

120
Docks, 24/7/00
Oil on canvas, 61 × 61 cm (24 × 24 in)

mind. There are the birds, too, and the beasts and insects, and the ever-present sea half a mile away, across the fields below the house. Again, as particular work or circumstance requires, he will work either in the studio from studies made in the field, or directly from the subject out in the landscape. He does so indeed, even when working on the largest scale, pegging the canvas out on the ground. To get the necessary longer view of what he has done, and to measure the progress of the work, he will scramble up the cliff or bank behind him, or climb a convenient tree or ladder, or clamber on to the roof of his car. In making these huge paintings, he uses acrylic paint for its practical, quick-drying and flexible qualities in rolling the canvas up and taking it home.

Jackson will walk across the canvas, as he must to reach all parts of its surface, accepting and absorbing into the fabric of the paint whatever debris Nature chooses to cast upon it – leaves, twigs, mud and sand, and the occasional avian tribute, to say nothing of his own footprints. For chance, and the acceptance of chance, and his intuitive response to it are central to his working philosophy. Here the incidental record and the found object play crucial roles. He will write notes on the canvas of things that he has seen or have happened as he works, not as any self-conscious exercise, but rather in the manner of the naturalist annotating his record. He takes back to the studio things that have caught his eye where he has been at work, all manner of junk, such as tins, plastic bottles, bones, rusted metal, roots, shells, stones and twigs. They may serve him as a local marker or imaginative trigger, or a simple souvenir perhaps, or as an object to be formally integrated into the work now back in the studio, stretched up and ready to be developed as he sees fit. What emerges from this idiosyncratic process is work not just fraught with a strong, numinous sense of the spirit of place, but also oddly accurate in its description, for all that on the surface the handling might well seem abstracted to a degree – a loose, broadly stated, intuitive expressionism.

He is constantly drawing and taking visual notes in the sketchbooks he always carries with him. He will work up the image on any old scrap of board or card he has to hand, whether it is of the widest landscape or the closest view of hedge or undergrowth. The medium of the moment is sometimes a matter of convenience, but at others a practical choice. He finds oil paint richer in feel and palette, whereas acrylic has a subtler range, close to watercolour in principle, if not in scale. It invites, perhaps, a more radical handling, with its capability for bleeding and puddling and soaking through the canvas. He will switch arbitrarily

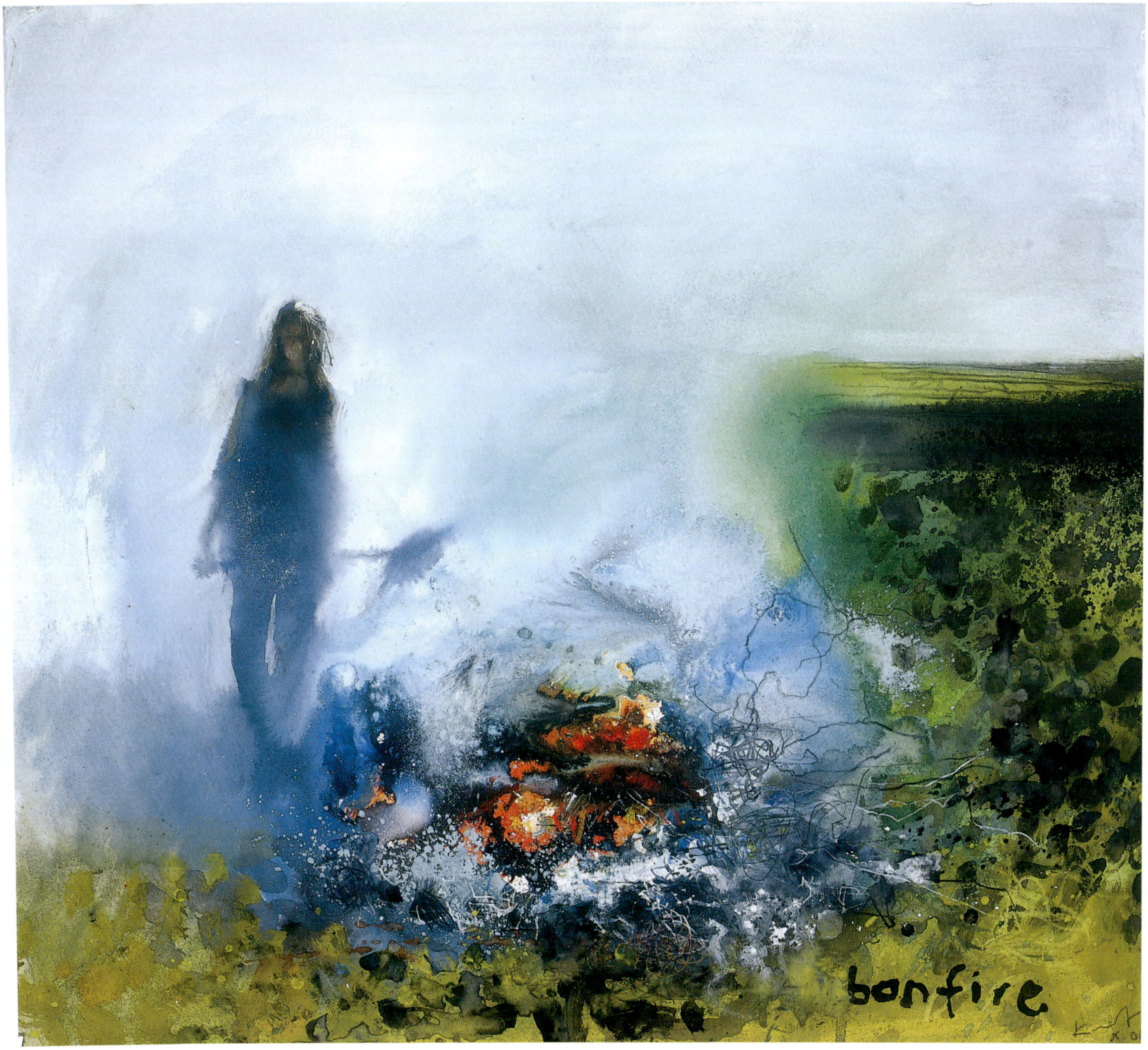

121
Bonfire, October 2006
Mixed media, 57 × 62 cm (22.5 × 24.5 in)

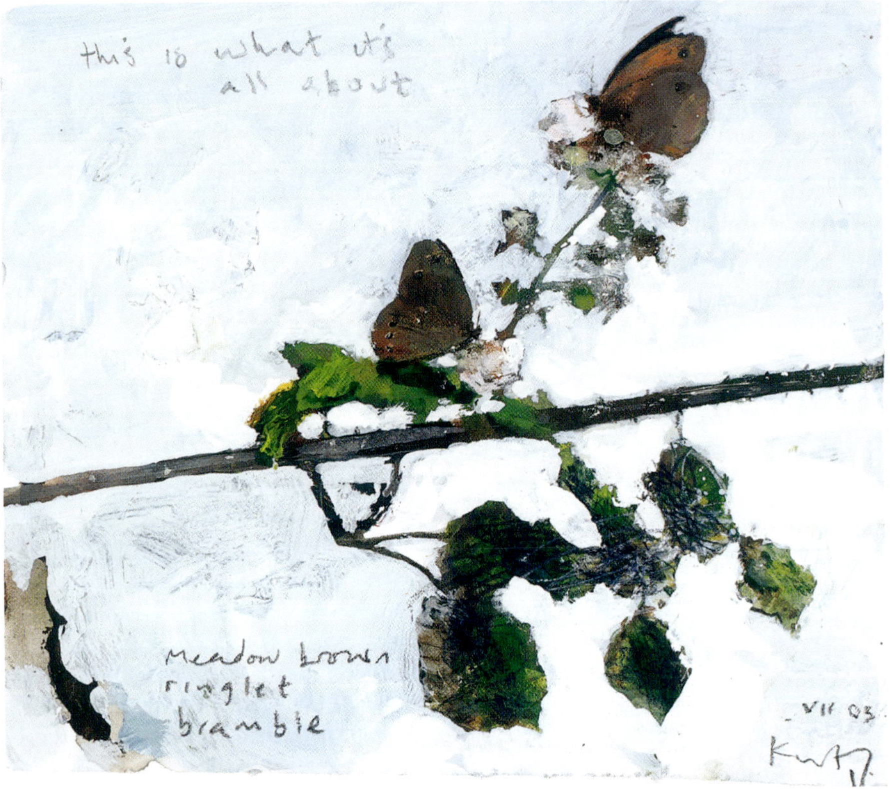

122
Ringlet, meadow brown, bramble, July 2005
Acrylic, 17 × 20 cm (6.5 × 8 in)

from the one to the other, simply for a change and the sake of freshness, with no predetermination of outcome or expectation.

At the heart of this is a physical engagement, which is of central importance to all he does, whether it is etching, painting, collage or sculpture. It is a quality that is often expressed quite unselfconsciously, in that physical incorporation into the work of elements or material found on site, or in the physical gestures of its making – mud on the mine walls (mining), plastic bottles fished from the River Avonmouth (pollution); leaves, twigs and bootprints (*passim*).

The sculpture is perhaps more direct in its making even than the painting, in being more incidental a concern, a matter of acting on an opportunity rather than an abiding preoccupation. He will twist a coil of old and rusty metal into a tangle of thorn branches, or add to it a stabilising, stone-like clay base that he has modelled and fired himself. Lately he has taken to investing actual foliage or branches with a plaster mould, to be thus burnt off in the kiln, after the fashion of the classic lost-wax technique, leaving the now-empty mould to be filled with bronze. His latest, most ambitious plan is to do this on a large scale, taking a wind-ravaged hawthorn from one of the prehistoric stone 'hedges' around his house, high in the flank of the hill above the sea, across the valley from St Just.

All in all, for Kurt Jackson the business of making Art, of whatever kind, is a bit like cooking, or gardening, both of which he approaches in the same, openly creative way, exhibiting an ever-flexible approach as to materials and what may work, and an open-minded curiosity as to the result. If it's not delicious, it will at the very least be interesting, and suggest something further: the garden may seem a wilderness, but it is a cultivated wilderness, for the vegetables grow and the wild flowers blossom; birds nest in the thicket and the frogs soon discover the pond. Nature indeed is the mother and inspiration of it all. As the noble poet says, in 'Childe Harold's Pilgrimage', 'There is a pleasure in the pathless woods, | There is a rapture on the lonely shore, |... I love not man the less, but Nature more.'

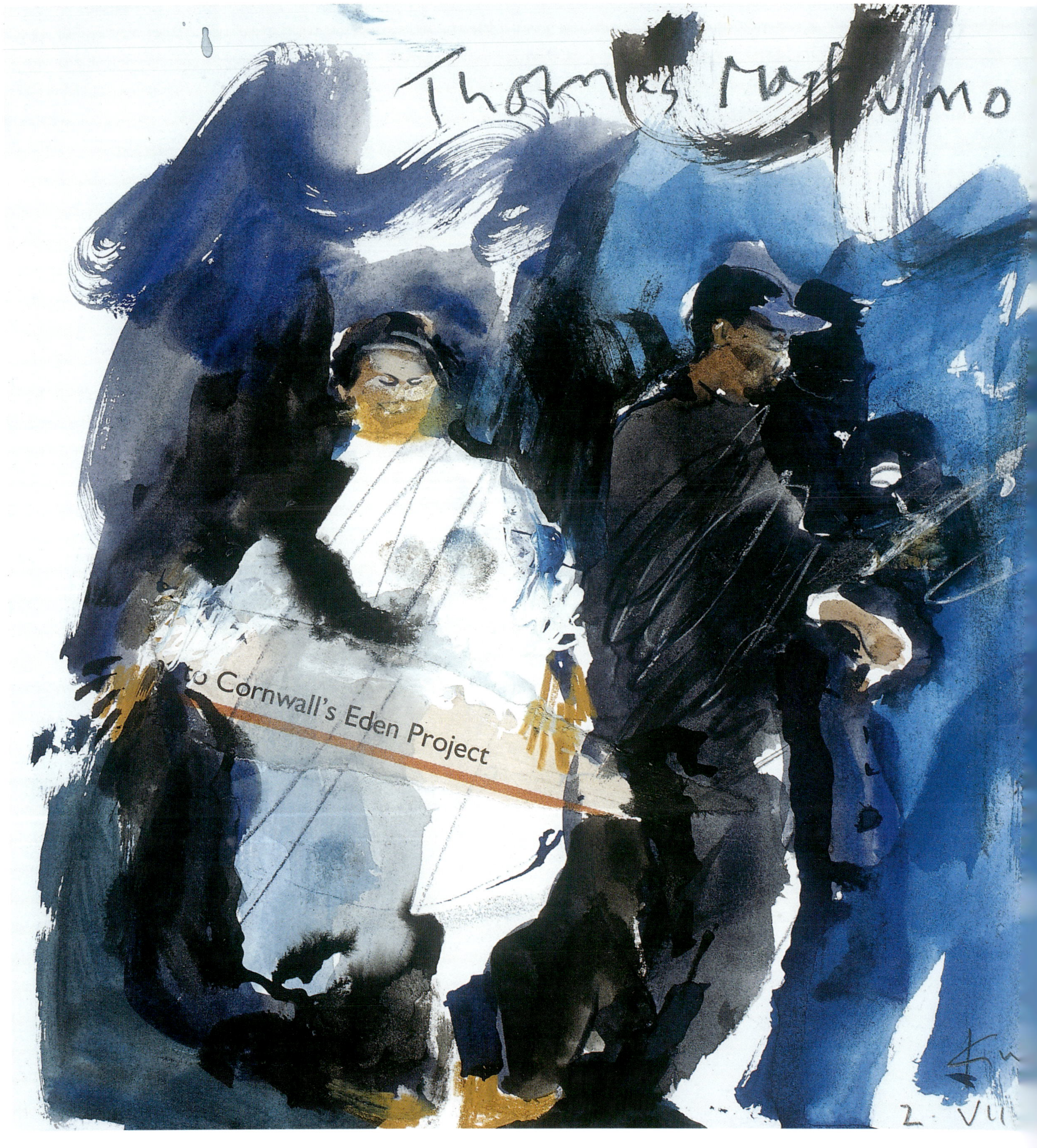
Cornwall's Eden Project

10 Kurt Jackson: Facing the Music

Tim Smit

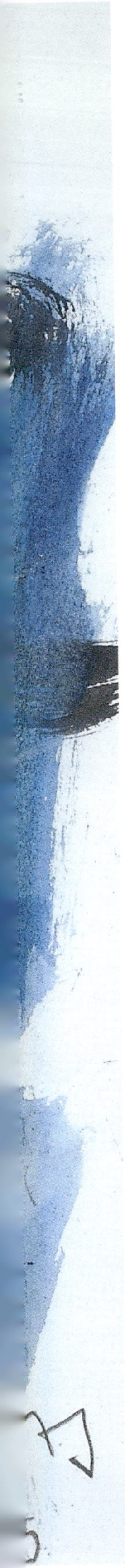

123
Thomas Mapfumo, 2005. [Africa Calling, Eden]
Mixed media on paper, 25 × 24 cm (10 × 9.5 in)

Memorable days do not come much better than this. The Eden Project arena was jumping and the stage was packed with musicians from all over Africa, playing their part in raising awareness of poverty at the Live 8 concert. Youssou N'Dour and Peter Gabriel were hosting the concerts and N'Dour had coined the Eden leg of the tour 'Africa Calling'. The day was 2 July 2005. On the side of the stage, with the stamina of a Dervish, stood Kurt Jackson, alternately sweating in the middle of the hubbub and then ducking the rain, which spitefully tried to dampen enthusiasm all day. He was working like a man possessed to capture every nuance of the performances that grew with intensity up until the address by Nelson Mandela from a stage across the world in South Africa – which was viewed by the emotional cast of 120 musicians and a crowd of almost 7,000 people, craning their necks and hanging on to his every word on a day that they hoped would persuade the leaders of the G8 countries to contribute to the 'Make Poverty History' campaign.

It was appropriate that Jackson should have been the artist in residence on this day. 'Africa Calling' could have been the subtitle to his life. Many of the elements drawn together that day had been the drivers that shaped his identity, such as music, Africa and charity. Since his early teens, he had attended concerts, starting with a Hawkwind gig, moving on to the free festivals at Stonehenge and graduating to the early green gatherings, Womad and his beloved Glastonbury. He first attended this iconic music festival as an ordinary punter, before becoming an institution as the artist in residence, which offered him unparallelled access to the artists and events that have shaped the course of popular music over the last 20 years. If you ask him what music he likes, he will give you a breathtaking sweep, from rock to folk, to reggae and African music; he even plays opera and classical music in his studio.

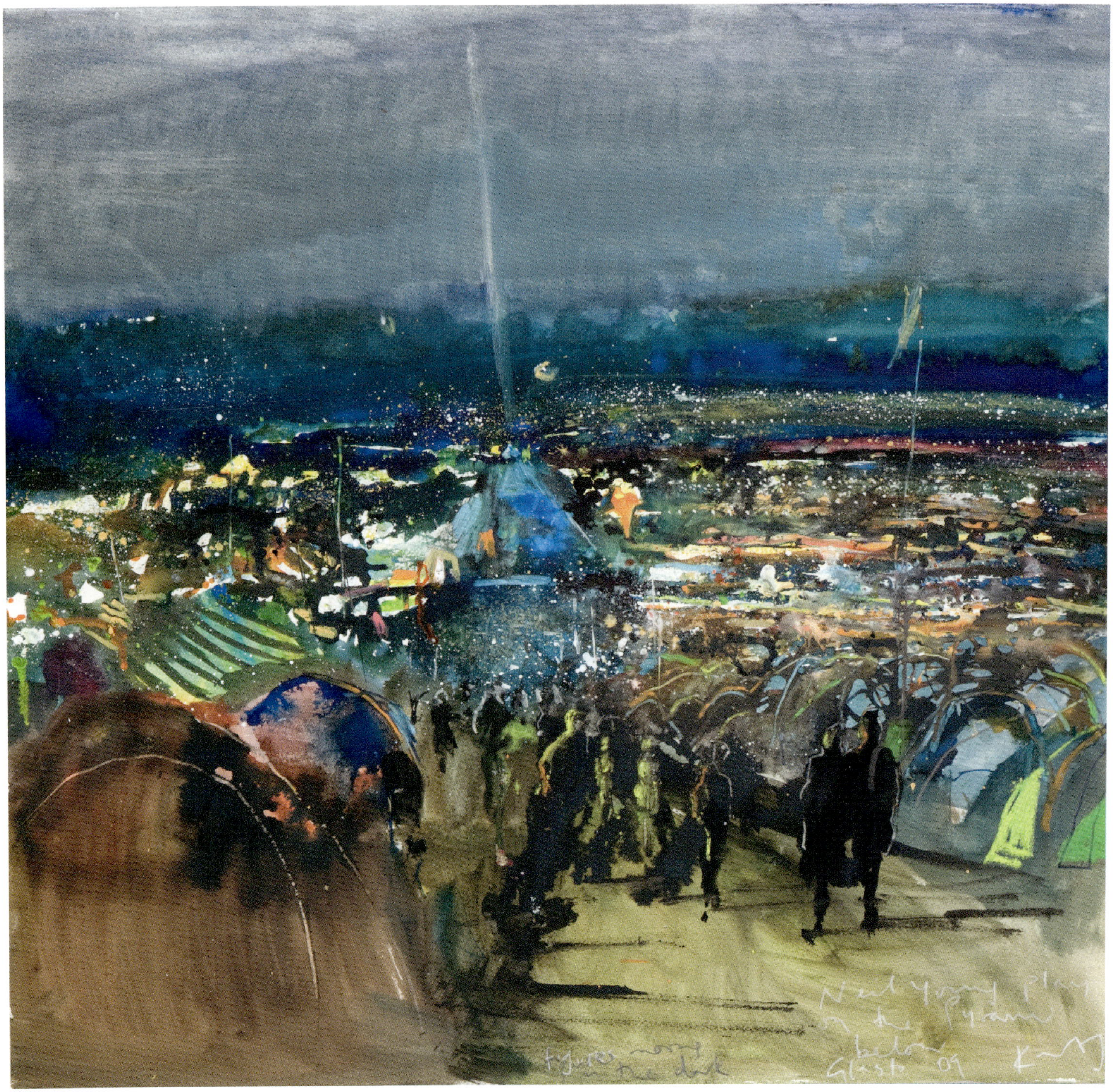

124

Figures moving in the dark, Neil Young playing on the Pyramid Stage below, Glastonbury, 2009

Mixed media, 57 × 58 cm (22.5 × 23 in)

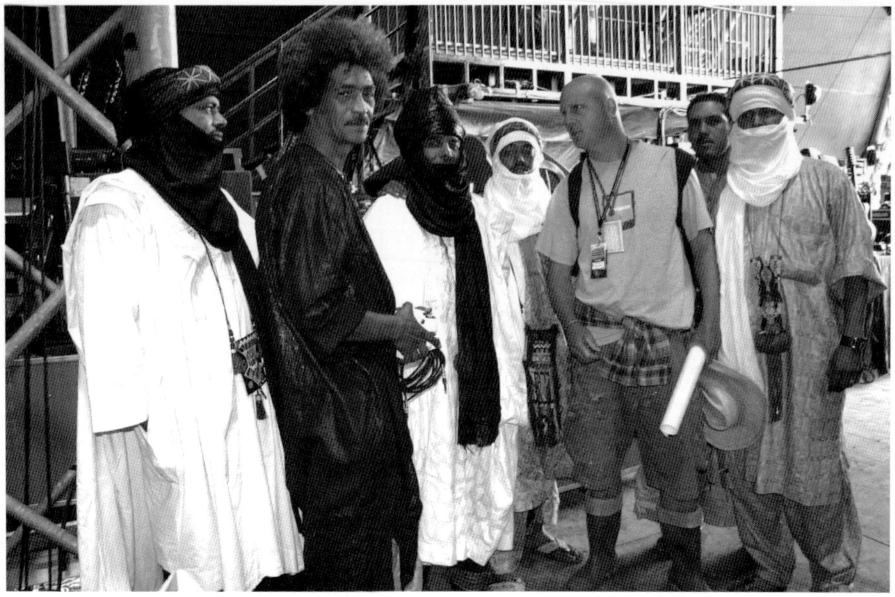

125
With Tinariwen, 2009

Africa would shape Jackson's career when, on graduating from Oxford, he and Caroline set out to explore the Sub-Saharan region. He was overwhelmed by the extreme sensations that he found there. The endless aridity, with its palette of baked earth tints and hues, and the myriad adaptations of the peoples to their surroundings, from the mud cities of Mali to the nomadic herders, the Tuareg, who so influenced his taste in music. The impressions segued into the sharpest of counterpoints, the rivers that oozily meander through the landscapes, bringing as their companions the rich abundance of the forest with its cornucopia of wildlife and ecological diversity. It was this shock that brought him to the realisation that the sketchbooks, which were forever being brought into service to capture what he saw and felt in drawings and paintings, were the sign of his true vocation. It was here that Kurt and Caroline would forge the most extraordinary bond. He with his compulsion to paint would become the willing servant to his art.

His mother, a lifelong supporter of Oxfam and his father, a Quaker committed to contributing to the community, would shape Jackson's views of the world. From his teenage years, he was putting on fundraising concerts and setting up jumble sales to raise much-needed funds for his chosen charities, groups doing what he considered to be vital work. Brought up to take action and not to sit on the sidelines, he believed that if you do not like something, then demonstrate. If someone needs help, raise a collection. When he established himself as one of the country's leading painters, it did not change him. He recalls the months on the dole, the building jobs, the struggle to bring up children in Boscastle in North Cornwall, where for seven years the harvest from the allotment and the collection of free firewood from the woods were a necessary supplement to a meagre income. Thereafter would come St Just, in the far southwest of the country, where

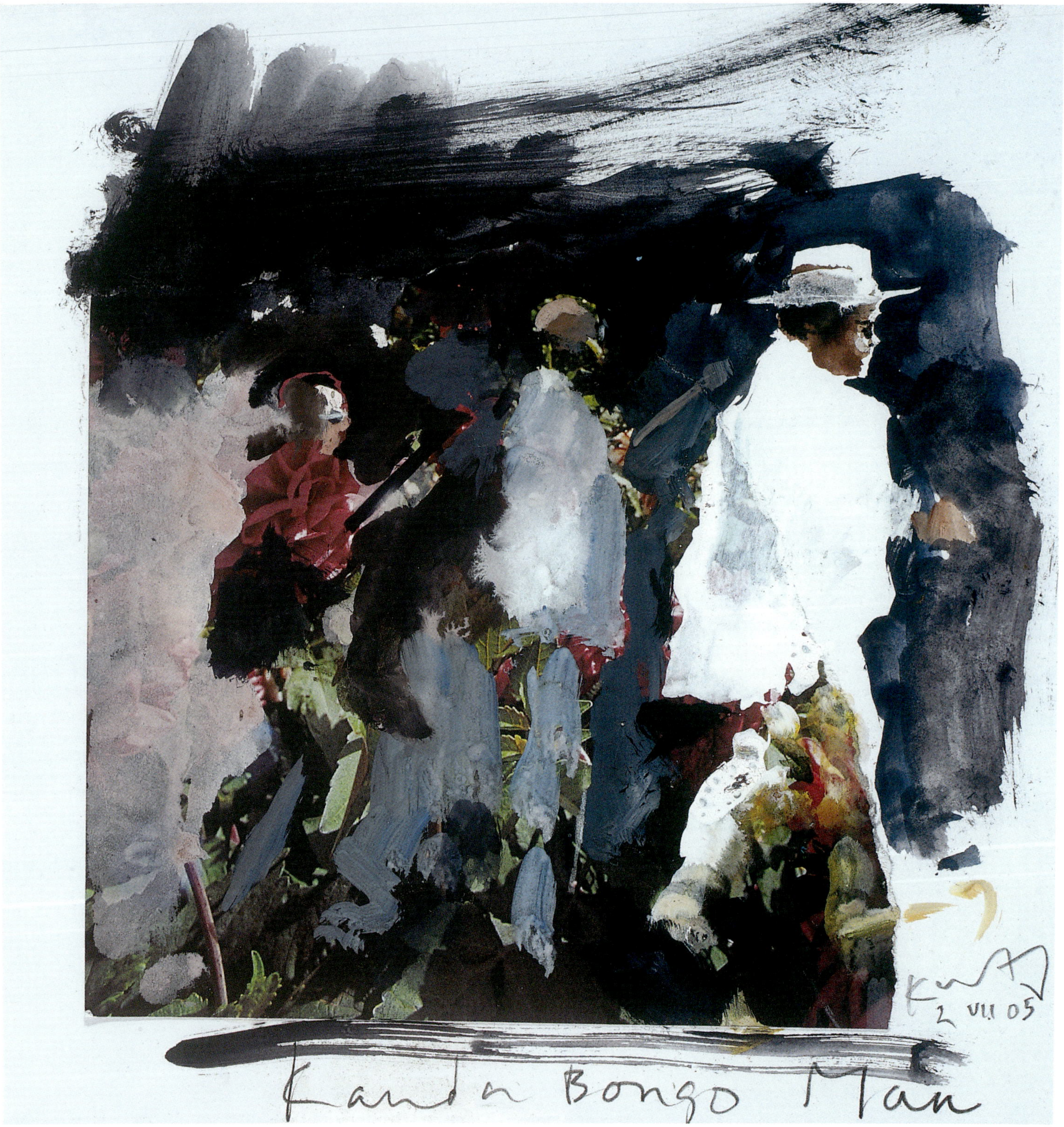

126
***Kanda Bongo Man*, 2005. [Africa Calling, Eden]**
Mixed media on paper, 25 × 24 cm (10 × 9.5 in)

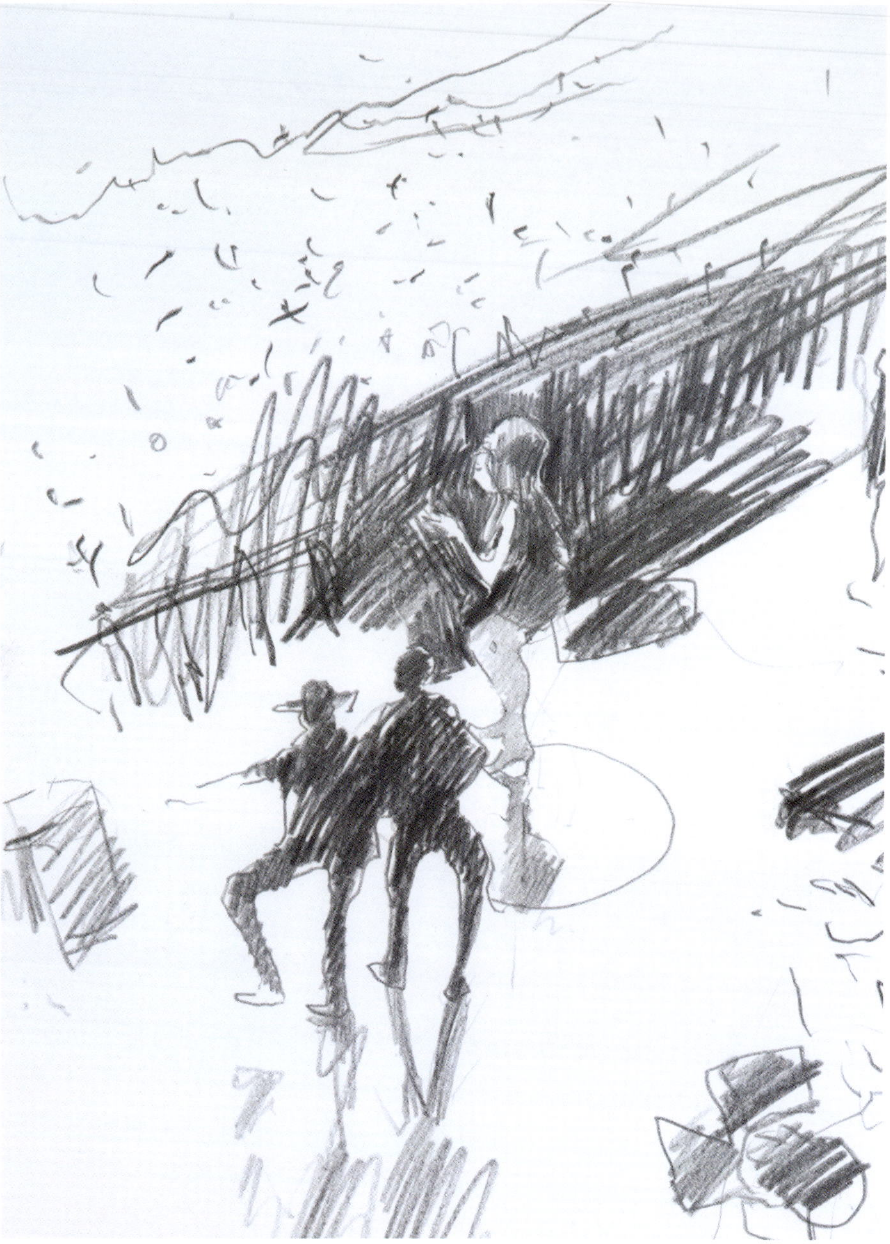

127
Amy Winehouse on the Pyramid Stage, 2008
Pencil, 41.5 × 29.5 cm (16.5 × 11.5 in)

his career would blossom and allow the scratchings of the past to be viewed in a romantic sepia tint, but the experience shaped the family and led them to savour success with a deep gratitude.

Jackson has created something of a tithe on his work. The Glastonbury work is sold to raise funds for Greenpeace, WaterAid and Oxfam. When he painted at 'Africa Calling', the works were donated to raise funds for 'Gardens for Life', a programme that links schools in India, Kenya and the UK in creating allotments. From his mainstream exhibitions he always selects a few choice pieces to be sold, and many charities have benefited from his generosity over the years: Survival International (Kurt and Caroline are ambassadors), Friends of the Earth (for whom

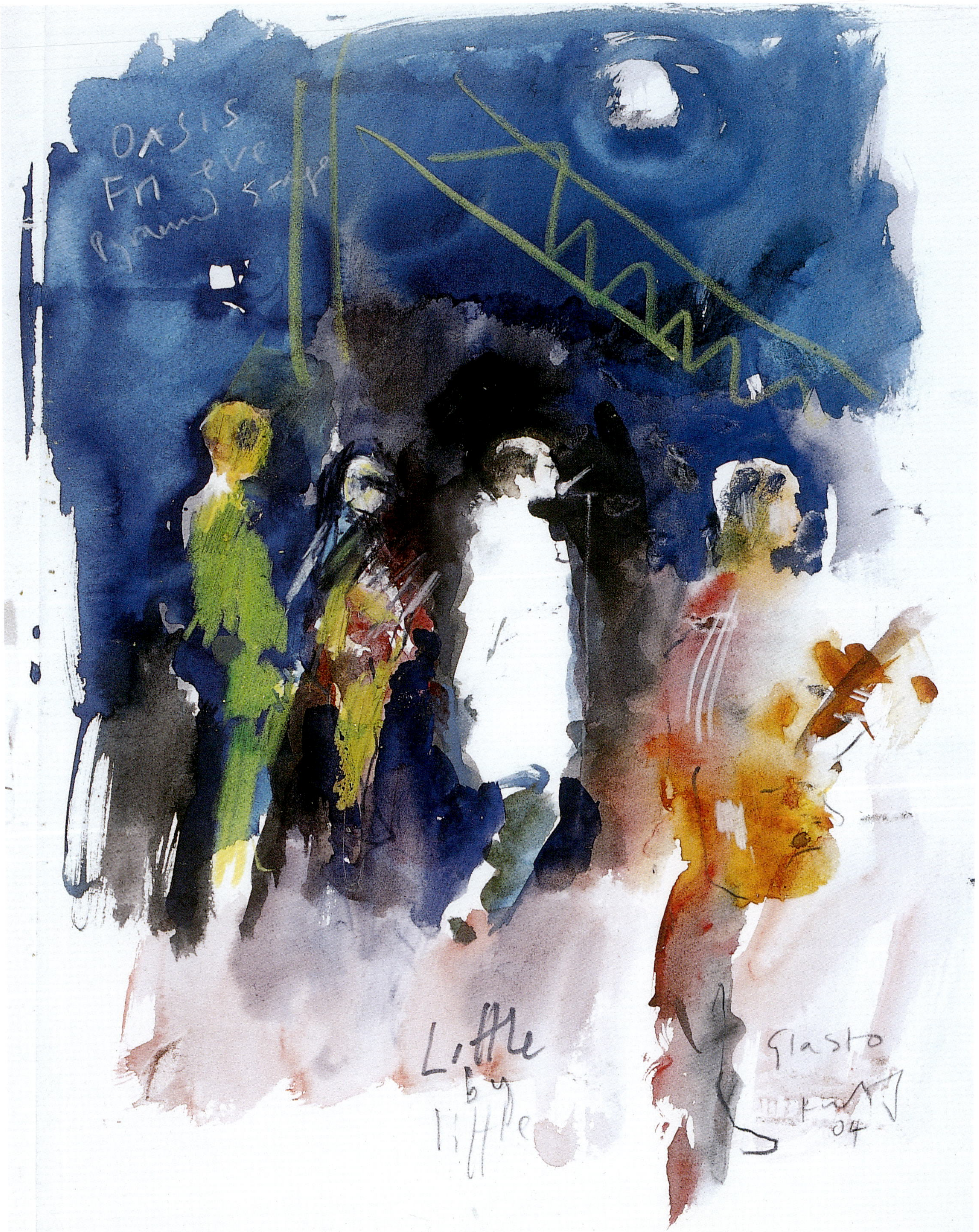
OASIS
Fri eve
Pyramid stage
Little
by
little
Glasto
04

the artist painted a collection in a threatened landscape – the East Anglian Fens) and the Cornwall Wildlife Trust (it is vital to keep things local).

One of the threads running through Jackson's work is his interest in people's connection to the land: how they have shaped or have been shaped by the narratives of their occupations. This is not about a romanticised primitivism, a desire to see a world that was, through a mist of nostalgia, but is rather based on a sense of meaning that people need to have in order to belong. The artist as outsider is only relevant to him as a symbol of the zone he needs to inhabit to capture the moment, but there is no radical intent to shock, or to be noticed for his personal behaviour. His elegiac paintings of the French landscape and regions in Scotland, Greece and Spain carry a simple story of the need to nurture access to the land and the traditions that give this meaning. This is his bedrock, it is this that defines culture – rootedness. This theme is carried into a much darker vein, literally and metaphorically, in his studies of miners working underground, such as *Jeff Tonkin operating the drill rig, Dolcoath South, South Crofty, 1995* (plate 18) and *Through Deep Adit into Geevor, June 2007* (plate 5). Here again he is describing their essential nature rather than making character studies of people as portraiture.

So, we might ask, how is it that an artist famed for his studies of the natural world makes forays into the world of urban angst and transient mythologies of popular music, which suggest the opposite of being rooted? In all his other works, people are defined by the nature of their activities, as miners, fishermen, farmers and even surgeons. When Jackson does music, something changes. Imagine you are living in a tent, surrounded by happy drunks, or you are on stage with some of the biggest bands in the world, looking out over crowds that are measured in their tens and sometimes hundreds of thousands of people. There is music of great intensity, there are light shows, and the artists vary from a gentle folk to thrash punk rockers. The personalities vary, from jobbing musicians who are content doing a day's work to deluded, saviour-like figures who whip their followers up into a frenzy: ego, vanity and messianic fervour are all on display. Forced to think on your feet, you face the challenge of trying to capture the essence of a vital event that is just out of reach. How do you paint the surface? How do you convey what it is like to be there in the din, almost in touching distance of madness, with the pressure to record it now?

Looking over Jackson's work in music is fascinating. He will tell you that mood is more important than a recognisable likeness and portraiture is not his intention, but rather that he aims to capture the life force of the moment. Although it is easy

128
Oasis, Little by Little, Friday evening, Pyramid Stage, Glastonbury, 2004
Mixed media, 35 × 28 cm (14 × 11 in)

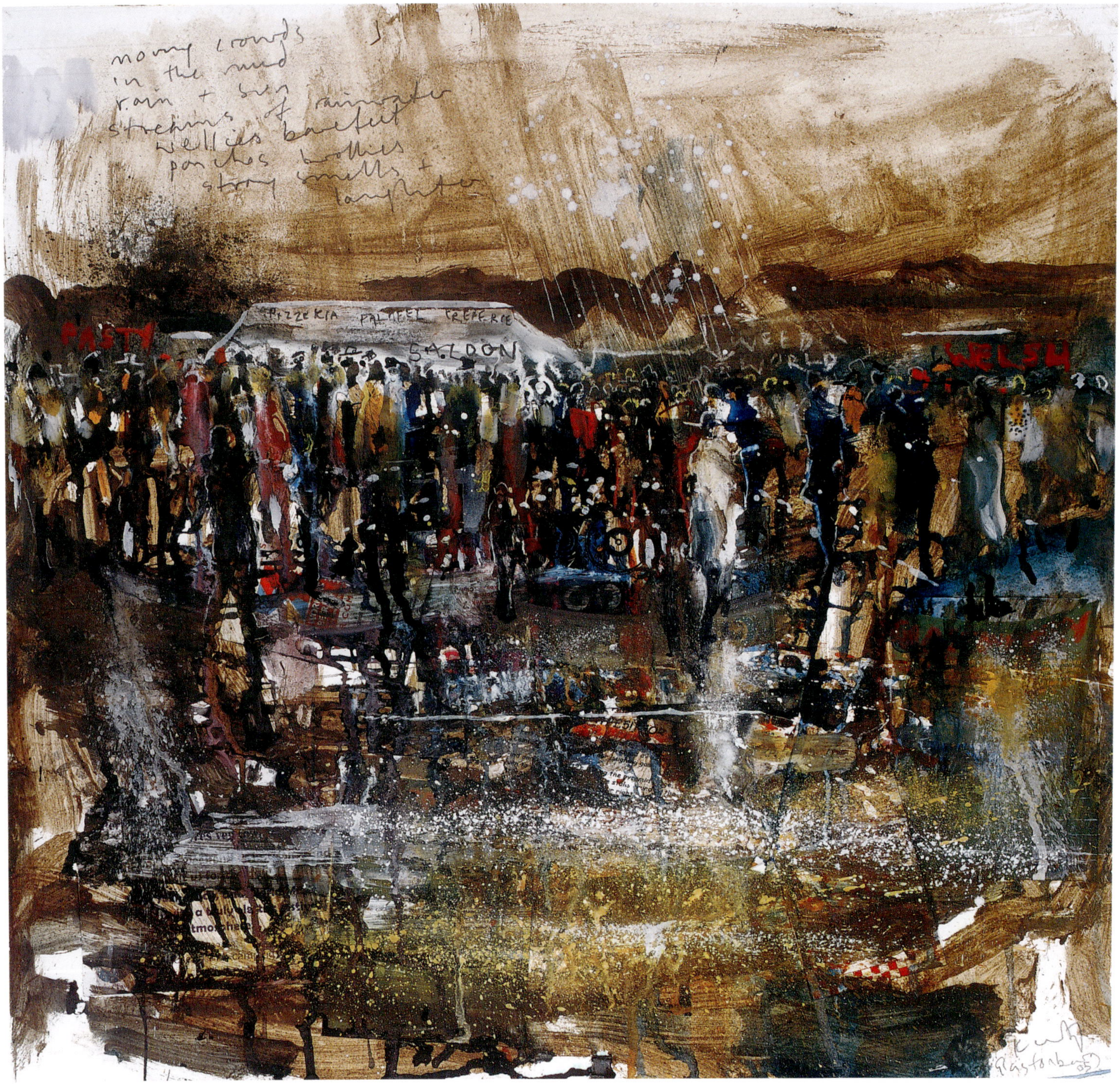

129

Moving crowds in the mud, rain and sun. Streams of rainwater. Wellies, bare feet, ponchos and brollies. Strong smells and laughter, Glastonbury, June 2005

Mud, collage and mixed media, 57 × 59 cm (22.5 × 23 in)

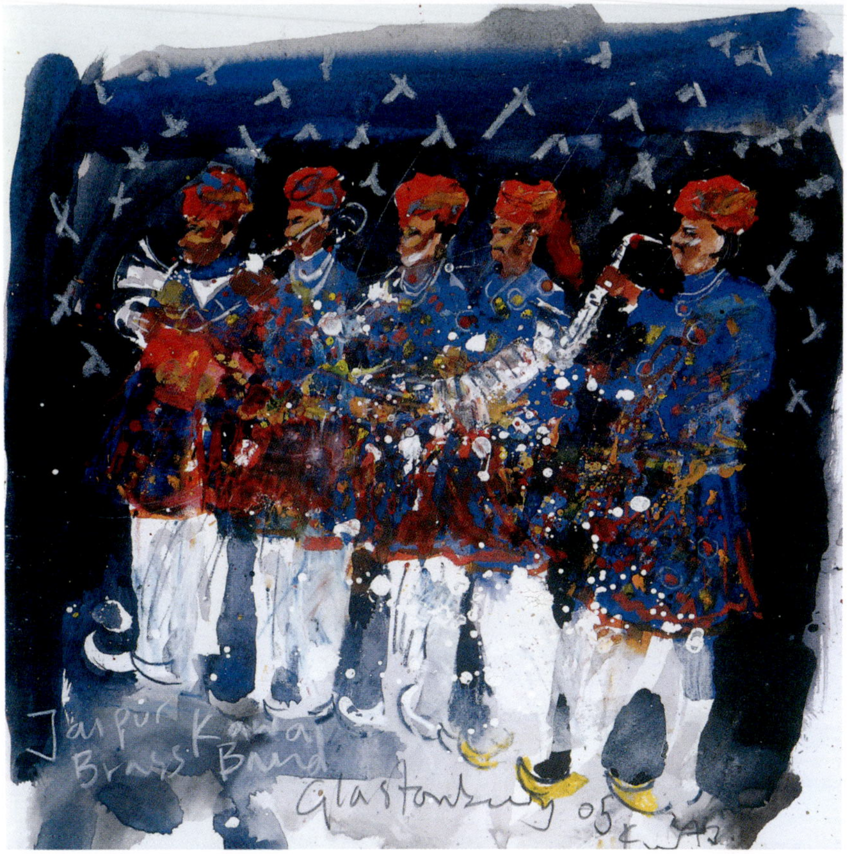

130
Jaipur Kawa Brass Band, Glastonbury, June 2005
Mixed media, 25 × 24 cm (10 × 9.5 in)

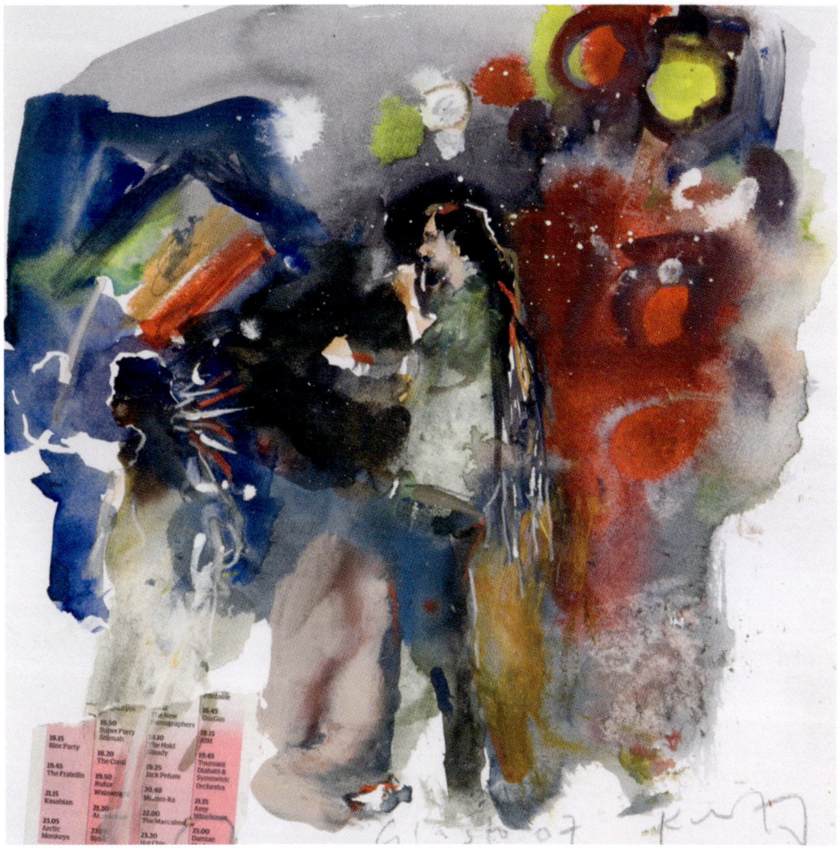

131
Damian Marley, Glastonbury, 2007
Mixed media and collage, 25 × 14.5 cm (10 × 5.5 in)

to cast such a phrase in a pretentious light, his paintings illustrate the energy that this dimension brings to his practice. What is extraordinary about his best artworks is that the characters are so alive. The medium on which the work is executed adds immediacy: in the case of 'Africa Calling', the collage of newsprint highlighted the urgent need to fight poverty and in the 'Glastonbury' series, mud defined the earthy nature of the experience shared by festival goers.

By chance, I attended the 2009 exhibition 'Madness and Modernity' at the Wellcome Collection, London, in which a number of works dating from early nineteenth-century Austria were on display, representing the evolution of psychoanalysis in relation to the arts in Vienna. A series of unusual paintings were on show, by Egon Schiele, Gustav Klimt and Oskar Kokoschka, in which the artists experimented with 'auras' and hot spots in their attempt to convey the nature of the person. On reflection, it is this search for colour and movement in the portraiture that gives an impressionistic view of the subjects, but at the same time imbues them with a sense of rhythm and relative heat. The whole conveys a highly unusual reference point to the passion of the artist.

It is interesting to see how Jackson translates the music into the palette of his work. The acoustic, solitary performer has a more brooding and gentle patina than, say, the punk act captured in explosive chaos. The painter gives the African Tuareg band Tinariwen a sinuous treatment, which captures the desert and the dust, yet does not hide the anomaly of electric instrumentation, instead creating a Mad Max moment that is global in its context. I believe that the richest irony in his musical work is that the one form he seems to shy away from is jazz, yet, if you were to ask someone to create paintings that describe the essence of jazz, you could be looking at the artist in question. Miles Davis would have loved this art.

Where to now for the man who has covered almost every musical form from every possible angle, from the stage, from the crowd, from the artist's perspective, working in almost every media? Those familiar with Kurt Jackson's landscapes, with their signature commentary etched on canvas, may hanker for a musical equivalent. Come on Kurt, how about creating some big stuff with musical notation across it to satisfy those whose second language is music? One thing is for sure, this magnificent obsessive will continue to surprise and delight. All lovers of live music and its joyous, melancholy, explosive, caressing and mystifying qualities are in his debt.

Biographical note

Born in Blandford, Dorset, 21 September 1961

BSc (Honours) degree in Zoology at St Peter's College, University of Oxford

DLitt (Honorary), University of Exeter

Lives and works near St Just-in-Penwith, Cornwall

Exhibitions and events

Selected solo exhibitions

2010 'River', Plymouth City Art Gallery
'Ardnamurchan', Dovecot Studios, Edinburgh

2009 'Forest Gardens', Messum's, London
'Glastonbury Festival' charity auction, Guardian Newsroom, London
'River Avon, Part 2', Victoria Art Gallery, Bath
'Enesow – An Exploration of the Islands of Cornwall', Lemon Street Gallery, Truro, Cornwall

2008 'The Lights of West Cornwall', Messum's, London
'Wicken, A Threatened Landscape', charity auction for Friends of the Earth, Foyles Gallery, London
'The Solent Project', St Barbe Museum and Art Gallery, Lymington (touring exhibition)
'The Solent Project', Gosport Arts Centre, Hampshire (touring exhibition)
Quay Arts Centre, Isle of Wight
'The Tamar', Lemon Street Gallery, Truro, Cornwall
'The Mining Paintings', Geevor Mine Gallery, Cornwall
'Theatre Five', charity exhibition for MSF, Royal College of Surgeons, London

2007 'Caroline and the Veg Patch', Messum's, London
'River Avon Part 1', Victoria Art Gallery, Bath
'Glastonbury Festival' charity auction, The Hospital, Covent Garden
'The Cornish Crow', Lemon Street Gallery, Truro

2006 Messum's, London
'Porth', Catmose Art Gallery, Rutland
'Neil's Place', Dundas Street Gallery, Edinburgh
'The Thames Project', South Hill Park, Bracknell, Berkshire
'Ponds, Pools and Puddles', Lemon Street Gallery, Truro, Cornwall

2005	Messum's, London
	'Porth', Royal Albert Memorial Museum and Art Gallery, Exeter and Canterbury City Art Gallery
	'The Painted Etchings', Newlyn Art Gallery, and Dundas Street Gallery, Edinburgh
	'Glastonbury Festival' charity auction
	'Three Woods', St Barbe Museum and Art Gallery, Lymington, and Royal Cornwall Museum and Art Gallery, Truro, Cornwall
	'The Cornish Estuary', Lemon Street Gallery, Truro, Cornwall
2004–05	Paddington Station installation
2004	Messum's, London
	'Porth', Newlyn Art Gallery, Cornwall (touring exhibition)
	'Porth', Worcester City Art Gallery, Worcestershire (touring exhibition)
	'Porth', King's Lynn Arts Centre, Norfolk (touring exhibition)
	'The Paps of Jura', RGI Kelly Gallery, Glasgow (touring exhibition)
	'The Paps of Jura', Dundas Street Gallery, Edinburgh (touring exhibition)
	'Two Woods', Victoria Art Gallery, Bath
	'The Cornish Hedge', Lemon Street Gallery, Truro, Cornwall
2003	Messum's, London
	'Glastonbury Festival' charity auction, Guardian Newsroom, London
	'St Michael's Way', Lemon Street Gallery, Truro, Cornwall
2002	'Scilly', Lemon Street Gallery, Truro, Cornwall
	Messum's, London
	'Delabole Slate Quarry', Penzance Geology Museum, Cornwall (touring exhibition)
	'Delabole Slate Quarry', Slate Valley Museum, New York, US (touring exhibition)
	'Delabole Slate Quarry', Helen Day Art Centre, Vermont, US (touring exhibition)
	'Delabole Slate Quarry' with works by Richard Long, Falmouth Art Gallery, Cornwall
	'Cill Riallaig', Royal Cornwall Museum and Art Gallery, Truro
2001	Messum's, London
2000	Messum's, London
	Origin Gallery, Dublin
	University of Exeter
1999	Messum's, London
	Origin Gallery, Dublin
1998	Origin Gallery, Dublin
	Royal Cornwall Museum, Truro
1998–99	'Carnsew', Falmouth Art Gallery, Cornwall (touring exhibition)
	'Carnsew', Worcester City Art Gallery, Worcestershire (touring exhibition)
	'Carnsew', Cornwall Geological Museum, Penzance (touring exhibition)
	'Carnsew', Lancashire Mining Museum, Salford (touring exhibition)
1998	Messum's, London
	'La Cornouaille', Concarneau Town Hall, Brittany (held as part of town's exchange with Cornwall)
1997	Darlington Art Centre, Durham
	Rheda-Wiedensbrück, Germany
1995–97	'South Crofty', Camborne School of Mines, Cornwall (touring exhibition)
	'South Crofty', Penzance Geological Museum, Cornwall (touring exhibition)
	'South Crofty', Plymouth City Art Gallery (touring exhibition)
	'South Crofty', Doncaster Museum (touring exhibition)
1986–95	North Cornwall Museum and Art Gallery
1984	Robinson College, Cambridge

Selected group exhibitions

2008	'Africa Calling', Falmouth Art Gallery
2007	Presentation of paintings to Cornwall County Council collection
	Art Miami, US, with Lemon Street Gallery
	Exhibition at Kew Gardens
2000–10	London Art Fair
2000–10	Royal West of England Academy
	Penlee House Gallery and Museum, Penzance, Cornwall

1994-2008	Newlyn Society of Artists
1994-97	Penwith Society of Artists
	City Gallery, Leicester
	Hastings Museum
1994	Rheda, Wiedensbrück, Germany
1982	Three-man exhibition with brother and father, Maltings Gallery, Weathampstead, Hertfordshire

Awards and Residences

2009	Elected honorary ambassador of Survival International
2007	Awarded honorary doctorate for contribution to the arts by the University of Exeter
	Residency at Treliske Hospital operating theatre, Truro, Cornwall
2005	Artist in Residence on Greenpeace ship 'Esperanza'
	'Live 8' at Eden Project, Artist in Residence
2004–07	Chair of Newlyn Society of Artists
2000	Elected Academician, Royal West of England Academy
1999–2009	Glastonbury Festival, Artist in Residence
1997 & 1999	Artist in Residence in Cill Riallaig, Ireland

Broadcasts

2005	'Kurt Jackson, A Picture of Cornwall', BBC1 South West
	'Kurt Jackson, A Picture of the South West', BBC3
1998	'A Place in My Heart', Carlton TV

Public collections

Camborne School of Mines
Cill Rialaig Arts Centre, Kerry, Ireland
Concarneau Town Council, Brittany
Cornwall County Council
Crown Court, Truro
Cornwall University, Tremough
Darlington Arts Centre, Darlington
Exeter University
Falmouth Art Gallery, Falmouth
Lancashire Mining Museum
Ministry of Works, Republic of Ireland
National Museum of Germany, Nurenburg
Penlee House Museum, Penzance
Porthcurno Cable and Wireless Museum, Penzance
Plymouth City Museum and Art Gallery, Plymouth
Royal Cornwall Museum and Art Gallery, Truro
Royal West of England Academy, Bristol
Slate Valley Museum, New York, US
The Steiner School, Hanover
St Barbe Museum and Art Gallery, Lymington
Tate Britain
Victoria and Albert Museum
Victoria Art Gallery, Bath
Worcester City Museum and Art Gallery

Select bibliography

Barrett, Jeff, Turner, Robin and Walsh, Andrew (eds) *Caught By The River – A Collection of Words on Water*, Octopus Publishing, London 2009

Benington, Jonathan, *The Avon Project,* Lemon Street Gallery, Cornwall, 2009

Cocker, Mark, 'Encounter: The visions of Kurt Jackson' in 'The New Nature Writing', *Granta*, vol.102, London, 2008, pp.22–26.

Collins, Ian and Admiral Sir Jock Slater, *The Lights of West Cornwall*, Messum's, London, 2008

Crace, Jim, *Enesow*, Lemon Street Gallery, Cornwall, 2009

Cross, Tom, *Catching the Wave: Art and Artists in Contemporary Cornwall,* Halsgrove Publishing, Somerset, 2002

Dubois, Marc, *Theatre Five*, Lemon Street Gallery, Cornwall, 2008

Gaskell, Ronald and Jackson, Kurt, *The Cape,* Truran, Cornwall, 2002

Jackson, Kurt, *Sketchbooks*, Truran, Cornwall, 2003–04

Jackson, Kurt, *The Solent Project*, St Barbe Museum and Art Gallery, Hampshire, 2008

Jackson, Kurt, *Three Woods*, St Barbe Museum and Art Gallery, Hampshire, 2005

Mabey, Richard, *Forest Gardens*, Messum's, London, 2009

Mallett, Francis, *Paintings of Cornwall and The Scillies*, White Lane Press, Devon, 1999

McCullough, Christopher and Packer, William, *The Cornish Crow: An Vran Kernewek*, Lemon Street Gallery, Cornwall, 2007

Nixon, Giles and Wallace, Catherine, *Carnsew, A Working Granite Quarry in Cornwall,* Falmouth Art Gallery, Cornwall, 1999

O'Brien, JA, *South Crofty, The Last Working Tin Mine in Cornwall,* Camborne School of Mines, Cornwall, 1996

Packer, William, *Caroline and the Vegetable Patch,* Messum's, London 2007

Smit, Tim, *The Thames Project*, Lemon Street Gallery, Truro, Cornwall, 2006

Taylor, John Russell, *Porth*, Newlyn Art Gallery, Cornwall, 2004

Think Books, *Icons of England*, Think Publishing, London, 2008

Warburton, Josephine, *The Mining Paintings*, Pendeen Community Heritage, Cornwall, 2008

Index

Acknowledgements and credits

All images reproduced in this book are courtesy of Kurt Jackson and the Lemon Street Gallery. Art photography is by Simon Cook. Portrait photography is by Caroline Jackson, with the exception of plate 35 which is by Chloe Jackson.

The artist would like to thank the following for enabling this book to come together: Caroline Jackson for her companionship, encouragement and extensive archival work; the team at Lund Humphries (Nigel Farrow, Lucy Clark, Miranda Harrison, Nicola Homer and Kevin Brown); and Louise Jones for her constant support and hard work.

Howard Jacobson's text, forming chapter 1 in this book, originally appeared in the *Independent* (Monday 16 January 2006). Grateful thanks for permission to reproduce it here.